Law and Human Behavior:

A Study in Behavioral Biology, Neuroscience, and the Law

Law and Human Behavior:

A Study in Behavioral Biology, Neuroscience, and the Law

By

Edwin Scott Fruehwald

VANDEPLAS PUBLISHING LLC

UNITED STATES OF AMERICA

Law and Human Behavior: A Study in Behavioral Biology,
Neuroscience, and the Law

Fruehwald, Edwin Scott

Published by:

Vandeplas Publishing LLC - July 2011

801 International Parkway, 5th Floor
Lake Mary, FL. 32746
USA

www.vandeplaspublishing.com

ISBN: 978-1-60042-144-0

Dedication

I dedicate this book to my father, Edwin J Fruehwald, who taught me to love knowledge.

Table of Contents

Chapter One

Introduction

There is no denying, at this point, that Darwin's idea is a universal solvent, capable of cutting into the heart of everything in sight.

Daniel C. Dennett[1]

Behavioral biology is the next frontier for legal thought.[2] In the next few years, behavioral biology will become as important for the analysis of law as economics has been for the last several decades. Professor John Monahan has declared, "the question I want to raise is whether evolutionary psychology [a branch of behavioral biology] . . . could play the same central role in legal scholarship for the next thirty years that economics has played for the past thirty."[3] Similarly, Professors Gottschall and Wilson have observed, "choose any subject relevant to humanity–philosophy, anthropology, psychology, economics, political science, law, even religion–and you will find a rapidly expanding interest in approaching the subject from an evolutionary perspective."[4] Likewise, Professor Joseph Carroll has stated, "Darwinian psychology is on the verge of achieving a paradigm–that is, a consensus about the necessary minimum of conceptual elements that enter into an understanding of 'human nature.'"[5] Finally Professors Goetz and Shackelford have proclaimed, "as prejudicial barriers are overcome, as more evolutionary psychology work is conducted, and as hypothesized psychological mechanisms are substantiated in other disciplines, evolutionary psychology will emerge as the metatheory for psychology."[6]

To ignore the insights of behavioral biology in legal analysis is to create a legal

1

system based on crucially incomplete information.[7] Professor Paul Thagard has declared, "[t]he Brain Revolution requires a substantial change in widely accepted theories and concepts."[8] Professor Owen Jones has similarly asserted, "the extraordinary growth of behavioral biology renders obsolete any law-relevant model of human behavior that fails to integrate life science perspectives with social science ones, and . . . this deficiency can be remedied, in part, through . . . evolutionary analysis in law."[9] As Professor Jones has noted, the law will learn a great deal from the insights of behavioral biology in three ways: (1) "anything law achieves, it achieves by effecting changes in human behavior," (2) "evolutionary processes (such as natural and sexual selection) exert influences on the behavioral predispositions of all living organisms," and (3) "if better behavioral models can yield more effect legal tools, and if human behavior is influenced by evolutionary processes, then greater knowledge of how evolutionary processes influence behavior may improve law's ability to regulate it."[10] He has added: "If legal thinkers are charged with regulating behaviors, and, if understanding the causes of behaviors aids in regulating them, then familiarity with behavioral biology should be important to legal thinkers."[11]

　　　Yet, legal scholars, following social scientists, have generally disregarded human behavior in legal analysis, instead often analyzing law as a social construct.[12] This "Standard Social Science Model" of the mind considers the mind "a blank slate, or general, all-purpose computer in which all content is produced by external (social and cultural) influences."[13] This blank slate view of the mind, however, has been thoroughly debunked.[14] As Professor E. O. Wilson has averred, "much of the history of philosophy up to the present day has consisted of failed models of the brain."[15] Similarly, Professor Catherine Salmon has observed, "[m]any mainstream humanists have had a tendency to assume that human nature is constructed, that everything is nurture and nothing is nature. Recent research in cross-cultural anthropology and psychology suggests that this is incorrect, that almost everything that is important about human behavior and psychology has developed through a combination of nature and environment."[16]

　　　Although research in behavioral biology dates back to the 1950s,[17] scholars have only recently applied its insights to fields outside of science. For example, literary scholars have applied behavioral biology methods to the analysis of texts,[18] art scholars have applied it to art,[19] and a music scholar has used cognitive science to study music.[20] As will be seen in the notes throughout this book, there have also been numerous studies where legal scholars have applied the insights of behavioral biology to the law.

This author believes that there was a nascent legal system on the savannah,[21] where innate behavioral rules were enforced by devices such as force, reputation, and ostracism. Others who have studied law through the lens of behavioral biology hold similar opinions. For example, Professor Jeffrey Stake believes that there is a "property" instinct that helped mankind survive.[22] Similarly, a group of scholars thinks that humans have shared institutions of justice.[23] Likewise, Professor Michael Guttentag asserts that humans share a "law instinct"–"a protean system of legal rules to organize social behavior."[24] Finally, Professor Hendrik Gommer thinks that the very concept or system of law has a counterpart in biological mechanisms.[25]

In this book, I will present the general principles of behavioral biology and neuroscience, then apply these principles to topics in the law. Chapter Two will discuss the tenets of behavioral biology and neuroscience. Chapter Three will then apply these principles to Postmodern Legal Thought, demonstrating that this approach to jurisprudence is based on a faulty view of human nature. Chapter Four will show how reciprocal altruism, a central characteristic of human nature, can illuminate the basis of contract. Chapter Five will demonstrate how a system of rights can be predicated on innate human nature. Chapter Six will analyze three constitutional law cases using behavioral biology. Finally, the Conclusion will show why it is important to base law on a correct view of human nature.

Before concluding this Introduction, I would like to emphasize that the current use of behavioral biology to study law and human nature should not be confused with earlier applications of evolutionary theories to society. Behavioral biology is not Social Darwinism; today's biologists see evolution as a directionless process that has no goal. As Professor Pinker has pointed out, "Darwin's theory of evolution was commonly misinterpreted as an explanation of intellectual and moral progress rather than an explanation of how living things adapt to an ecological niche."[26] Furthermore, eugenics is not part of the behavioral biology agenda. As Professor Pinker has remarked, "eugenics for much of the twentieth century was a favorite cause of the left, not the right."[27] He has added, "[p]rogressives loved eugenics because it was on the side of reform rather than the status quo, activism rather than laissez-faire, and social responsibility rather than selfishness."[28]

I would also like to acknowledge the importance of several organizations that have helped develop the field of law and behavioral biology. Margaret Gruter founded the Gruter Institute for Law and Behavioral Research in 1981.[29] The Society for Evolutionary Analysis in Law (SEAL), centered at Vanderbilt University, has a valuable website for law and behavioral biology scholars, and they hold yearly conferences.[30] Finally, the MacArthur Law and Neuroscience Project has recently begun to investigate the complex issues that neuroscience raises for the criminal justice system.[31]

Notes

1. DANIEL C. DENNETT, DARWIN'S DANGEROUS IDEA: EVOLUTION AND THE MEANINGS OF LIFE 521 (1995).

2. Behavioral biology as used on this study means "[e]volutionary processes (such as natural selection and sexual selection)–together with environmental and physical inputs–built the brains that yield behaviors." Owen D. Jones, *Evolutionary Analysis in the Law: Some Objections Considered*, 67 Brook. L. Rev. 207, 211 (2001) [hereinafter Jones, *Evolutionary Analysis*]. For introductions to behavioral biology, *see* STEVEN PINKER, HOW THE MIND WORKS (1997), DAVID M. BUSS, EVOLUTIONARY PSYCHOLOGY: THE NEW SCIENCE OF THE MIND (3d ed. 2008), and TIMOTHY H. GOLDSMITH, THE BIOLOGICAL ROOTS OF HUMAN NATURE (1991). Areas of study related to and overlapping with behavioral biology include cognitive science, evolutionary psychology, evolutionary biology, sociobiology, cognitive anthropology, neuroscience, etc. These terms are often used interchangeably with behavioral biology. For a detailed history of cognitive science see William Bechtel, Adele Abrahamsen, and George Graham, *The Life of Cognitive Science, in* A COMPANION TO COGNITIVE SCIENCE 1-104 (William Bechtel & George Graham eds., 1998); *see also* PAUL THAGARD, MIND: INTRODUCTION TO COGNITIVE SCIENCE (1996).

3. John Monahan, *Symposium: Violence in the Family: Could "Law and Evolution" Be the Next "Law and Economics?"* 8 VA. J. SOC. POL'Y & L. 123 (2000); *see also* Jones, *Evolutionary Analysis, supra*, at 207 ("Evolutionary analysis in law represents, in large measure, an effort to inform legal thinking with behavioral biology, in much the same way that we try to inform legal thinking with economics or psychology."); John O. McGinnis, *The Human Constitution and Law: A Prolegomenon*, 8 J. CONTEMP. L. ISSUES 211, 211 (1997).

4. Jonathan Gottshall and David Sloan Wilson, *Introduction: Literature–A Last Frontier in Human Evolutionary Studies, in* THE LITERARY ANIMAL: EVOLUTION AND THE NATURE OF THE NARRATIVE xvii (Jonathan Gottshall and David Sloan Wilson eds., 2005).

5. Joseph Carroll, *Human Nature and Literary Meaning: A Theoretical Model Illustrated with a Critique of* Pride and Prejudice," *in* THE LITERARY ANIMAL: EVOLUTION AND THE NATURE OF NARRATIVE 77 (Jonathan Gottschall and David Sloan Wilson eds., 2005); *see also* Leda Cosmides & John Tooby, *Evolutionary Psychology, Moral Heuristics, and the Law, in* HEURISTICS AND THE LAW 183 (Gerd Gigerenzer & Christoph Enge eds., 2006) ("The cognitive revolution provided, for the first time in human history, a precise language for describing mental mechanisms, as programs that process information.").

6. Aaron T. Goetz & Todd K. Shackelford, *Modern Application of Evolutionary Theory to Psychology: Key Concepts and Clarifications*, 119 AM. J. PSYCH. 567, 567 (2006).

7. Professor Jones has declared: "Any model of behavior that ignores the biology of behavior–through the effect of evolutionary processes on brain function–is materially incomplete." Jones, *Evolutionary Analysis*, *supra*, at 214.

8. PAUL THAGARD, THE BRAIN AND THE MEANING OF LIFE 65 (2010).

9. Owen D. Jones, *Time-Shifted Rationality and the Law of Law's Leverage: Behavioral Economics Meets Behavioral Biology*, 95 N.W. U.L. REV. 1141, 1143 (2001).

10. Jones, *Evolutionary Analysis*, *supra*, at 208-09.

11. *Id.* at 215.

12. *See* Chapter Three for a detailed discussion.

13. Carroll, *supra*, at 80; *see also* STEVEN PINKER, THE BLANK SLATE: THE MODERN DENIAL OF HUMAN NATURE 55 (2002).

14. Professor Rubin has declared: "The notion that humans are born as blank slates (*tabula rosa* to use Locke's Latin phrase) is no longer intellectually respectable among serious people." PAUL RUBIN, DARWINIAN POLITICS: THE EVOLUTIONARY ORIGIN OF FREEDOM ix (2002); *accord* Jim Chen, *Law as a Species of Language Acquisition*, 73 WASH. L.J.1263, 1272 (2001) ("[W]e stand on the brink of a century whose principal intellectual project may consist of overthrowing the Social Science Model. . ."); E. O. Wilson, *Foreword from the Scientific Side*, in THE LITERARY ANIMAL: EVOLUTION AND THE NATURE OF NARRATIVE viii (Jonathan Gottschall and David Sloan Wilson eds., 2005) ("The blank-slate model could be tested empirically. It lost."); Dylan Evans, *From Lacan to Darwin*, in THE LITERARY ANIMAL: EVOLUTION AND THE NATURE OF NARRATIVE 52 (Jonathan Gottschall and David Sloan Wilson eds., 2005) ("The cognitive revolution swept through psychology in the 1960s, replacing the behaviorist paradigm that had held sway since the 1920s."); *see generally* PINKER, *supra*; *see also* Sharon Street, *A Darwinian Dilemma for Realist Theories of Value*, 127 PHIL. STUD. 109, 109 (2006) ("[R]ealist theories of value prove unable to accommodate the fact that Darwinian forces have deeply influenced the content of human values.").

15. E. O. Wilson, *supra*, at viii; *see also* Gail L. Heriot, *The Symposium on Law: Human Behavior and Evolution: An Introduction*, 8 J. CONTEMP. L. ISSUES 1, 1 (1997) ("Law must be accommodated to the fixed aspects of human nature; they cannot be refitted to accommodate law.").

16. Catherine Salmon, *Crossing the Abyss: Erotica and the Intersection of Evolutionary Psychology and Literary Studies*, in THE LITERARY ANIMAL: EVOLUTION AND THE NATURE OF NARRATIVE 244 (Jonathan Gottschall and David Sloan Wilson eds., 2005).

17. Evans, *supra*, at 52.

18. *See generally* Gottshall and Wilson, *supra*.

19. *E.g.,* DAVID LEWIS-WILLIAMS, THE MIND IN THE CAVE: CONSCIOUSNESS AND THE ORIGINS OF ART (2002); ELLEN DISSANAYAKE, ART AND INTIMACY: HOW THE ARTS BEGAN (2000); Nancy A. AIKEN, THE BIOLOGICAL ORIGINS OF ART (1998).

20. *E.g.,* OLIVER SACKS, MUSICOPHILIA: TALES OF MUSIC AND THE BRAIN (2008).

21. The savannah is intended to refer to the environment in which homo sapiens evolved. It is also sometimes referred to as the Environment of Evolutionary Adaptedness or the EEA.

22. Jeffrey Evans Stake, *The Property 'Instinct,'* 359 PHIL. TRANSACTIONS ROYAL SOC'Y LONDON 1763 (2004). I will discuss Stake's theories in detail in Chapter Five.

23. Robinson et. al., *The Origins of Shared Intuitions of Justice*, 60 VAND. L. REV. 1653 (2007). I will discuss these scholars theories in detail in Chapter Three.

24. Michael D. Guttentag, *Is There a Law Instinct?*, 87 WASH. U.L. REV. 269 (2009). I will discuss Guttentag's theories in detail in Chapter Three.

25. Hendrik Gommer, *The Molecular Concept of Law*, 7 UTRECHT L. REV. 141, 158 (2011).

26. PINKER, *supra*, at 15.

27. *Id.* at 153. H.G. Wells, George Bernard Shaw, Winston Churchill, Beatrice and Sidney Webb, Harold Laski, and Virginia Woolf were advocates of eugenics. OPHELIA BENSON & JEREMY STRANGROOM, WHY TRUTH MATTERS 85 (2007).

28. PINKER, *supra*, at 153.

29. http://www.gruterinstitute.org.

30. http://law.vanderbilt.edu/seal.

31. http://lawneuro.org.

Chapter Two

An Introduction to Behavioral Biology and Neuroscience

Is it not reasonable to anticipate that the our understanding of the human mind
would be aided greatly by knowing the purpose for which it was designed?

G.C. Williams[1]

I. An Introduction to Brain Science

Behavioral biologists believe that the mind is the brain.[2] In other words, they reject a dualistic view that the mind is separate from the body–that there is a soul or similar entity that controls thought and behavior separate from the physical.[3] Thus, perception, memory, learning, morality, and everything else we associate with the mind are physical processes that occur in the brain.

Professor Pinker has succinctly summarized how the brain functions: "Brain cells fire in patterns."[4] These brain cells (neurons) work by passing on electrical charges to neurons that are connected to them by synapses.[5] The firing neuron sends a chemical signal called a neurotransmitter across the synaptic gap to other neurons.[6] These signals either excite the neurons by increasing their electrical activity or inhibit their activity.[7] Neurons interact to create complex representations, concepts, and processes.[8] Professor Thagard has compared brain activity to "a bunch of jamming jazz musicians whose coordinated playing emerges from their dynamic interactions."[9]

The brain's physical processes create behavior. Behavioral biologists study human behavior using a multitude of scientific methods. Evolutionary psychologists examine how subjects react while playing various "games," such as the prisoners' dilemma or the ultimatum game.[10] Psychologists also analyze how brain deformities alter human behavior,[11] while other scientists study childhood development.[12] Comparative anthropologists investigate behavior across cultures.[13] Biologists study other living creatures to see how their behavior sheds light on human behavior.[14] Finally, neuroscientists examine the brain using techniques, such as fMRI scans,[15] and they also investigate the brain's chemistry.[16]

These scientists use established scientific methods in studying human behavior. For example, "[t]he researcher first formulates a hypothesis about an evolved psychological mechanism and then generates testable predictions about the attributes or design features of that mechanism that have not previously been discovered or documented."[17] In other words, the hypotheses are subjected to confirmation or falsification.[18]

Behavioral biologists study human behavior largely from an evolutionary perspective; they believe that evolution has "endowed humans with a universal complex mind . . ."[19] Behavioral biologists connect patterns of "genes through neural activity to brain circuitry and behavior."[20] They think that the human brain evolved similarly to human physical characteristics, such as opposable thumbs and walking erect.[21] In other words, the human brain evolved through natural selection "to make decisions that enhance reproductive success."[22] Likewise, "complex functional human psychology and behavioral traits are the results of adaption through natural selection."[23]

In studying evolution's effect on human behavior, behavioral biologists look at both ultimate and proximate causes. The ultimate explanation is "understanding the evolved function of a psychological mechanism"–"why it exists," and the proximate explanation is "*how* the mechanism works."[24] The how causes involve "the immediate mechanistic logistics of physiology and biochemistry as well as an organism's unique developmental history that lead to particular behavioral outcomes."[25] Ultimate causes concern "the aggregate reproductive consequences of behavior over evolutionary time."[26] For instance, the proximate causes of a male robin's singing in the spring include "hormonal changes triggered by the lengthening of successive days, the activation of particular motor neurons to the vocal apparatus, and each bird's individual experience of songs heard and songs practiced."[27]   The ultimate causes of the singing include claiming territory, advertising health, and attracting mates, traits that contribute to the robin's survival and reproductive success.[28]

Natural selection and sexual selection are the main forces behind evolution. Concerning natural selection, one scholar has stated: "Differential reproduction of genetically different forms, or evolutionary selection, is the only candidate for the principal guiding force of evolutionary change."[29]   Under natural selection, genes compete with other alleles (variations of the gene), and "those alleles that are better at securing the reproductive success of their organisms are likely to spread in the gene pool at the detriment of others."[30] As Professor Hauser has noted: "Natural selection builds organisms with complex design features based on a nonrandom but directionless process. Poorly-designed variants are eliminated, better-designed ones favored."[31] Similarly, "[i]n evolutionary theory, an 'adaption' is a biological trait, physiological, psychological, or behavioral, shaped by natural selection to enhance the fitness of members of a species."[32] As Professor McGinnis has observed, "[s]ince resource acquisition ability was important to the genetic fitness of our ancestors, traits that contributed to this ability were selected over time in any given population."[33]   In other words, both body parts and behaviors evolved to deal with particular problems.[34]

A simple and uncontroversial example of a psychological adaption is humans' fear of snakes, which is contained in specialized neural circuitry.[35]   Snakes were potentially dangerous to human survival, and a neural mechanism (fear) evolved to capture human attention to snakes more than harmless objects.[36] Stated differently: "The functional outputs of evolved fear adaptions, such as freezing, fighting, and fleeing, are specifically designed to solve the adaptive problem posed by these evolutionary threats to survival."[37]

Sexual selection is also important to evolution because it mixes genes and selects for and against genes. Sexual selection is the competition for mates and reproductive opportunities.[38] Human males and females make different contributions to reproduction, with females making the most valuable contribution in that they provide the egg (eggs are larger than sperms), internal fertilization, gestation, and lactation and they bear most of the responsibility for raising their offspring.[39] Because females contribute the most important resources and they can have only a limited number of offspring due to gestation, males must compete for females.[40] Males who are better at attracting mates reproduce and continue their genes, while males that cannot attract mates do not.[41] Thus, nature selects against those males who are not good at attracting mates. Characteristics that attract females indicate traits that the mate will produce strong offspring, traits such as physical attractiveness, social status, good health, and intelligence, and traits that show that the male will help the female raise the child and be a good-faith mate, traits such as kindness, faithfulness, and the ability to obtain resources.[42] While male preferences in a mate overlap with female preferences, there are significant differences because of the different investments in and benefits from mating.[43] Males prefer mates who are attractive (an indicator of being young and healthy and having good genes), make commitments, and would be a good mother.[44]

Behavioral biologists believe that evolution developed a modular brain, with each module having a specialized function (domain-specific reasoning procedures), that these modules interact to produce a thought or an action, and that they can "reinforce or cancel one another out, according to context."[45] Professor Hauser has stated, " [t]he logic of natural selection suggests that the mind is equipped with specialized reasoning abilities, designed to solve specific adaptive problems."[46] Similarly, Professor Gazzaniga has declared: "[T]hink of a module as a hardwired (innate) mechanism that unconsciously directs you to think or act in a certain way, that directs your attention to such states as belief, desire, and pretense, and then allows you to learn about these mental states."[47] Professor Pinker has described how these modules interact: "[A]n urge or habit coming out of one module can be translated into behavior in different ways–or suppressed altogether–by some other module."[48] Professor Gazzaniga has argued that "[t]hese modules produce specific intuitive concepts that have allowed us to create the societies we live in."[49] Two neuroscientists at USC have theorized that the mind works more like the internet than a top-down command center; the brain uses loops, not lines.[50] Finally, neuroscientists have observed the modularity of the human mind with fMRI scans.[51]

Behavioral biologists do not believe that our actions are genetically predetermined.[52] The human genome project has shown that humans do not possess enough genes so that they can directly determine a particular behavior.[53] Humans have approximately 30,000 genes, and these genes are recipes for proteins.[54] Some genes are promoter genes, which switch other genes on and off and allow for the great variety scientists see in living things.[55] In other words, a genetic code is more like a recipe than a blueprint.[56]

Instead of being genetically predetermined, behavior "comes from an internal struggle among mental modules with differing agendas and goals."[57] Moreover, how genes interact is determined by the environment they inhabit.[58] In addition, our mental mechanisms help us learn culture.[59] Thus, our behavior is a combination of competing innate mechanisms reacting to the environment combined with our learning of culture, which is facilitated by our innate mechanisms.[60] In other words, "[o]ur brains have evolved to the point where we are capable of rebelling against our selfish genes"[61] and making responsible decisions.

II. The Selfish Gene, Kin Altruism, and Reciprocal Altruism

An essential concept in behavioral biology is the notion of the selfish gene. Natural selection occurs at the level of the gene (the "replicators"), with the organism being the "vehicle" that contains the genes.[62] Behavioral biologists believe that genes are ruthlessly selfish; they are only interested in their survival.[63] The first goal of the selfish gene is its survival, and the second is reproduction.[64] As Professors Grady & McGuire have observed, "individuals have a biological incentive to behave selfishly when the benefit is greater than the cost to others discounted by the other's degree of relatedness. . ."[65] In fact, a creature that contained a gene to help the species, rather than itself, would quickly be selected against.[66] Thus, "[i]ndividuals, not groups, are the functional units through which genes act, and social norms become adaptive only because they confer a net benefit to individuals."[67] Consequently, legal studies should generally focus on the individual, not the group.

However, the existence of the selfish gene does not mean that individuals are always selfish. At least two types of altruism developed that produce human cooperation–kinship altruism and reciprocal altruism. The first type of altruism is kinship altruism (kin selection). Genes can survive by altruism to kin; kin (children, siblings, cousins, nephews, etc.) share some of the same genes as the original organism.[68] "[S]ince relatives share genes, any gene that inclines an organism toward helping a relative will increase the chance of survival of a copy of itself that sits inside the relative, even if the helper sacrifices its own fitness in the generous act."[69] As Professor Alexander has stated, "[i]t is surely no accident that all human societies studied everywhere on earth are centered on extensive kinship systems that operate so as to match their circumstances to reproductive interests, no accident that humans everywhere know in amazing detail who their relatives are and how related they are and that they also have strong opinions on how much help they should be receiving–or giving."[70] Therefore, in general, "natural selection can be expected to favor behaviors that enhance the reproductive success of near relatives."[71] As one can see from the above, kin altruism is a consequence of gene selection, not group selection.[72]

The other type of altruism is reciprocal altruism (mutual cooperation or tit-for-tat), where both parties gain through an interaction.[73] Professor Alexander has described the process as: "[w]henever benefit givers obtain a net reward for giving a benefit, they will evolve to give more of the benefits, and to do so at less expense to themselves thereby gaining greater rewards. Benefit receivers will evolve to extract more of the benefits, and to use them more effectively, thus favoring the givers of more and greater benefits."[74] When the benefit comes from a nonrelative, it can be used to further reproduction or the organism's survival.[75] As Professor Pinker has pointed out, "[r]eciprocal altruism can evolve because cooperators do better than hermits or misanthropes."[76] Thus, reciprocal altruism comes from the need to obtain goodwill from one's peers whose goodwill an individual may need at another time.[77] Accordingly, "reproductive success can be improved by mutual support, even among nonrelatives."[78] "The paradigmatic example of reciprocal altruism is food sharing, which human beings engage in far more than any other species, and which was almost certainly essential to the survival of our hominid ancestors in their African Savannah niche."[79]

Reciprocal altruism succeeds because humans are "risk takers"; they make long-term investments and are willing to invest without immediate return.[80] As Professor Alexander has observed, "[m]odern humans invest this way almost continually, often not expecting returns for decades, or even expecting returns only for their descendants after they themselves are dead."[81] Professor Hauser has theorized that risk taking occurs because humans have strong inhibitory control.[82] He has written that humans "can not only inhibit a desire to immediate gratification, but we can use our capacity for self-control to block previously learned rules, thereby opening up opportunities to set up new social norms."[83] Reciprocal altruism also works because humans have developed an innate sense of trust–"the willingness to behave in such a way that only makes sense if you believe that others will reciprocate any benefits you extend to them."[84] Finally, reciprocal altruism requires that the cooperators be able to recognize and remember each other.[85] Humans may have developed moral sentiments that predispose them not to cheat, so that others will see that they are trustworthy.[86]

Because reciprocal altruistic interactions will only continue "as long as they continue to yield greater returns than less risky investments,"[87] reciprocal altruism has developed methods for policing transactions and punishing cheaters. As Professor Hösle has noted, "it makes perfect sense that an altruist who in a situation of conflict, due to the scarcity of resources, has to choose between two different recipients of her charitable activities selects that person who is more likely to continue with altruist activities."[88] Moreover, humans have evolved specialized methods of detecting and responding to cheating (non-reciprocators), and our emotions are involved in this process.[89] As Professor Mayton has commented, "[w]hen the punishment feature of reciprocal altruism is suppressed, the disposition to act generously to others is generally stunted."[90] Furthermore, studies have shown that humans have enhanced memory for the faces of untrustworthy individuals.[91] In addition, "[o]ne of the greatest advantages a human can have in social matters is superior ability at building mental scenarios that describe most or all possibilities in upcoming or ongoing interactions with parties having somewhat different life interests."[92] More specifically, Professor Hauser has averred, "it is likely that evolution equipped us with a specialized ability to work through the cost-benefit analysis of social contract."[93] Finally, humans have an interest in their reputation and the reputations of others, and this presents an individual with another way to detect reciprocators and cheaters.[94]

Neuroscientists have supported the existence of reciprocal altruism using fMRI scans, and they have observed that reciprocal altruism involves specific neural networks, thus corroborating Professors Cosmides and Tooby's theory of special designs in the brain that deal with specific evolutionary problems.[95] In one study, neuroscientists used an fMRI to scan 36 women as they played an Iterated Prisoners' Dilemma game[96] with another woman.[97] They concluded:

> Mutual cooperation was associated with consistent activation in brain areas that have been linked with reward processing: nucleus accumbens, the caudate nucleus, ventromedial frontal/orbitofrontal cortex, and rostral anterior cingulate cortex. We propose that activation of this

neural network reinforces reciprocal altruism, thereby motivating
subjects to resist the temptation to selfishly accept but not reciprocate
favors.[98]

Another study, by a related group of neuroscientists again using an Iterated Prisoners'
Dilemma Game, demonstrated that "unreciprocated cooperation was associated with
increased activity in bilateral anterior insula, left hippocampus, and left lingual gyrus
compared with reciprocated cooperation."[99]   Furthermore, "functional connectivity
between anterior insula and lateral orbitofrontal cortex (OFC) in response to
unreciprocated cooperation predicated subsequent defection by the player."[100] Moreover,
a related group of neuroscientists discovered that "unfair offers elicited activity in brain
areas related to both emotion (anterior insula) and cognition (dorsolateral prefrontal
cortex)."[101]   Finally, neurobiologists have concluded that the neuroactive hormone
oxytocin "responds to the receipt of a social signal of trust and is statistically related to
trustworthy behavior."[102]

In sum, reciprocal altruism needs three conditions to remain stable and evolve:
1. Small costs to giving and large benefits to receiving;
2. A delay between the initial and reciprocal act of giving, and
3. Multiple opportunities for interacting, with giving contingent upon receiving.[103]

III. Universals

Behavioral biologists have discovered neuro-cognitive universals that transcend
cultures. These universals exist because "[s]ome designs [evolutionary adaptions]
outreproduce others until they become universal in the population."[104]   Similarly,
Professor Carroll has observed, "[h]uman universals or species typical norms of behavior
are merely behavioral patterns so firmly grounded in the logic of human history that they
are characteristic features of all cultures."[105]

For example, linguist Noam Chomsky has argued that a universal grammar
underlies all human language.[106] Chomsky considers the language faculty a "module"
of the mind,"[107] and he has declared, "[t]he language faculty is a distinct system of the
mind/brain, with an initial state so common to the species . . . and apparently unique to
it in essential respects."[108]   He has further stated: "UG [universal grammar] is a

characteristic of these innate, biologically determined principles, which constitute one component of the human mind–the language faculty."[109] Chomsky has replied to those who look externally for mankind's language abilities: "A more fruitful approach shifts the main burden of explanation from the structure of the world to the structure of the mind."[110] He has asserted that "[t]o come to know a human language would be an extraordinary intellectual achievement for a creature not specifically designed to accomplish this task. A normal child acquires this knowledge on relatively slight exposure and without specific training."[111]

Chomsky has suggested what is true of language is also true in other areas in which human beings acquire knowledge,[112] and behavioral biology has confirmed this by demonstrating universals in many areas. Professor Pinker has declared: "Universal mental mechanisms can underlie superficial variation across cultures."[113] Likewise, he has stated, "[b]ehavior may vary across cultures, but the design of the mental programs that generate it need not vary."[114] Thus, "familiar categories of behavior–marriage customs, food taboos, folk superstitions, and so on–certainly do vary across cultures and have to be learned, but the deeper mechanisms of mental computation that generate them may be universal and innate."[115]

Professor Brown has listed hundreds of universals in all societies, including classification, crying, daily routines, envy, etiquette, facial expressions, jokes, law, leaders, logical notions, play, and social structure.[116] Other universals that scientists have discovered include:

> The primacy of family ties in all human societies and the consequent appeal of nepotism and inheritance;
> The limited scope of communal sharing in human groups, the more common ethos of reciprocity, and the resulting phenomenon of social loafing and the collapse of contributions to public goods when reciprocity cannot be implemented;
> The universality of dominance and violence across human societies . . . and the existence of genetic and neurological mechanisms that underlie it;
> The universality of ethnocentrism and other forms of group-against-group hostility across societies, and the ease with which such hostility

can be aroused in people within our society;

The partial heritability of intelligence, conscientiousness, and antisocial tendencies, implying that some degree of inequality will arise even in perfectly fair economic systems, and that we therefore face an inherent tradeoff between equality and freedom;

The prevalence of defense mechanisms, self-serving biases, and cognitive dissonance reduction, by which people deceive themselves about their autonomy, wisdom, and integrity;

The biases of human moral sense, including a preference for kin and friends, a susceptibility to a taboo mentality, and a tendency to confuse morality with conformity, rank, cleanliness, and beauty.[117]

Most importantly, behavioral biologists believe that human nature is universal.[118] As Professor de Waal has declared: "Why not assume that our humanity, including the self-control to form a liveable society, is built into us?"[119]

IV. Sexual Selection and Related Topics

As mentioned in Part I, sexual selection is a major element of evolution and, thus, human behavior. Sexual reproduction is important because it mixes the genes; every human child gets half her genes from her father and half from her mother.[120] Mixing the genes is important because it helps offspring adapt to changed conditions, especially quickly adapting parasites such as bacteria and viruses.[121]

As noted earlier, males and females have different sexual strategies. Males and females use each other for mutual exploitation: a man uses his mate to produce children and continue his genes and a woman uses her mate to make children and help her care for them.[122] A female invests the most in rearing the young because of gestation, which cuts down on her mating opportunities.[123] She looks for a mate that will make a good father, which means that she can be choosey.[124] On the other hand, a male has more time to search for other mating opportunities, and a male is less choosey concerning a mate.[125]

Pair-bonding, the mother-child bond, and parental love are a universal part of human nature. As Professor Wilson has written, "the human family may have originated as an adaption to particular environmental conditions."[126] "Evolution favored male-female bonds not for the emotional pleasure per se–although such pleasure constitutes the actor's motivation and reinforcement–but rather because bonded males and females constituted a complimentary pair with the mutually important goal of raising their offspring."[127] Moreover, "[t]he most distinctive feature of the sexual bond, one of overriding significance for social organization, is that it transcends sexual activity."[128] Pair-bonds are especially important because human females have concealed ovulation, and "[o]nly frequent copulation with the same female over the length of her cycle will lead to a high possibility of paternity."[129] In fact, some scientists think "that the human species may not have remained viable were it not for the evolution of love."[130]

The mother-child bond must be maintained longer in humans than in other primate species because of the longer period of human dependency.[131] Unlike most other mammals, human fathers also have strong parental bonds with their children.[132] Consequently, the savannah version of the nuclear family is an evolutionary trait because it allowed couples to raise more offspring, thus passing on the couple's genes.[133]

The hormone oxytocin may play a large role in pair-bonding, the parent-child bond, and parental love. Professor Damasio relates that mating in prairie voles causes the release of oxytocin in affect-related brain regions.[134] This, in turn, creates a life-long monogamous attachment and parent-child bonds. When experimenters suppressed oxytocin production, the pair-bond and parent-child bonds were eliminated.

All things being equal, parents will invest equally in their offspring because each carries 50% of their genes.[135] However, things in nature are not always equal. For example, a mother will sometimes let a runt starve so that she can give her resources to her children who are more likely to survive.[136] Similarly, if a parent can feed only one of two children, the parent will probably feed the older child because the parent has already invested more in that child.[137] On the other hand, if the older sibling can fend for himself, a mother may wean the sibling so that she can devote her resources to a younger child.[138]

"Family planning" is also part of evolution. Very high birth rates lead to high death rates due to starvation and other related causes.[139] Consequently, natural selection limits the number of offspring to take advantage of limited food and other resources by not passing down genes for high birth rates since individuals with these genes do not often live to adulthood.[140]

An example of the application of the above principles concerns the dangers from step-fathers to children from infanticide.[141] In evolutionary times, mammalian fathers sometimes killed the unrelated children of their new mates because it enhanced their reproductive success.   There is a contraceptive effect from constant nursing in mammalian females. Thus, by killing the unrelated children of his new mate, a male increased his reproductive success because his new mate could bear offspring for him. This tendency continues today, with step-fathers killing their wives' children more often than natural parents. Professor Jones and Goldsmith note, however, that policy makers should be cautious in using such findings; a cost-benefit analysis should be applied to the analysis.[142] In creating a policy to deal with this problem, the legislature needs to balance the number of infant deaths that could be prevented by legislation against the costs of stigmatizing innocent step-fathers.

V. The Universal Grammar of Morality

Behavioral biologists believe that morality (our sense of right and wrong) is a universal characteristic that is hardwired into human brains (a "universal moral grammar") and that aided survival.[143] As Professor Dwyer has stated: "Universal moral grammar provides the cognitive resources that make possible the acquisition of moral capacities."[144] Moral judgements are generally intuitive and unconscious (prerational); they often occur automatically and allow humans to make rapid judgements.[145] For example, humans developed an innate incest taboo that causes an individual to be sexually uninterested in a person that he or she lived with as a child, a trait which developed to discourage the genetic costs of inbreeding.[146] However, there are times when abstract moral reasoning is required, such as when conflicting moral judgments are involved.[147] Moreover, occasionally strong consequentialist reasoning can overcome personally harmful moral intuitions, such as when a crying baby endangers the survival of an entire group. [148] In addition, individuals often work out moral dilemmas with others; morality is partly a social process.[149]

Professor Greene makes an analogy between a camera that has automatic and manual settings and morality.[150] A camera with both automatic and manual settings provides both efficiency and flexibility. It allows a photographer to usually rely on automatic for a normal picture, but he can use the manual settings when he wants something fancy. Our human brain is similar with automatic settings–the emotions–and manual–our conscious reasoning. Our emotions help us react quickly to the myriad of minor actions that occur incessantly, while our conscious reasoning helps us deal with life's challenges in a more flexible way–problems that are too difficult to deal with using "gut" reactions. In sum, much of our morality is based on moral intuition, but man is also capable of conscious moral decision-making and sometimes morality develops through a social process.[151]

Morality doesn't derive from a single module in the brain; rather, it is produced by several modules in combination.[152] FMRI scans have revealed that "when people confront certain kinds of moral dilemmas, they activate a vast network of brain regions, including areas involved in emotion, decision-making, conflict, social relations, and memory."[153] Professors Haidt and Joseph have proposed that there are five moral modules: 1) harm/care ("a sensitivity to or dislike of signs of pain and suffering in others"), 2) fairness/reciprocity, 3) authority/respect ("a set of concerns about navigating status hierarchies, e.g., anger towards those who fail to display proper signs of deference and respect"), 4) boundaries between in-groups and out-groups (coalitions), and 5) purity/sanctity ("relating to the emotion of disgust").[154]

In addition, fMRI scans show the effects of emotion on moral reasoning. People distinguish between types of moral dilemmas (such as direct versus indirect harm) based on the regions of the brain activated.[155] For example, when direct physical harm is involved (e.g., pushing one person off a footbridge to stop a trolley from killing five people–the "footbridge problem"), most individuals have an emotional reaction that causes them to think intuitively and come to an immediate conclusion that this action is wrong.[156] The brain region involved in this process is the ventromedial prefontal cortex, which integrates affective responses (emotion) with higher cognition.[157] However, when indirect harm but the same outcome is involved (e.g., throwing a switch to shift a trolley from killing five people to a track that kills one–the "trolley problem"), individuals have a different response with a different part of the brain being involved, and they often exhibit a utilitarian reaction in which one person is sacrificed to save five.[158] This suggests that intuitive moral responses involve emotion, and they active different parts of the brain than utilitarian reasoning.[159]

Humans can recognize the emotional states of others, and they "have the ability to form theories with some degree of accuracy what those desires, intentions, beliefs and mental states are."[160] In other words, humans have "the ability to observe behavior and then infer the unobservable mental state that is causing it."[161] This is "a theory of mind"–"a more-or-less automatic understanding of what it means to be someone else."[162] Most significantly, "human nature provides a yardstick to identify suffering in any member of our species."[163]

"Individuals recognize actions made by others because the pattern of firing neurons [mirror neurons] made when observing an action is similar to the pattern produced to generate that action."[164] Professors Casebeer and Churchland have described how mirror neurons work:

> The behavior of the "mirror neurons" suggests that when seeing the other make the movement, the premotor cortex generates incipient motor commands to match the movement. It is possible that these signals can be detected as intentions, albeit off-line intentions, which are used to interpret what is seen (e.g., "he intends to share food").[165]

In other words, an individual understands an action because he has a template in his brain for that action based on his own movements;[166] humans put themselves in the other person's place.[167] Moreover, social cognition depends on the ability to form triadic mental representations of mental states–You, Me, and This (an object), which allows sharing attention to an object and collaborating on a shared goal ("shared intentionality").[168]

Mirror neurons help us understand the emotions of others.[169] For example, fMRI scans suggest that "the understanding of facial expressions of disgust in someone else involves the activation of the same part of the brain that normally is activated during the experience of the same emotion."[170] Understanding the emotions of others helps us navigate our lives; "[i]f our brains were not able to discriminate at an emotional level events perceived, remembered, or imagined, it would be almost impossible for us to deal with even the most banal of the situations that we have to face daily."[171] Furthermore, "[b]y being able to feel what others feel, we are also able to respond compassionately to their emotional states."[172]

There are specific neural circuits in the brain that allows one to distinguish between oneself and others (self-awareness).[173] This self is both physical and psychological.[174] Professor Gazzaniga has stated that "the sense of self arises out of distributed networks in both hemispheres. It is likely that both hemispheres have processing specializations that contribute to a sense of self, and that sense of self is constructed by the left-hemisphere interpreter on the basis of the input from the distributed networks."[175] Professor Iacoboni has elaborated: "The mirror neurons embody both the interdependence of self and other–by firing for the actions of both–and the independence we simultaneously feel and require, by firing more powerfully for actions of the self."[176] In addition, the brain may have "super mirror neurons," which are involved in creating a proper sense of the self.[177]

Our self-awareness and theory of mind contribute to our moral judgments of responsibility.[178] According to Professor Hauser, "[s]elf-knowledge is a prophylactic, a protective skin that can empower us to avoid temptations or, more mundanely, avoid saying or doing the wrong thing at the wrong time."[179] Similarly, empathy ("a matching up of the emotions in the displayer and observer") derives from our self-awareness, mirror neurons, and theory of mind.[180] "[I]ndividuals can think about what someone else feels, imagine what they would feel in the same situation, work out what would make them feel better, and from this deduce how to make the other person feel better."[181] More specifically, "the perception of someone's suffering evokes an altruistic motivation directed toward the ultimate goal of reducing the suffering."[182] However, empathy is not just automatic, it can be affected by such factors as "the affective link to the other person, the perceived fairness of the other, the subject's appraisal of whether the reason the other person is suffering is justified, the frequency of a person's prior exposure to pain inducing situations and the intensity of the inflicted pain."[183]

Finally, not all moral emotions are "nice."[184] Emotions involving shaming, ostracism, and revenge are part of human nature.[185] Similarly, disgust protects against disease (lack of purity).[186] Even fear is an essential moral emotion because it can affect our moral choices.[187]

The mind also has cognitive limitations–"[t]here are things it cannot do, cannot learn, and cannot comprehend."[188] Our cognitive abilities developed for survival–"[i]f an organism repeatedly comes across the same situation, any individual that evolves a mechanism to understand or predict the results of the situation is going to have a survival advantage."[189] Consequently, our cognitive limitations exist because mankind didn't need all skills on the primate savannah. These limitations apply to moral reasoning: "From an evolutionary perspective, the survival of the animal depends on its maintaining its inner milieu within a very narrow range of values."[190] In other words, strong moral relativism does not exist.

VI. Cultural Differences

Culture provides the details of human behavior. As Professor Dawkins has declared, "[a]mong animals, man is uniquely dominated by culture. . . ."[191] The development of culture aided survival during evolutionary times in light of differing geography, ecology, and social circumstances.[192] The mind learns because it has innate mechanisms for learning.[193] Learning aided survival because it allowed humans to adopt to unpredictable environments.[194] Thus, "[n]urture is reinforcing nature, not opposing it."[195] In fact, children tend to pick the nurture that suits their nature.[196] Most importantly, both are important for survival: "Learning implies plasticity; whereas instinct implies preparedness."[197] Finally, Judge Hoffman has argued: "Perhaps all behaviors are represented in the brain by a set of probability distributions which are then continuously influenced by the interaction between ultimate causes (the initial probabilities evolution built into our brains) and proximate causes (the particular environmental challenges brains are called upon to solve)."[198] In sum, evolutionary psychology eliminates dichotomies, such as nature versus nurture, in favor of an interactivity framework.[199]

While categories of behavior, such as law, marriage, taboos, etc., are universal and innate, the details of behaviors (the content) do vary across cultures and have to be learned.[200] These differences are usually due to different conceptions of the facts, rather than difference in fundamental principles.[201] For example, all cultures proscribe murder, but the exceptions to murder vary by culture (factual disagreements as to what murder is). A more detailed example concerns honoring the dead as related by Herodotus.[202] The ancient Greeks honored their fathers by cremating them. In contrast, the Callatiae ate their fathers dead bodies, and the Persians put their corpses on high towers and let the vultures devour them. These cultures each considered the practices of the others to be abhorrent. Yet, they were all performing the same fundamental, universal act–honoring their fathers.

Similarly, although there is a narrow range of possible moral systems,[203] the details of morality do differ among cultures and individuals.[204] Professor Hauser has observed, "[a] mature individual's moral grammar enables him to unconsciously generate and comprehend a limitless range of permissible and obligatory actions within the native culture, to recognize violations when they arise, and to generate intuitions about punishable violations."[205]   Or, as Professor Graefrath has asserted: "We have to distinguish between the *ethos* of a community, which tells us what people in this community regard as obligatory, and *morality proper*, which tells us what is obligatory without reference to what a community's customs happen to be."[206]

Man learns the details of a culture through imitation by exposure to that culture's social norms.[207]   The ability to imitate others is innate and often unconscious.[208]   As Professor Hauser has observed, "[t]he role of experience is to instruct the innate system, pruning the range of possible moral systems down to one distinctive moral signature."[209] More specifically, mirror neurons create a connection between the observation and imitation of an action.[210]   Under this process, "the action as observed and as executed must share the same neural code and that this is the *sine qua non* condition for imitation."[211]   Furthermore, the aforementioned triadic mental representations are important for learning culture.[212]

According to one theory, cultural differences occur in the realization of morality because different cultures stress different aspects of Haidt's and Joseph's five modules.[213]   There are three areas of moral concern under these modules: 1) the ethic of autonomy (suffering and reciprocity), which is concerned with an individual's rights, freedoms, and welfare, 2) the ethic of community (hierarchy and coalitional boundaries), which is concerned with protecting families, communities, and nations, and 3) the ethic of divinity (the concern for purity), which involves the spiritual self and physical and mental purity.[214]   An environmental trigger activates the input into these modules; they then elicit moral emotions, and moral intuition (output) ensues.[215]

VII. Behavioral Biology, Society, and the Social Contract

Mankind flourished because it was able to come together into social groups, which produced a survival advantage (reciprocal altruism on a large scale). Professor Barash has asserted: "The basic concept of "society assumes give and take, often called a 'social contract,' whereby individuals make what is essentially a deal with society at large. Each will forego certain selfish, personal opportunities in exchange for profiting from the cooperation of others."[216] Professor Gazzaniga has proposed that "all those social relationships we worry about intensely are merely by-products of behavior originally selected to avoid our being eaten by predators."[217] Groups that cooperate internally prevail over selfish groups for survival.[218] As Professor Gazzaniga has declared: "Without all those others, without our alliances, we die."[219] For example, cooperation in hunting was important for human evolution because it created a supply of meat for protein and energy that allowed humans to grow big brains.[220] Furthermore Professor Hauser has observed: "What has allowed us to live in large groups of unrelated individuals that often come and go is an evolved faculty of the mind that generates universal and unconscious judgments concerning justice and harm."[221]

Professor Ridley has gone further and conjectured that the sudden takeoff of the last 45,000 years was due to "collective intelligence"–"the notion that what determines the inventiveness and rate of cultural exchange of a population is the amount of interaction between individuals."[222] He has stated, "[o]nce human progress started, it was no longer limited by the size of human brains. Intelligence became collective and cumulative."[223] This collective intelligence was brought about by exchange–trade, and trade lead to centralized institutions.[224] Also, more dense societies had more collective intelligence.[225]

One of the advantages of living in groups is division of labor and specialization. As Professor Ridley has declared: "Specialization is the means by which exchange encourages innovation: In getting better at making your product or delivering your service, you come up with new tools."[226] Of course, this specialization is one of the hallmarks of individuality.[227]

Man can live in large groups because humans are innately able "to monitor social behavior in large groups so that we may access the value of cooperation, the risk of noncooperation, and so on."[228] Under the social contract, most "people don't mind paying 'their fair share,' once they are convinced that (1) it is in fact fair, and (2) others are doing the same."[229] On the other hand, people stop cooperating when others are cheating.[230] Cheating violates and undermines the social contract.

Societies must, therefore, be able to control cheaters (freeriders) and prevent excessive status-seeking. Of course, this applies to government officials, as well as citizens, because under behavioral biology government officials are the servants of the people.[231] Punishment is the glue that holds societies together; without punishment, society would fall apart.[232] Animals expend energy (use resources) to reduce or avoid punishment.[233] For example, "laws against racism do have an effect because one of the more appealing aspects of human nature is that people calculate the consequences of their activities."[234] When individuals are punished, "the individuals in the group benefit because they are less likely to be subject to violence, theft, or cheating,"[235] thus increasing their chances of surviving and reproducing. For example, gossip, which affects reputation, may have evolved as an early way to restrain cheaters by limiting their reproductive opportunities and opportunities for cooperation.[236] Similarly, as Professor Haidt has averred: "the combination of language and a full theory of mind made it possible for large groups of non-kin to reap the benefits of cooperation by monitoring each other's behavior (with gossip), shunning or punishing cheaters, and rewarding team players. . ."[237] In large groups, incarceration is often an effective means of punishment because incarceration limits the cheater's reproduction chances.

Behavioral biologists believe that the human brain has a special module to detect social cheaters.[238] For example, facial expressions and voice tone can often reveal a cheater because of the effect of the underlying emotions.[239] Similarly, humans' shared emotions, which are triggered when cheating occurs, motivates societies to punish cheaters.[240] People even punish cheaters when it is costly to themselves (altruistic punishment) because punishing cheaters promotes cooperation and it is a fitness indicator for sexual selection.[241] Alternatively, it might be immoral not to punish cheaters. Significantly, the cost of punishing cheating is reduced when undertaken by a group.[242] Moreover, because culture is learned through observation and is passed from generation to generation, punishment becomes a behavioral-cultural norm, thus allowing "the outcome of punishment to be learned without personal transgression."[243] In addition, punishment and law help to create trust within the group.[244] In sum, law and punishment help maintain reciprocal altruism within a group when the opportunity for personal interaction is impossible because of the group's size.[245]

VIII. Cautionary Notes

Behavioral biologists do not believe that what is natural is necessarily good or that nature creates "musts."[246] What was adaptive on the savanna may no longer be proper today.[247] Obviously, violence was part of our evolutionary past, but this is not a human behavioral trait that we want to encourage in our modern world. In addition, "[t]he proper evolutionary use of a domain may be quite different from its current use."[248] Consequently, as Professor Wilson has noted, our innate characteristics "have to be played like a musical instrument, with some parts stressed to produce results of great beauty and pleasure (by terms of the human limbic system) and other parts sublimated and averted."[249] Therefore, "[t]he step from *is* to *ought* requires a special justification."[250] For instance, "if there is a kind of 'natural' tendency for male domination, but we find it morally obligatory that females have the same moral status as males, biological knowledge can help us determine what the most promising course of action will be to counter the 'natural' tendency that we cannot justify."[251] On the other hand, "[n]ature may. . . limit what is morally possible, and suggest ways in which humans . . . are motivated into action."[252]

One reason to base law on biology is that it is easier to adopt a positive natural trait than repress it since it is part of the human behavioral system.[253] As Professor McEwan has noted, "[i]f there are human universals that transcend culture, then it follows that they do not change, or they do not change easily."[254] Or as Professor Ridley has stated, "[n]urture always reinforces nature; it rarely fights it."[255] More specifically, "[s]hared institutions of justice are not easily altered, regardless of their source. . . . It is unlikely that the shared intuition that serious wrongdoing should be punished can be changed through social engineering, at least not through methods short of the kind of coercive indoctrination that liberal democracies find unacceptable."[256] Therefore, it would be easier and more efficient to enforce positive human traits, than repress them.

Equally important, normative statements about law should be predicated on facts; "ought" needs to be grounded in "is." As Professors Haidt & Bjorklund have declared: "If moral facts are anthropocentric facts, then it follows that normative ethics cannot be done in a vacuum, applicable to any rational creature anywhere in the universe."[257] Furthermore, "[w]hen not properly grounded, entire schools of metaethics can be invalidated by empirical studies. . .,"[258] and, as will be discussed in detail in the Conclusion, wrong views of human behavior have caused great human suffering. Consequently, theories about law should not contradict scientific facts, but rather be grounded in science.

Notes

1. GEORGE C. WILLIAMS, ADAPTION AND NATURAL SELECTION 16 (1966).

2. PAUL THAGARD, THE BRAIN AND THE MEANING OF LIFE 42-66 (2010).

3. *Id.*

4. *Id.* at 44.

5. *Id.*

6. *Id.* at 44-45. In other words, electricity does not actually pass across the synaptic gap; the chemical neurotransmitter sends the signal.

7. *Id.* at 45.

8. *Id.* at 8.

9. *Id.* at 46.

10. *E.g.*, MICHAEL S. GAZZANIGA, HUMAN: THE SCIENCE BEHIND WHAT MAKES US UNIQUE 133-34 (2008) and other articles cited in this study. More specifically, "[e]volutionary psychology uses all the standard methods of investigation available to psychologists, including laboratory experiments, observational techniques, questionnaires, physiological techniques, mechanical recording devices, genetic methods, and brain imaging techniques. . . [as well as] comparative analyses across specie, ethnographic records, archeological records, paleontological data, and life-history data." Jamie C. Conifer et. al., *Evolutionary Psychology: Controversies, Questions, Prospects, and Limitations*, 65 AM. PSYCHOLOGIST 110, 112 (2010).

11. *E.g.*, GAZZANIGA, *supra*, at 119-20 and other articles cited in this study.

12. *E.g.*, GAZZANIGA, *supra*, at 165-68 and other articles cited in this study.

13. *E.g.*, Raffaele Caterina, *Comparative Law and the Cognitive Revolution*, 78 TUL. L. REV. 1501 (2004) and articles cited therein.

14. *E.g.*, GAZZANIGA, *supra*, at 38-75 and other articles cited in this study.

15. *E.g.*, GAZZANIGA, *supra*, at 124-26, 168-71 and other articles cited in this study.

16. *E.g.*, GAZZANIGA, *supra*, at 175-76 and other articles cited in this study.

17. Confer et. al., *supra*, at 112.

18. *Id.* at 112-113. "[H]undreds of empirical studies have been conducted to test a variety of evolutionary psychology hypotheses." *Id.* at 113.

19. STEVEN PINKER, THE BLANK SLATE: THE MODERN DENIAL OF HUMAN NATURE 55 (2002); *see also* MARC D. HAUSER, MORAL MINDS: HOW NATURE DESIGNED OUR UNIVERSAL SENSE OF RIGHT AND WRONG 291 (2006) ("The logic of natural selection suggests that the mind is equipped with specialized reasoning abilities designed to solve specific adaptive problems."); *see also* Frans de Waal, *Does Evolution Explain Human Nature?* Obviously, Says the Monkey, *in* DOES EVOLUTION EXPLAIN HUMAN NATURE 4 (John Templeton Foundation 2009). Most human characteristics, including behavioral traits, developed millions of years ago when our ancestors were hunters and gathers. Bailey Kuklin, *Peril Invites Rescue: An Evolutionary Perspective*, 35 HOFSTRA L. REV. 171, 178 (2006) [hereinafter Kuklin, *Rescue*].

20. Edward O. Wilson, *Foreword* to DONALD PFAFF, THE NEUROSCIENCE OF FAIR PLAY: WHY WE (USUALLY) FOLLOW THE GOLDEN RULE ix (2007) [hereinafter Wilson, *Fair Play Foreword*].

21. Bernd Graefrath, *Darwinism: Neither Biologistic nor Metaphysical, in* DARWINISM & PHILOSOPHY 364, 367-68 (Vittorio Hösle & Christian Illies eds., 2005) ("Darwinism gives a most plausible biological explanation of the origins of the human brain with all its capacities." *Id.* at 368); Sharon Street, *A Darwinian Dilemma for Realist Theories of Value*, 127 PHIL. STUD. 109, 113 (2006). For example, Professor Hauser believes that humans possess an innate morality, which is "more like growing a limb than sitting in Sunday school and learning about vices and virtues. . ." HAUSER, *supra*, at xviii; *see also* PINKER, *supra*, at 55; Leda Cosmides & John Tooby, *Cognitive Adaptions for Social Exchange, in* THE ADAPTED MIND: EVOLUTIONARY PSYCHOLOGY AND THE GENERATION OF CULTURE 19, 163 (Jerome H. Barkow, Leda Cosmides, & John Tooby eds., 1992); William D. Casebeer & Patricia S. Churchland, *The Neural Mechanisms of Moral Cognition: A Multiple Aspect Approach to Moral Judgment and Decision-Making*, 18 BIOLOGY & PHIL. 169, 170 (2003).

22. GAZZANIGA, *supra*, at 19; *see also* PINKER, *supra*, at 303 ("These psychologists have argued that human thinking and decision making are biological adaptions rather than engines of pure rationality.").

23. Confer et. al., *supra*, at 110 ("psychological adaptions too have evolved because they solved problems related to survival and reproduction. . ."); Paul H. Robinson et. al., *The Origins of Shared Intuitions of Justice*, 60 VAND. L. REV. 1633, 1644 (2007).

24. Confer et. al., *supra*, at 111.

25. Owen D. Jones & Timothy H. Goldsmith, *Law and Behavioral Biology*, 105 COLUM. L. REV. 405, 454-55 (2005).

26. *Id.* at 455.

27. *Id.*

28. *Id.*

29. Richard D. Alexander, *Evolutionary Selection and the Nature of Humanity, in* DARWINISM & PHILOSOPHY 301, 325 (Vittorio Hösle & Christian Illies eds., 2005). "Although natural selection is not the only mechanism of evolution (e.g., mutation, migration, genetic drift), it is the primary means of modification and the only evolutionary force capable of producing functional organization." Aaron T. Goetz & Todd K. Shackelford, *Modern Application of Evolutionary Theory to Psychology: Key Concepts and Clarifications*, 119 AM. J. PSYCH. 567, 570 (2006).

30. Kuklin, *Rescue, supra*, at 178. "A gene is a region of DNA that occupies a specific location on a chromosome." GAZZANIGA, *supra*, at 33.

31. HAUSER, *supra*, at 312; *see also* Cosmides & Tooby, *supra*, at 167 ("If a change in an organism's design allows it to outreproduce the alternative design in the population, then that design change will become more common–*it will be selected for*."). In addition, "the fitness of a gene is determined, at least partially, by its ability to coordinate well with the other genes it finds itself with in its particular genome." Bailey Kuklin, *Evolution, Politics and Law*, 38 VAL. U.L. REV. 1129, 1135 (2004) [hereinafter Kuklin, *Politics*].

32. Brian Boyd, *Evolutionary Theories of Art, in* THE LITERARY ANIMAL: EVOLUTION AND THE NATURE OF NARRATIVE 147, 148 (Jonathan Gottschall & David Sloan Wilson eds., 2005); *see also* Cosmides & Tooby, *supra*, at 164 ("[C]omplex adaptions are constructed in response to evolutionarily long-enduring problems. . ."). Psychological adaptions "are information-processing circuits that take in delimited units of information and transform that information into functional output designed to solve a particular adaptive problem." Confer et. al., *supra*, at 111.

33. John O. McGinnis, *The Human Constitution and Constitutive Law: A Prolegomenon*, 8 J. CONTEMP. LEGAL ISSUES 211, 223-24 (1997).

34. MATT RIDLEY, THE RED QUEEN: SEX AND THE EVOLUTION OF HUMAN NATURE 14 (2003) [hereinafter RIDLEY, RED QUEEN].

35. Confer et. al., *supra*, at 111.

36. *Id.*

37. *Id.*

38. Kuklin, *Peril, supra*, at 194-95.

39. *Id.*; PINKER, *supra*, at 252; RICHARD DAWKINS, THE SELFISH GENE 146 (2006).

40. Kuklin, *Peril, supra*, at 196-97; PINKER, *supra*, at 252 ("Males compete, females choose; males seek quantity, females quality.").

41. Kuklin, *Peril, supra*, at 205; RIDLEY, RED QUEEN, *supra*, at 14.

42. Kuklin, *Peril, supra*; *see also* ANTHONY WALSH, BIOSOCIOLOGY: AN EMERGING PARADIGM 209, 211 (1995).

43. Kuklin, *Peril, supra*, at 197-98.

44. *Id.* at 198; RIDLEY, RED QUEEN, *supra*, at 16.

45. GAZZANIGA, *supra*, at 52 (It appears our brains have neuronal circuits that have developed over evolutionary time that do indeed do specific jobs." *Id.* at 127.); Wilson, *Fair Play Foreword, supra*, at x; Robinson et. al., *supra*, at 1659-60; PINKER, *supra*, at 40, 219; Cosmides & Tooby, *supra*, at 209. Professor Ridley has stated that "[n]eurologists can produce battalions of case histories to support the idea that particular parts of the mind correspond to particular parts of the brain with little variation all over the world." MATT RIDLEY, THE AGILE GENE: HOW NATURE TURNS ON NURTURE 64 (2003).

46. HAUSER, *supra*, at 291. Professor Pinker thinks we have at the least 1) an intuitive physics, 2) an intuitive version of biology or natural history, 3) an intuitive engineering, 4) an intuitive psychology, 4) a spatial sense, 5) a number sense, 6) a sense of probability, 7) an intuitive economics, 8) a mental database and logic, and 9) language. PINKER, *supra*, at 220-221. Professor Rubin has pointed out that specialized modules developed because a general purpose mind that could deal with everything on the savannah was too costly. PAUL RUBIN, DARWINIAN POLITICS: THE EVOLUTIONARY ORIGIN OF FREEDOM 27 (2002).

47. GAZZANIGA, *supra*, at 52.

48. PINKER, *supra*, at 40.

49. GAZZANIGA, *supra*, at 128.

50. Richard H. Thompson & Larry W. Swanson, Hypothesis-Driven Structural Connectivity Analysis Supports Network Over Hierarchical Model of Brain Architecture, 107 PNAS 15235 (2010).

51. GAZZANIGA, *supra*, at 9 ("Brain imaging studies have revealed that specific parts of the brain are active for specific types of information."); Robinson et. al., *supra*, at 1659-64; HAUSER, *supra*, at 220-23; Casebeer & Churchland, *supra*, at 178-79; *see generally* GIACOMO RIZZOLATTI & CORRADO SINIGAGLIA, MIRRORS IN THE BRAIN–HOW OUR MINDS SHARE ACTIONS AND EMOTIONS (2008); MARCO IACOBONI, MIRRORING PEOPLE: THE NEW SCIENCE OF HOW WE CONNECT WITH OTHERS (2008). FMRI scans measure brain activity by examining blood flow in the brain. For a more detailed explanation of the fMRI, see IACOBONI, *supra*,

at 59-60.

52. Confer et. al., *supra*, at 120 ("Evolutionary psychology forcefully rejects a genetic determinism stance. . ."); PINKER, *supra*, at 112-13, 174-85.

53. PINKER, *supra*, at 74, 75-78. Professor Ridley has written: "Genes work in huge teams and build the organism and its instincts not directly but through a flexible process of development." RIDLEY, AGILE GENE, *supra*, at 129.

54. RIDLEY, AGILE GENE, supra, at 26.

55. *Id.* at 31-33; *see also id.* at 235 ("genes come with DNA switches"). This means that different species may have the same gene, but they function differently because promoter genes cause them to turn on or off for different lengths of time. *Id.* at 45.

56. *E.g.*, Robinson et. al., *supra*, at 1641; RIDLEY, AGILE GENE, *supra*, at 24.

57. Pinker, *supra*, at 40; *see also* RIDLEY, AGILE GENE, *supra*, at 273 (The cause of behavior lies in a circular, not a linear, system.); Owen D. Jones, *Evolutionary Analysis in the Law: Some Objections Considered*, 67 Brook. L. Rev. 207, 214-15 (2001) ("Brains exist because natural selection has favored information-processing, behavior-biasing machines, the benefits of which (measured in contributions to genetic fitness) have historically exceeded the costs (measured in, for example, energy, as well as the material necessary for building and running a large and energy-hungry brain.").

58. Confer et. al., *supra*, at 120 (Evolutionary psychology supports an "interactionist framework that invokes the role of the environment at every step of the casual process."); Alexander, *supra*, at 308; DAWKINS, *supra*, at 37.

59. PINKER, *supra*, at 39.

60. As E. O. Wilson has observed, "[h]uman behavior is determined by neither genes nor culture but instead by a complex interaction of these two prescribing forces, with biology guiding and environment specifying." E. O. Wilson, *Foreword from the Scientific Side, in* THE LITERARY ANIMAL: EVOLUTION AND THE NATURE OF NARRATIVE viii (Jonathan Gottschall and David Sloan Wilson eds., 2005) [hereinafter Wilson, *Foreword.*]; *see also* Jones, *supra*, at 211 ("[S]ome of the different behaviors we observe, from different individuals, can be traced not to different genes, but rather to widely-shared species-typical information processing algorithms that encounter different environmental contexts."); E. Donald Elliot, *Law and Biology: The New Synthesis*, 41 ST. LOUIS L.J. 595, 598 (1997).

61. DAWKINS, *supra*, at xiv.

62. *Id.* at ix, 11. Dawkins has stated that that "[w]e are survival machines–robot vehicles blindly programmed to preserve the selfish molecules known as genes." *Id.* at xxi. Professor Ridley has noted that "[c]ooperating to build a body is [an] effective survival strategy for genes." RIDLEY, RED QUEEN, *supra*, at 93.

63. PINKER, *supra*, at 199; *see generally* DAWKINS, *supra*.

64. Alexander, *supra*, at 309.

65. Mark F. Grady & Michael T. McGuire, *A Theory of the Origin of Natural Law*, 8 J. CONTEMP. LEGAL ISSUES 87, 93 (1997).

66. RIDLEY, RED QUEEN, *supra*, at 16.

67. Morris B. Hoffman, *The Neuroeconomic Path of the Law*, 359 PHIL. TRANS. R. SOC. LOND. B. 1667, 1674 (2004); *see also* DAVID P. BARASH, THE SURVIVAL GAME: HOW GAME THEORY EXPLAINS THE BIOLOGY OF COOPERATION AND COMPETITION 216 (2003) ("It is now widely acknowledged that evolution does not operate for the good of species, but rather, via the disparities in success of different individuals and–better yet–of competing genes."); HAUSER, *supra*, at 311 ("From the gene's eye-view, the way to think about the evolution of moral behavior is to think selfishly.").

68. Alexander, *supra*, at 311; *see also* HAUSER, *supra*, at 311 ("We act nicely to kin because our genetic posterity is wrapped up in theirs.").

69. PINKER, *supra*, at 242. For example, the chances of a brother and sister sharing a gene is 50%. DAWKINS, *supra*, at 90.

70. Alexander, *supra*, at 311. Of course, nepotism can be a serious problem in public life. PINKER, *supra*, at 245.

71. GOLDSMITH, *supra*, at 39; *see also* Kuklin, *Politics*, *supra*, at 1137.

72. DAWKINS, *supra*, at 94.

73. Alexander, *supra*, at 325; PINKER, *supra*, at 243, 255 ("Altruism can also evolve when organisms trade favors." *Id.* at 243.); James K. Rilling et. al., *A Neural Basis for Social Cooperation*, 35 NEURON 395, 403 (2002) ("Cooperative social interactions with nonkin are persuasive in all human societies and generally emerge from relationships based on reciprocal altruism.") [hereinafter Rilling et. al., *Social Cooperation*]. Professor Hauser has noted that "[h]umans appear to be uniquely endowed with a capacity that enables large-scale cooperation among unrelated individuals, and to support stable relationships that rely on reciprocity." HAUSER, *supra*, at 411.

74. Alexander, *supra*, at 325; *see also* Vittorio Hösle, *Objective Idealism and Darwinism*, *in* DARWINISM & PHILOSOPHY 216, 228 (Vittorio Hösle & Christian Illies eds., 2005) ("If the ratio of the gain in inclusive fitness to loss in inclusive fitness exceeds the reciprocal of the average coefficient of relationship, then such a behavior may evolve because it is in the selfish gene's interest. Analogously, reciprocal altruism can occur if, and only if, the diminution of fitness linked to the altruistic act is more than compensated for by the advantages the organism receives when it is the beneficiary of the altruistic act."); Neel P. Parekh, *Note: When Nice Guys Finish First: The Evolution of Cooperation, the Study of Law and the Ordering of Legal Regimes*, 37 U. MICH. J. L. REFORM 909, 925 (2004) ("Game theorists who embraced the neo-Darwinian dictates of micro-evolution have shown that organisms that cooperate prevail over those who do not."). Professor Street has observed that reciprocal altruism evolved just like other human traits: "Just as we may see a reflexive mechanism as effecting a pairing between the circumstances of a hot surface and the response of withdrawing one's hand, so may we view this evaluative judgment as effecting a pairing between the circumstances of one's being helped and the response of being helped in return." Street, *supra*, at 127. The point is that both promoted the reproductive success of those who had these traits. *Id.* at 127-28.

75. Alexander, *supra*, at 327; DAWKINS, *supra*, at 2.

76. PINKER, *supra*, at 243.

77. TIMOTHY H. GOLDSMITH, THE BIOLOGICAL ROOTS OF HUMAN NATURE 119 (1991) ("Your interests, both reproductive and somatic, are best served if you have the goodwill of your peers because you are more likely to be assisted in the future.").

78. Kuklin, *Rescue*, *supra*, at 187. Neel Parekh has stated that "[t]he brain actively embodies those algorithms required to negotiate the environment of evolutionary adoption." Parekh, *supra*, at 914-15 (2004).

79. Rilling et. al., *Social Cooperation*, *supra*, at 395.

80. Alexander, *supra*, at 328.

81. *Id.*

82. HAUSER, *supra*, at 411.

83. *Id.*

84. Terrence Chorvat & Kevin McCabe, *The Brain and the Law*, 359 PHIL. TRANS. R. SOC. LOND. B 1727, 1729 (2004).

85. DAWKINS, *supra*, at 189.

86. GAZZANIGA, *supra*, at 131.

87. Alexander, *supra*, at 328; James K. Rilling et. al., *The Neural Correlates to the Affective Response to Unreciprocated Cooperation*, 46 NEUROPSYCOLOGIA 1256, 1256 (2007) ("The evolutionary stability of this system depends on recognition of and discrimination against non-reciprocators, and the human mind is apparently specialized for detecting non-reciprocators) [hereinafter Rilling et. al., *Neural Correlates*]; William Ty Mayton, *Birthright Citizenship and the Civic Minimum*, 22 GEO. IMMIGR. L.J. 221, 256 (2008).

88. Hösle, *supra*, at 229; *see also* Parekh, *supra*, at 936.

89. Rilling et. al., *Neural Correlates*, *supra*, at 1263, 1265; HAUSER, *supra*, at 272, 287 ("[H]umans are good at detecting free riders, cheaters who try to take advantage of the goodwill of others." *Id.* at 272); Alexander, *supra*, at 329; PINKER, *supra*, at 243, 255 (Humans "remember each other as individuals . . . ., and they have an eagle eye and a flypaper memory for cheaters." *Id.* at 255); James K. Rilling et. al., *Opposing BOLD Responses to Reciprocated and Unreciprocated Altruism in Putative Reward Pathways*, 15 NEUROREPORT 2539, 2543 (2004) ("Our results are therefore consistent with the hypothesis that the mesolimbic dopamine system computes errors in predicting about whether a social partner will reciprocate an act of altruism. This error signal may teach us to seek out reciprocators and avoid nonreciprocators as social partners.") [hereinafter Rilling et. al., *Putative Reward Pathways*]; Alan G. Sanfey et. al., *The Neural Basis of Economic Decision-Making in the Ultimate Game*, 300 SCIENCE 1755, 1755 (2003) ("[S]ignificantly heightened activity in anterior insula for rejected unfair offers suggests an important role for emotions in decision-making."); Valerie E. Stone et. al., *Selective Impairment of Reasoning about Social Exchange in a Patient with Bilateral System* Damage, 99 PROC. NAT'L ACAD. SCI. USA 11531 (2002) ("[H]umans' cognition architecture reliably develops functionally distinct procedures designed for reasoning about social exchange and detection of cheaters." *Id.* at 11535); *see also* Cosmides & Tooby, *supra*, at 205-06.

90. Mayton, *supra*, at 256; *see also* Chorvat & McCabe, *supra*, at 1735 ("It is likely that punishment of violations will always have to be part of the arsenal of any government authority, because of the heterogeneity of the population.").

91. Rilling et. al., *Neural Correlates*, *supra*, at 1257; Barash, *supra*, at105 ("Our species is even equipped with brain regions specialized for recognizing the faces of others, and it is at least possible that face recognition is itself crucial to reciprocating, TIT-FOR-TAT systems.").

92. Alexander, *supra*, at 329; *see also* HAUSER, *supra*, at 216 ("In the case of altruism, we imagine what someone else's mental state will be like if we do something nice for them."); Joseph Carroll, *Human Nature and Literary Meaning: A Theoretical Model Illustrated with a Critique of* Pride and Prejudice," *in* THE LITERARY ANIMAL: EVOLUTION AND THE NATURE OF NARRATIVE 87 (Jonathan Gottschall and David Sloan Wilson eds., 2005). Similarly, Professor Hauser has written, "[a]lthough seemingly quite straightforward, reciprocity requires substantial psychological machinery, including the capacity to quantify costs and benefits, store these in memory, recall prior interactions, time the returns, detect and punish cheaters, and recognize the contingencies between giving and receiving." HAUSER, *supra*, at 380.

93. HAUSER, *supra*, at 274.

94. Kuklin, *Peril*, *supra*, at 192-93 ("[T]he person with a history of altruistic behavior is more likely to reciprocate, as are friends and acquaintances."); Alexander, *supra*, at 328; PINKER, *supra*, at 243; *see also* Parekh, *supra*, at 946-49.

95. Rilling et. al., *Neural Correlates*, *supra*, at 1256; Samuel McClure et. al., *Separate Neural Systems Value Immediate and Delayed Monetary Rewards*, 306 SCIENCE 503 (2004); Rilling et. al., *Social Cooperation*, *supra*, at 395; Rilling et. al., *Putative Reward Pathways*, *supra*, at 2539; Sanfey et. al., *supra*, at 1755; Kevin McCabe et. al., *A Functional Imaging Study of Cooperation in Two-Person Reciprocal Exchange*, 98 PROC. NAT'L ACAD. SCI. 11832 (2001).

96. The authors describe a reiterated Prisoner's Dilemma game as:

> In this game, two players independently choose to either cooperate with each other or not, and each is awarded a sum of money that depends upon the interaction of both players' choices in that round. There are four possible outcomes of a round: player A and player B cooperate (CC), player A cooperates and player B defects (CD), player A defects and player B cooperates (DC), or player A and player B defect (DD). The payoffs for the outcomes are arranged such that DC > CC > DD > CD, and CC > (CD + DC)/2. Each cell of the payoff matrix [not included] corresponds to a different outcome of a social interaction. DC represents the situation where player A opts for noncooperation and player B cooperates so that player A benefits at player B's expense. CD is the converse. CC involves mutual cooperation, and DD involves mutual noncooperation. Rilling et. al., *Social Cooperation*, *supra*, at 395.

97. *Id.*

98. *Id.*

99. Rilling et. al., *Neural Correlates*, *supra*, at 1265.

100. *Id.*

101. Sanfey et. al., *supra*, at 1755.

102. Paul J. Zak et. al., *The Neurobiology of Trust*, 1032 ANNALS N.Y. ACAD. SCI. 224, 226 (2004).

103. HAUSER, *supra*, at 254.

104. Cosmides & Tooby, *supra*, at 170; *see also* Robinson et. al, *supra*, at 1683 ("Evolutionary explanations, dependent as they are on evolutionary evolved mechanisms that all humans share, fit naturally with human universals.").

105. Carroll, *supra*, at 91.

106. *E.g.*, NOAM CHOMSKY, KNOWLEDGE OF LANGUAGE: ITS NATURE, ORIGINS, AND USE (1986) [hereinafter CHOMSKY, KNOWLEDGE OF LANGUAGE]; CHOMSKY, REFLECTIONS ON LANGUAGE (1975). "There seems no doubt now that language is an instinct, or at least has a strong genetic component. In fact the evidence is so strong, one wonders why it was ever doubted." PETER WATSON, THE MODERN MIND: AN INTELLECTUAL HISTORY OF THE 20ᵀᴴ CENTURY 695 (2000).

107. CHOMSKY, KNOWLEDGE OF LANGUAGE, *supra*, at 12-13.

108. *Id.* at 25.

109. *Id.* at 24.

110. CHOMSKY, REFLECTIONS ON LANGUAGE, *supra*, at 13.

111. *Id.* at 4.

112. CHOMSKY, KNOWLEDGE OF LANGUAGE, *supra*, at 272; CHOMSKY, REFLECTIONS ON LANGUAGE, *supra*, at 13 ("Every 'theory of learning' that is even worth considering incorporates an innateness hypothesis.").

113. PINKER, *supra*, at 37 (emphasis deleted).

114. *Id.* at 41.

115. *Id.* at 39.

116. DONALD E. BROWN, HUMAN UNIVERSALS (1991), *summarized in* PINKER, *supra*, at 435-39.

117. PINKER, *supra*, at 294 (citations omitted).

118. RIDLEY, RED QUEEN, *supra*, at 101; *see also* STEVEN LUKES, MORAL RELATIVISM 54 (2008) ("Across all cultures humans seem to show the same automatic emotional responses to social interactions (indicated by facial expressions).").

119. De Waal, *supra*, at 5.

120. RIDLEY, RED QUEEN, *supra*, at 12. This process is called "meiosis," where the male selects the genes that go into the sperm and the female into the egg. *Id.* at 29-30.

121. *Id.* at 57, 65-67.

122. *Id.* at 19, 175.

123. *Id.* at 133, 178.

124. *Id.* at 138.

125. *Id.* at 133.

126. EDWARD O. WILSON, ON HUMAN NATURE 138 (1978) [hereinafter WILSON, ON HUMAN NATURE].

127. WALSH, *supra*, at 202.

128. WILSON, ON HUMAN NATURE, *supra*, at 137.

129. WALSH, *supra*, at 205.

130. *Id.* at 202.

131. *Id.* at 207; RIDLEY, RED QUEEN, *supra*, at 191.

132. WALSH, *supra*, at 209 ("Most primate fathers are unable to identify their offspring, let alone form a bonded relationship with them." *Id.* at 211.).

133. *Id.* at 211.

134. Antonio Damasio, *Does Moral Action Depend on Reasoning? Yes and No, in* DOES MORAL ACTION DEPEND ON REASONING? 46-47 (John Templeton Foundation 2010).

135. DAWKINS, *supra*, at 125. "Parental investment is any investment by the parent in the individual offspring that increases the offspring's chance of surviving at the cost of the parent's ability to invest in other offspring." GAZZANIGA, *supra*, at 86.

136. DAWKINS, *supra*, at 125.

137. *Id.*

138. *Id.* at 129.

139. *Id.* at 111-12.

140. *Id.* at 117.

141. Jones & Goldsmith, *supra*, at 432-438.

142. *Id.*

143. Street, *supra*, at 109, 113-114; HAUSER, *supra*, at xvii, 36, 53-54, 419-20; PINKER, *supra*, at 187-88, 193; Casebeer & Churchland, *supra*, at 170 ("[M]oral reasoning will involve a series of cognitive acts that issue in a conclusion (either implicit or explicit) about what one *ought* to *do* or *think*."); Jonathan Haidt, *The Emotional Dog and Its Rational Tail: A Social Intuitionist Approach to Moral Justice*, 108 PSYCHOL. REV. 814 , 814 (2001) ("Institutionalism in philosophy refers to the view that there are moral truths . . ."); 1 CHARLES DARWIN, THE DESCENT OF MAN, AND SELECTION IN RELATION TO SEX 166 (1871) ("Advancement in the standard of morality will certainly give an immense advantage to one tribe over another."); *see also* Sam HARRIS, THE MORAL LANDSCAPE: HOW SCIENCE CAN DETERMINE HUMAN VALUES 56 (2010) ("Because moral virtue is attractive to both sexes, it might function as a kind of peacock's tail, costly to produce and maintain, but beneficial to one's genes in the end.").

144. Susan Dwyer, *How Good is the Linguist Analogy?*, *in* 2 THE INNATE MIND: CULTURE AND COGNITION 247 (Peter Carruthers et. al. eds., 2007).

145. GAZZANIGA, *supra*, at 118; HAUSER, *supra*, at xvii, 2, 67, 425 ("[W]e are endowed with a moral instinct, a faculty of the human mind that unconsciously guides our judgments concerning right and wrong, establishing a range of learnable moral systems, each with a set of shared and unique signatures." *Id.* at 425); Casebeer & Churchland, *supra*, at 185; Haidt, *supra*, at 814 ("In the social intuitionist model it becomes plausible to say, 'I don't know, I can't explain it, I just know it's wrong."). Professor Haidt added: "Affective evaluation occurs so quickly, automatically, and persuasively that it is generally thought to be an integral part of perception." Haidt, *supra*, at 819. He continued that "[t]hese flashes of intuition are not dumb; as with the superb mental software that runs visual perception, they often hide a great deal of sophisticated processing occurring behind the scenes." Jonathan Haidt & Fredrik Bjorklund, *Social Intuitionists Answer Six Questions About Moral Psychology*, *in* 2 MORAL PSYCHOLOGY 188 (W. Sinnott-Armstrong ed., 2006).

146. GAZZANIGA, *supra*, at 116-17; Robinson et. al., *supra*, at 1645-46.

147. Casebeer & Churchland, *supra*, at 185; Haidt, *supra*, at 817. Professor Haidt has asserted that "[t]he social intuitionist model, therefore, is not an antirationalist model. It is a model about the complex and dynamic ways that intuition, reasoning, and social influences interact to produce moral judgement." Haidt, *supra*, at 829; *see also* Street, *supra*, at 120, 123 ("The view I am suggesting by no means involves thinking of us as automatons who simply endorse whatever evaluative tendencies are implanted in us by evolutionary and other forces." *Id.* at 123); Cass R. Sunstein, *Moral Heuristics*, 28 BEHAV. & BRAIN SCI. 531, 533 (2005)

("System I proposes quick answers to problems of judgment, and System II operates as a monitor confirming or overruling these judgments."). Professors Mullen and Skitka have suggested that people "tend to shift into a more thoughtful and analytical mode of reasoning when they experience something negative or unexpected. . . ." Elizabeth Mullen & Linda J. Skitka, *Exploring the Psychological Underpinnings of the Moral Mandate Effect: Motivated Reasoning, Group Differentiation, or Anger?*, 90 J. PERSONALITY & SOC. PSYCH. 629, 631 (2006).

148. LUKES, *supra*, at 51.

149. Haidt & Bjorklund, *supra*, at 192-93.

150. Joshua Greene, *Does Moral Action Depend on Reasoning? Less Than It Should*, *in* DOES MORAL ACTION DEPEND ON REASONING? 27-30 (John Templeton Foundation 2010).

151. Chris D. Firth and Tania Singer, *The Role of Social Cognition in Decision Making*, 363 PHIL. TRANS. R. SOC. B. 3875, 3883 (2008). They add that "decisions dictated by reason are not always good, while decisions dictated by emotion are not always bad." *Id.* at 3884.

152. DONALD W. PFAFF, THE NEUROSCIENCE OF FAIR PLAY: WHY WE USUALLY FOLLOW THE GOLDEN RULE 4 (2007); Robinson et. al., *supra*, at 1662; Haidt & Bjorklund, *supra*, at 203; Chorvat & McCabe, supra, at 1728; Casebeer & Churchland, *supra*, at 172, 188.

153. HAUSER, *supra*, at 222; *see also* Casebeer & Churchland, *supra*, at 172; *see generally*, Jorge Moll et. al., *The Neural Correlates of Moral Sensitivity: A Functional Magnetic Resonance Imaging Investigation of Basic and Moral Emotions*, 22 J. NEUROSCI. 2730 (2002); Joshua Greene & Jonathan Haidt, *How (and Where) Does Moral Judgement Work*, 6 TRENDS COGNITIVE SCI. 517 (2002).

154. Haidt & Bjorklund, *supra*, at 203.

155. Joshua D. Greene et. al., *An fMRI Study of Emotional Engagement in Moral Judgment*, 293 SCIENCE 2105, 2106-07 (2001); *see also* Haidt & Bjorklund, *supra*, at 200.

156. Greene et. al., *supra*, at 2105-07; Haidt & Bjorklund, *supra*, at 200.

157. Greene et. al., *supra*, at 2106-07; Haidt & Bjorklund, *supra*, at 200.

158. Greene et. al., *supra*, at 2106-07; Haidt & Bjorklund, *supra*, at 200.

159. Professor Gommer has argued that "[e]motion is the evolutionary calculator that makes an estimation of our reproductive chances." Hendrik Gommer, *The Molecular Concept of Law*, 7 UTRECHT L. REV. 141, 147 (2011).

160. GAZZANIGA, *supra*, at 48.

161. *Id.* at 49; *see also* PINKER, *supra*, at 166 ("The faculties underlying empathy, foresight, and self-respect are information-processing systems that accept input and commandeer other parts of the body and brain.").

162. Ian McEwan, *Literature, Science, and Human Nature*, *in* THE LITERARY ANIMAL: EVOLUTION AND THE NATURE OF NARRATIVE 5 (Jonathan Gottschall & David Sloan Wilson eds., 2005); Casebeer & Churchland, *supra*, at 176-78; *see also* Rebecca Saxe, *Uniquely Human Social Cognition*, 16 CURRENT OPINION NEUROBIOLOGY 235 (2006) (Neuroscientific evidence suggests that social cognition is connected with at least five brain regions. In other words, theory of mind is modular with different parts of the mind supplying different aspects of TOM.).

163. PINKER, *supra*, at 172.

164. GAZZANIGA, *supra*, at 63; *see also* IACOBONI, *supra*, at 4; HAUSER, *supra*, at 224 (The mirror neuron system plays an essential role in moral judgments.); *see generally* RIZZOLATTI & SINIGAGLIA, *supra*; *see also* Giacomo Rizzolatti & Corrado Sinigaglia, *The Functional Role of the Parieto-Frontal Mirror Circuit: Interpretations and Misinterpretations*, 11 Nature Reviews Neuroscience 264-274 (2010) (a reply to criticisms of mirror neuron theory). One researcher has "suggested that the discovery of mirror neurons promise[s] to do for neuroscience what the discovery of DNA did for biology." IACOBONI, *supra*, at 8.

165. Casebeer & Churchland, *supra*, at 176; *see also* IACOBONI, *supra*, at 119 ([M]irror neuron areas help us understand the emotions of other people by some form of inner imitation); Haidt, *supra*, at 825.

166. IACOBONI, *supra*, at 5.

167. PFAFF, *supra*, at 79; *see also* RIZZOLATTI & SINIGAGLIA, *supra*, at xii ("Emotions, like actions, are immediately shared; the perception of pain or grief, or of disgust experienced by others activates the same areas of the cerebral cortex that are involved when we experience those emotions ourselves.").

168. Saxe, *supra*, at 237; *see also* Michael Tomasello et. al., *Understanding and Sharing Intentions: The Origins of Cultural Cognition*, 28 BEHAV. & BRAIN SCI. 675 (2005).

169. RIZZOLATTI & SINIGAGLIA, *supra*, at 173-93.

170. GAZZANIGA, *supra*, at 168. For a discussion of several brain scan studies involving mirror neurons, see RIZZOLATTI & SINIGAGLIA, *supra*, at 115-38.

171. RIZZOLATTI & SINIGAGLIA, *supra*, at 174.

172. IACOBONI, *supra*, at 114.

173. GAZZANIGA, *supra*, at 189; *see also* Jean Decety & Claus Lamm, *Empathy Versus Personal Distress: Recent Evidence from Social Neuroscience, in* THE SOCIAL NEUROSCIENCE OF EMPATHY 199, 209 (Jean Decety & William Ickes eds., 2009) ("[S]ocial neuroscience has demonstrated that the self and other are distinguished at both the behavioral and neural levels.").

174. GAZZANIGA, *supra*, at 189.

175. *Id.* at 308.

176. IACOBONI, *supra*, at 133.

177. *Id.* at 202-03.

178. HAUSER, *supra*, at 182. As Professors Haidt and Bjorklund have written: "Reasoning requires affective channeling mechanisms." Haidt & Bjorklund, *supra*, at 195.

179. HAUSER, *supra*, at 183.

180. HAUSER, *supra*, at 194; *see also* RIZZOLATTI & SINIGAGLIA, *supra*, at 185-93; IACOBONI, *supra*, at 5, 109. A group of neuroscientists have theorized that empathy has both cognitive and affective components. Simone G. Shamay-Tsoory, *Empathetic Processing: Its Cognitive and Affective Dimensions and Neuroanatomical Basis, in* THE SOCIAL NEUROSCIENCE OF EMPATHY 216 (Jean Decety & William Ickes eds., 2009); *see also* Decety & Lamm, *supra*, at 209.

181. HAUSER, *supra*, at 352.

182. Haidt, *supra*, at 824.

183. Firth & Singer, *supra*, at 3877.

184. GAZZANIGA, *supra*, at 130.

185. *Id.* at 131.

186. *Id.* at 137.

187. PFAFF, *supra*, at 22-23.

188. GAZZANIGA, *supra*, at 127; Haidt & Bjorklund, *supra*, at 183.

189. GAZZANIGA, *supra*, at 251.

190. Casebeer & Churchland, *supra*, at 175; *see also* Hoffman, *supra*, at 1669 ("[T]here is indeed a relatively fixed and immutable set of right and wrong human behaviors.").

191. DAWKINS, *supra*, at 3. He has added, "[n]atural selection favors genes that control their survival machines in such a way that they make the best use of their environment." *Id.* at 66.

192. Robinson et. al., *supra*, at 1640; Robin Bradley Kar, *The Deep Structure of Law and Morality*, 84 TEX. L. REV. 877, 887 (2006); PINKER, *supra*, at 60, 68; *see generally* JARED DIAMOND, GUNS, GERMS, AND STEEL (1997) ("History followed different courses for different people because of differences among peoples' environments, not because of biological differences among people themselves." *Id.* at 257.).

193. RIDLEY, AGILE GENE, *supra*, at 245; Wilson, *Forward*, *supra*, at viii; PINKER, *supra*, at 35, 39, 60-63 ("[T]here can be no learning without innate circuitry to do the learning."); Kuklin, Politics, *supra*, at 1172 ("[T]he ability to learn is an evolved trait.").

194. DAWKINS, *supra*, at 57.

195. RIDLEY, AGILE GENE, *supra*, at 55. He also believes that "[n]urture is affected by genes, just as much as nature is." *Id.* at 181.

196. *Id.* at 59. Ridley has written that "[e]ach child soon realizes what he or she is good at and bad at–compared with the others in the group. The child then trains for the role and not for others. . ." *Id.* at 257.

197. RIDLEY, RED QUEEN, *supra*, at 313.

198. Hoffman, *supra*, at 1672.

199. Confer et. al., *supra*, at 116.

200. PINKER, *supra*, at 39; *see also* Caterina, *supra*, at 1513 ("[W]e can say that perception of the world, recognition of certain discontinuities in the world, preceded, and do not follow, cultural elaboration."). Professor Ridley has noted, "it is hard to conceive how people can learn (be plastic) without sharing assumptions (being prepared)." RIDLEY, RED QUEEN, *supra*, at 314.

201. LUKES, *supra*, at 80.

202. *Id.* at 29-30.

203. PINKER, *supra*, at 35 ("Universal mental mechanisms can underlie superficial variation across cultures."); HAUSER, *supra*, at 74, 420-21 ("The universal moral grammar is a theory about the principles that enable children to build a large but finite range of distinctive moral systems." *Id.* at 421.); Jones & Goldsmith, *supra*, at 424 ("All species have proclivities to learn some behaviors far more easily than others.").

204. Variations among cultures do not create cultural relativism. First, as noted, all cultures share many universals. Second, also as noted, the cultural variations are created by innate structures in the mind that permit cultural learning. Finally, as Professor Arnhart has pointed out, "for any given set of circumstances, there are naturally better and worse ways to satisfy the natural desires of human beings." LARRY ARNHART,

DARWINIAN NATURAL RIGHT: THE BIOLOGICAL ETHICS OF HUMAN NATURE 39 (1998).

205. HAUSER, *supra*, at 44.

206. Graefrath, *supra*, at 370.

207. IACOBONI, *supra*, at 62; HAUSER, *supra*, at 422; PINKER, *supra*, at 63.

208. GAZZANIGA, *supra*, at 160; IACOBONI, *supra*, at 73. Imitation is "the capacity of an individual to replicate an observed act." RIZZOLATTI & SINIGAGLIA, *supra*, at 140.

209. HAUSER, *supra*, at 422; *see also id.* at 165.

210. GAZZANIGA, *supra*, at 177; *see also* RIZZOLATTI & SINIGAGLIA, *supra*, at 139-71.

211. RIZZOLATTI & SINIGAGLIA, *supra*, at 140.

212. *See* Tomasello, *supra*, at 675 ("The main point is that 1-year-old infants use their newly emerging skills of intention understanding not only to predict what others will do, but also to learn from them how to do things conventionally in their culture." *Id.* at 680.).

213. GAZZANIGA, *supra*, at 130; Haidt & Bjorklund, *supra*, at 209.

214. GAZZANIGA, *supra*, at 130; *see also* PINKER, *supra*, at 271; R.A. Shweder et. al., *The "Big Three" of Morality (Autonomy, Community, and Divinity), and the "Big Three" Explanations of Suffering*, in MORALITY AND HEALTH 119, 119-69 (A. Brandt & P. Rozin eds., 1997).

215. GAZZANIGA, *supra*, at 132.

216. BARASH, *supra*, at 129; *see also* Kar, *supra*, at 898 ("Social contract problems arise whenever we could all do better by agreeing to be bound by some standard of action if that were the price of having all (or a significant majority of) others be similarly bound."). As Professor Pinker has pointed out: "Peaceful coexistence, then, does not have to come from pounding selfish desires out of people. It can come from pitting some desires–the desire for safety, the benefits of cooperation, the ability to formulate and recognize universal codes of behavior–against the desire for immediate gain." PINKER, *supra*, at 169.

217. GAZZANIGA, *supra*, at 82. Professor Pinker has asserted that "[t]he modern theory of evolution falls smack into the social contract tradition." PINKER, *supra*, at 285.

218. GAZZANIGA, *supra*, at 82; *see also* Wilson, *Fair Play Foreword*, *supra*, at xi; BARASH, *supra*, at 133 ("In a world of social dilemmas, the pursuit of rational self-interest results in a bad payoff for everyone."); Robert Boyd et. al., *The Evolution of Altruistic Punishment*, 100 PROC. NAT'L ACA. SCI. U.S. 3531, 3531 (2003) ("It is plausible that more cooperative groups are less subject to extinction because they are more effective in warfare, more effective in coinsuring, more adept at managing common resources, or for similar reasons.").

219. GAZZANIGA, *supra*, at 83.

220. *Id.* at 88-89.

221. HAUSER, *supra*, at 60; *see also* Kar, *supra*, at 891.

222. Matt Ridley, *Humans: Why They Triumphed*, WALL ST. J. (MAY 22, 2010).

223. *Id.*

224. *Id.* He added, "[t]rade is to culture as sex is to biology." *Id.*

225. *Id.*

226. *Id.*

227. RIDLEY, AGILE GENE, *supra*, at 260.

228. GAZZANIGA, *supra*, at 80; HAUSER, *supra*, at 274 ("[I]t is likely that evolution equipped us with a specialized ability to work through the cost-benefit analysis of a social contract."). Professor Pinker has declared that "the logic of social contracts may have propelled the evolution of the mental faculties that keep us in these groups." PINKER, *supra*, at 285.

229. BARASH, *supra*, at 137.

230. Ben Seymour et. al., *The Neurobiology of Punishment*, 8 NATURE REVIEWS NEUROSCI. 300 (2007) ("In humans, however, punishment also appears to adopt an important role in promoting and preserving cooperation."); BARASH, *supra*, at 152; *see generally* Janice Nadler, *Flouting the Law*, 83 TEX. L. REV. 1399 (2005) ("When a person evaluates particular legal rules, decisions, or practices as unjust, the diminished respect for the legal system that follows can destabilize otherwise law-abiding behavior."). Professor Pinker has noted that individuals differ genetically in their selfish tendencies. PINKER, *supra*, at 261.

231. Ayn Rand had a similar view of the function of the government, identifying it with the Declaration of Independence. AYN RAND, THE VIRTUE OF SELFISHNESS 111-112, 120 (1963). She has stated, "[u]nder a proper social system, a private individual is legally free to take any action he pleases (so long as he does not violate the rights of others), while a government official is bound by law in every official act." *Id.* at 128.

232. GAZZANIGA, *supra*, at 129 ("If cheaters take over, reciprocity crumbles."); HAUSER, *supra*, at 77, 99, 390, 403-08 ("If the payoffs to defection are higher than the payoffs to cooperation, individuals defect." *Id.* at 77.); BARASH, *supra*, at 136 ("The best–perhaps the only–solution is for external contraints to force individuals to cooperate, because otherwise they won't."); Boyd et. al., *supra*, at 3533 ("[A]dding punishment sustains substantial amounts of cooperation in much larger groups."); *see generally* Özgür Gürerk et. al., *The Competitive Advantage of Sanctioning Institutions*, 312 SCIENCE 108 (2006) ("Profound empirical evidence shows that the possibility of sanctioning norm violators stabilizes human cooperation at a high level, whereas cooperation typically collapses in the absence of sanctioning possibilities."). Professor Haidt has observed that only man has "widespread third-party norm enforcement." Haidt, *supra*, at 826. Similarly, Justice Holmes stated: "If you want to know the law and nothing else, you must look at it as a bad man, who cares only for the material consequences which such knowledge enables him to predict, not as a good one, who finds his reasons for conduct, whether inside the law, or outside it, in the vaguer sanctions of conscience." Oliver Wendell Holmes, Jr., *The Path of the Law*, 10 HARV. L. REV. 457, 459 (1897).

233. Seymour et. al., *supra*, at 300.

234. RIDLEY, RED QUEEN, *supra*, at 8.

235. Robinson et. al., *supra*, at 1650.

236. GAZZANIGA, *supra*, at 94-97; *see also* HAUSER, *supra*, at 81; BARASH, *supra*, at 153 ("Also, don't overlook the role of social punishment, administered by other 'players' who stand to lose if someone in their group is stingy or a shirker.").

237. Haidt, *supra*, at 826.

238. GAZZANIGA, *supra*, at 99 ("[T]hat cheater detection device develops at an early age, operates regardless of experience and familiarity, and detects cheating but not *unintentional* violations." *Id.* at 100); HAUSER, *supra*, at 272, 276; BARASH, *supra*, at 267; Cosmides & Tooby, *supra*, at 205-06.

239. GAZZANIGA, *supra*, at 103; *see also* BARASH, *supra*, at 105, 180. Professor Harris has noted that the sclera of human eyes is white, which allows others to detect subtle changes in a person's gaze. HARRIS, *supra*, at 57.

240. Kar, *supra*, at 914.

241. Seymour, *supra*, at 306; GAZZANIGA, *supra*, at 82.

242. Robinson et. al., *supra*, at 1650-51.

243. Seymour, *supra*, at 304.

244. Chorvat & McCabe, *supra*, at 1734.

245. *Id.*

246. Graefrath, *supra*, at 370; HAUSER, *supra*, at 3. Darwin did not view evolution as necessarily leading to a positive end. Graefrath, *supra*, at 374. As Professor Pinker has observed: "The existence of inborn talents . . . does not call for Social Darwinism." PINKER, *supra*, at 150.

247. HAUSER, *supra*, at 417; *see also* Confer et. al., *supra*, at 119 ("[M]ismatches between modern and ancestral environments may negate the adaptive utility of some evolved psychological mechanisms.").

248. GAZZANIGA, *supra*, at 254; PINKER, *supra*, at 219.

249. Edward O. Wilson, Comparative Social Theory, *in* 1 THE TANNER LECTURES ON HUMAN VALUES 68-69 (Sterling M. McMurrin ed., 1980); *see also* Douglas A. Terry, *Don't Forget About Reciprocal Altruism: Critical Review of the Evolutionary Jurisprudence Movement*, 34 CONN. L. REV. 477, 502-03 (2002) ("[T]he function of law is to both condone and prohibit the manifestations of certain biological tendencies given to humans by natural selection."); GOLDSMITH, *supra*, at 67 (1991).

250. Graefrath, *supra*, at 370; *see also* PINKER, *supra*, at 164. However, although he is cautious concerning the link between the is to the ought, Professor Gommer has challenged the naturalistic fallacy (going from the is to the ought). Hendrik Gommer, *From the 'Is' to the 'Ought': A Biological Theory of Law*, 96 ARCHIV FÜR RECHTS- UND SOZIALPHILOSOPHIE 449 (2010). He argues that goodness is a biological phenomenon and that good can be defined as everything that promotes survival in a genetic sense. Another problem with the naturalistic fallacy is that it was based on dualism–that there is an external goodness against which to measure human morality. He, along with most behavioral biologists, rejects the notion of an external goodness. Under Gommer's notion, killing your neighbor is bad because it limits survival chances–the murder will be punished and he will not be able to cooperate with his neighbor. On the other hand, paying taxes is good because it helps society (it is a form of group altruism), thus helping the individual's survival changes.

251. Graefrath, *supra*, at 370; *see also* PINKER, *supra*, at 299 ("Because social conventions are not adopted to human nature alone, a respect for human nature does not require preserving all of them."); HAUSER, *supra*, at 3.

252. HAUSER, *supra*, at 4.

253. Neel Parekh has written, "[l]egal rules that ignore human realities prove inefficient." Parekh, *supra*, at 942 (2004). He has added that evolutionary analysis "directs that, where appropriate, a default rule should conform to instinctive behavior and reduce private and social costs." *Id.* at 943; *see also* Jones & Goldsmith, *supra*, at 413 ("We can consider the law effective when it gets its job done, and efficient when it does so with minimum waste.").

254. McEwan, *supra*, at 12; *see also* Wilson, *Forward*, *supra*, at ix ("Our cultures and values seem highly variable to us but in fact are very specialized and very epigaeic and diurnal mammalian.").

255. RIDLEY, RED QUEEN, *supra*, at 212.

256. Robinson et. al., *supra*, at 1687-88.

257. Haidt & Bjorklund, *supra*, at 214.

258. *Id.* at 215.

Chapter Three

Postmodern Legal Thought and Cognitive Science: Law as Wishful Thinking

To be useful to citizens and lawmakers, a claim about human nature needs
to be a claim about how the mind actually works. . .

Leda Cosmides & John Tooby[1]

Postmodernism is a major influence on contemporary jurisprudence. For example, a
recent survey showed that postmodern thinker Michael Foucault was the third most cited
philosopher in legal scholarship in 2007 and Jacques Derrida was ninth, with Karl Marx,
a significant influence on postmodernism, seventh.[2] Postmodernism has influenced
critical legal studies, feminism, pragmatism, critical race studies, and numerous other
areas of jurisprudence. It has also had an effect on doctrinal areas of the law. This
chapter will critique Postmodern Legal Thought using insights from behavioral biology.
As this chapter will show, Postmodernism is based on the denial of human nature, and
it has had a pernicious effect on the law.

Part I of this chapter will examine Postmodern Legal Thought. This Part will
include a traditional critique of Postmodernism and its most important element–strong
moral relativism. Parts II and III will illustrate how insights of behavioral biology
weaken the foundations of Postmodern Legal Thought. Part II will demonstrate how
behavioral biology has destroyed the Blank Slate (social constructionist) theory of human

nature upon which Postmodernism is based. Part III will show the existence of neurocognitive (innate) universals in the human mind, which destroys the strong moral relativism underlying Postmodernism. Finally, Part IV will present an alternative to Postmodernism's radical political theories, based on behavioral biology.

I. Postmodern Legal Thought

A. Postmodernism and Postmodern Legal Thought

Postmodernism is radically antifoundational and antitheoretical; there is no objective truth or morality.[3] As Professor Hutchinson has declared: "Postmodernism is a flat rejection of universal knowledge and an outright denial of essential truths."[4] Similarly, Professor Schanck has asserted, "there are no foundational principles from which other assertions can be derived; hence, certainty as the result of empirical investigation or deductive reasoning is impossible."[5] He has added: "[T]here can be no such thing as knowledge of reality; what we think is knowledge is always belief and can apply only to the context within which it is asserted."[6] Going further, Professor Ross has argued: "How can metaphysical theories and explanations taken seriously by millions be ignored or excluded by a small group of powerful people called scientists?"[7] Thus, Postmodernism "uses the techniques of metaphor, narrative, and storytelling for discovering surprising new insights; it justifies the use of 'situated' and 'local' critiques as a means for decentering foundational theories."[8]

Postmodernists developed this antifoundational, moral relativist viewpoint because they saw a diversity of morals among societies.[9] They thought that this diversity was fundamental (there is no universal moral deep structure) and not limited to surface differences.[10]

Because of their rejection of universals, Postmoderns stress the importance of context; moral relativism is the belief that moral norms are relative to time and place.[11] Drawing on Wittgenstein, Professor Williams has written, "understanding a rule system entails understanding the language game or form of life of which it is a part: rules function to explain the conventions commonly observed in playing the game. Breaking the rules is wrong only in the sense that, if you break enough rules consistently enough, you have ceased to play the old game and have invented a new one."[12]   Professors

Minow and Spelman have similarly declared: "Like others concerned with the failures of abstract, universal principles to resolve problems, we emphasize 'context' in order to expose how apparently neutral and universal rules in effect burden or exclude anyone who does not share the characteristics of privileged, white, Christian, able-bodied, heterosexual adult men for whom those rules were actually written."[13] Likewise, Professor Susan Williams has asserted, "truth is seen as made by human actors rather than discovered."[14] Furthermore, rather than relying on foundationalism, Postmodernists rely on contingent political arrangements of a particular community or group.[15] Finally, since Postmodernism is relativistic, one cannot judge other cultures and societies most be tolerant of other cultures' practices.[16]

Postmodernism rejects the Enlightenment concept of the autonomous self; rather, it views the self as socially imposed.[17] Professor Massey has declared: "The postmodern contention is that there is no coherent self that lies outside the disparate social discourses that inevitably construct us."[18] Professor Schanck has similarly averred, "The self is not and cannot be, an autonomous, self-generating entity; it is purely a social, cultural, historical, and linguistic creation."[19] Likewise, Professor Hutchinson has asserted, "[r]ather than think of the individual subject as a unitary and sovereign subject whose self-directed vocation is to bring the world to heel through exacting discipline of rational inquiry, postmodernism interrogates the whole idea of autonomous subjectivity and abstract reason; it places them in a constantly contingent condition of provisionality."[20] Finally, Professor Schalg has declared, "[f]or critical legal thinkers, as for Sartre, the perpetual problem is that the subject is always constrained by 'reified structures' and 'thingified social rules' and that everything turns into 'pods.'"[21] He has stated elsewhere: "It is this image of a decentered self (a self without stable center and a self that is no longer the center) that enables postmodern thinkers to speak of the contingent, mutable, and even fractured character of the self."[22]

Many postmodernists view individualism with horror.[23] Individualism is a social construct that walls us off from community.[24] Individuals are only interested in endless self-discovery and self-fulfillment.[25]

Finally, Postmodernism views reality as a social construct, with even the natural world being socially constructed.[26] Professor Litowitz has noted that the Postmodern reaction to the Enlightenment notion of "reason as a universal faculty held by all humans which could be used to articulate a set of rational, true beliefs" was "to argue that reason is not a uniform faculty in all humankind but is rather socially constructed. . ."[27] Similarly, Professors Farber and Sherry have observed, "these radical multiculturalists believe in particular that Western ideas and institutions are socially constructed to serve the interests of the powerful, especially straight, white men."[28] For example, Professor Schanck has stated: "Because language is socially and culturally constituted, it is inherently incapable of representing or corresponding to reality; hence, all propositions and all interpretations, even texts, are themselves social constructions."[29] Postmoderns believe that reality is constructed by the linguistic system in our minds and that communities with different languages live in distinct worlds.[30] Thus, Professor Massey has declared, "our minds grasp things not as they are 'in themselves' but only through concepts, signified by words."[31] In other words, language does not correspond to reality.[32]

Some Postmoderns are pragmatists who believe that, even in the absence of universal theory, they can determine what is right in individual cases.[33] Professor Williams has described Postmodern pragmatism as:

> A pragmatic approach abandons the search for a single viewpoint because it abandons the search for certainty that compels agreement. In its place, pragmatism substitutes an "edifying conversation" that views societal differences as food for thought. The pragmatist's search for a workable society is a search not for universal principles but for strategies through which a population, inevitably divided by differences over a broad range of their affairs, can seek a series of necessarily transient and provisional understandings.[34]

In other words, "[t]he realist says that statements about justice and other ethical matters can be true, but only locally so."[35]

Postmodernists often adopt a radical leftist approach to politics, and they frequently attack the Enlightenment notion of democracy.[36] Professor Litowitz has noted that "[p]art of the postmodern malaise derives from the impression that two hundred years of an 'Enlightened' quest for reason, truth, and rationality has led to the present state of gross inequality, class warfare, the death of any hope for socialism, two world wars (in this century alone), the threat of nuclear annihilation, sexism, racism, neurosis and other ills of the modern era."[37]   As Professor Hutchinson has declared: "By employing such a skeptical strategy, the political hope is to destabilize power, displace domination and dismantle hierarchy."[38] Professors Minow and Spelman have similarly argued, "[i]n the late twentieth century in the United States, those who urge contextual interpretation often point to the harmful effects of legacies of exclusion based on race, gender, class, or other group traits. They imply new normative directions for legal and political life."[39] Postmodernists believe that the selection of any theory is an assertion of power.[40]   Finally, Professor Cook has declared, "[p]ostmodern critique might be thought of as a strategy for bringing to the surface the suppressed narratives and voices drowned out by univocal projections of master narratives."[41]

Moreover, Postmodernists are often distrustful of popular sovereignty and consensus.[42] As Professor Pinker has observed:

> According to relativistic doctrines like "false consciousness," "inauthentic preferences," and "interiorized authority," people may be mistaken about their own desires. If so, it would undermine the assumptions behind democracy, which give ultimate authority to the preferences of the majority of a population, and the assumptions behind market economies, which treat people as the best judges of how they should allocate their resources.[43]

Some Postmodernists have proposed radical changes for the law. For instance, Professor Menkel-Meadow has advocated the elimination of the adversarial component of our legal system.[44] She has written,"[t]he adversary system is inadequate, indeed dangerous for satisfying a number of important goals of any legal or dispute resolution system."[45] She has elaborated: "Binary, oppositional presentation of facts in dispute are not the best way for us to learn the truth; polarized debate distorts the truth, leaves out important information, simplifies complexity, and obfuscates rather than clarifies."[46] Instead, "she "envision[s] a greater multiplicity of stories being told, of more open participatory and democratic processes, yielding truths that are concrete but contextualized, explicitly focused on who finds 'truth' for whose benefit."[47]

One of the most important legal schools that have been influenced by Postmodernism is Critical Legal Thought ("CLS").[48] Roberto Unger has announced:

"The critical studies movement has undermined the central ideas of modern legal thought and put another conception of law in their place. This conception implies a view of society and informs a practice of politics."[49] Similarly, Mark Tushnet has asserted, "CLS tries to put into question the deepest values of a society: Because there is nothing timeless about those values, we must simply decide to abandon them."[50] CLS claims to have been descended from the critical part of Legal Realism and the progressive tradition in American historiography that studies the role of interest groups in American society.[51]

CLS is essentially a leftist critique of traditional liberalism.[52] CLS stresses "cognitive relativism"–"the social and historical contingency of structures of thought."[53] Rather than examining the value orientation of a particular judge as the Legal Realists did, they study "the premises that mainstream opponents actually share."[54] In particular, it criticizes the supposed determinacy, objectivity, formalism, and neutrality of the existing legal order.[55]

A major tenet of CLS is that there is no distinction between law and politics.[56] Concerning this critique, Professor Tushnet has written, "when one understands the moral, epistemological, and empirical assumptions embedded in any particular legal claim, one will see that those assumptions operate in a particular setting in which the legal claim is made to advance the interests of some identifiable political grouping."[57] Professor Singer has declared, "[w]e have proposed instead that legal reasoning is a way of simultaneously articulating and masking political and moral commitment."[58] Professor Fiss has stated that CLS believes that "[j]udges speak the way they do because that is the convention of their profession and is needed to maintain their power, but their rhetoric is a sham."[59] Many CLS adherents believe the law/politics distinction prevents political change.[60] As Professor Horwitz has written: "Until we are able to transcend the American fixation with sharply separating law from politics, we will continue to fluctuate between the traditional polarities of American legal discourse, as each generation continues frantically to hide behind unhistorical and abstract universalisms in order to deny, even to itself, its own political and moral choices."[61]

CLS similarly rejects the distinction between public and private spheres.[62] CLS believes that the public/private distinction is a social construct, not a reflection of objective reality.[63] It believes that eliminating this distinction opens up new possibilities for human conduct.[64]

CLS often uses a technique it calls trashing (sometimes called unpacking or deconstruction).[65] Trashing has been defined as: "Take specific arguments very seriously in their own terms; discover they are actually foolish ([tragic]-comic); and then look for some (external observer's) order (not the germ of truth) in the internally contradictory, incoherent chaos we've exposed."[66]

CLS employs trashing to expose illegitimate power and hierarchies, which are social constructs.[67] Mark Kellman has argued: "From my vantage point, which is the view of 'micropractices,' the primary thrust of the CLS enterprise at an academic level should be to explore, in a very concrete, particular setting, the vital general point that status hierarchies are founded, at least in a significant part, on sham distinctions."[68] Duncan Kennedy has explored hierarchies in the context of the law school, arguing that law schools provide "ideological training for willing service in the hierarchies of the corporate welfare state."[69] He has further stated that "teachers convince students that legal reasoning exists, and is different from policy analysis, by bullying then into accepting as valid in particular cases arguments about legal correctness that are circular, question-begging, incoherent, or so vague as to be meaningless."[70]

CLS has also critiqued the liberal notion of rights.[71] Duncan Kennedy has asserted: "Rights discourse is internally inconsistent, vacuous or circular. Legal thought can generate equally plausible rights justifications for almost any result."[72] He has added that the rights discourse framework "makes it difficult even to conceptualize radical proposals such as, for example, decentralized democratic worker control of factories."[73] Peter Gabel has criticized rights as alienating: "If we now turn our attention to the nature of rights themselves, we can see how they represent the field of social interaction in the service of legalizing its alienated appearances."[74] CLS would replace a rights-based society with a communitarian one:

> That suggests the other agenda–the fashioning of communities where one need not hide behind the private for either protection or self-aggrandizement. Communities where relationships might be just "us, you and me, and the rest of us," deciding for ourselves what we want, without the alienating third of the state. In that setting, however remotely possible it may seem, we might even make group decisions about reproduction, replacing our persuasive alienation and fear of one and other with something more like mutual trust, or love.[75]

The writings of Richard Rorty, a pragmatic, antifoundationalist philosopher, present another Postmodern approach to law.[76] Rejecting Kantian universal notions such as the concept of human dignity, Rorty adopts a Hegalian view that morality is local.[77] He believes that modern society does not need Kantian universals to survive; democracy is freestanding without an objective foundation.[78]   Instead, Rorty adopts an "ethnocentric" approach to culture–every culture is contingent upon the principles and practices in that culture.[79] Rorty also rejects the notion that there is a central self called reason.[80] Rather, he views the moral self "as a network of beliefs, desires, and emotions with nothing behind it–no substance behind the attributes."[81]

In politics, Rorty criticizes both the left-wing's espousal of communism and the right-wing's attempts to roll-back welfare-state reforms to capitalism.[82] Rather, he sees the best alternative as "governmentally-controlled capitalism plus welfare statism" as can be seen in the governments of Holland, Sweden, and Ireland.[83]

Rorty's has described his pragmatic approach to law as:

> Good prophets say that if we all got together and did such and such we would probably like the results. They paint pictures of what this brighter future would look like, and write scenarios about how it might be brought about. When they finished doing that, they have nothing more to offer, except to say "Let's try it!"[84]

He has added that, when an audience asks for authority or legitimacy, "[p]ragmatism is having a philosopher on hand to murmur into your ear 'You have the right not to answer that question.'"[85] Concerning traditional approaches to legal thinking, he has stated, "[w]e liberals have to admit the force of Dewey's, Unger's and Casoriadis's point that such familiar language-games are themselves nothing more than 'frozen politics,' that they serve to legitimate, and make seem inevitable precisely the forms of social life (for example, the cycles of reform and reaction) from which we desperately seek to break free."[86]

Rorty rejects any use of foundationalism in the law, stating "[f]or Deweyans, the whole idea of an 'authority' is suspect. . . . He hoped we'd stop using the judicial vocabulary which Kant made fashionable among philosophers, and start using metaphors from town meetings, rather than from tribunals."[87] Rorty is also skeptical of the universalists' motives: "They [foundationalists] defend their proposals in terms of how much we would like the consequences of the change they propose–how glad we, or at least our descendants, will be that we made the change–but also by reference to the authority of that for which they speak."[88]

Although Rorty thinks that Pragmatism can stand for a visionary tradition, as seen in such cases as *Brown v. Bd. of Education*, he also sees the limits of pragmatism: "But as a pragmatist, I do not believe that legal theory offers us a defense against such [bad] judges–that it can do much to prevent another *Dred Scott* decision."[89] However, there is good in a pragmatic approach to law: "Dewey the pragmatic would have been delighted that the courts sometimes tell the politicians and voters to start noticing that there are people who have been told to wait forever until a consensus emerges–a consensus from which these people are effectively excluded."[90]

B. The Traditional Critique of Postmodern Legal Thought and Moral Relativism

Professor Litowitz has pointed out that Postmodern theorists generally view law from an external perspective–from outside the system, rather than from an internal viewpoint, which accepts the starting practices of that system.[91] Postmoderns tend to attack the existing legal system as a whole, rather than showing why the details have gone wrong. Thus, they emphasize the social construction of the existing legal system and the ideological basis behind that social construction. As Professor Minda has remarked, "postmodern criticism seems to challenge the very idea of law itself."[92] The problem with this is that to fix the problems with law under this external perspective requires the development of a completely new system. While most Postmoderns would not consider this a problem, as will be discussed in detail below, the inadequate nature of the constructive portion of the Postmodernist agenda has not produced an acceptable alternative.

The strong moral relativism of Postmodern Legal Thought creates internal inconsistencies.[93] Twentieth-century theories of moral relativism, especially those that advocate cognitive relativism or see reality as a social construct, share an essential problem–if there is no morality underlying law, then why is *any* practice or conduct wrong? Why is slavery wrong? Because someone says it is wrong? Under Postmodernism one person's morality is no more legitimate than another person's morality. Because the majority says it is wrong? The same problem exists. The morality of the majority is no more legitimate than the morality of the minority or for that matter the morality of an individual. Because everyone knows intuitively that it is wrong? This answer suggests some sort of natural morality or law within us, and it contradicts the essential notion of moral relativism.

The simple answer is that when there is no Truth, but rather truths, there is no basis for saying that slavery, racism, discrimination, female circumcision, or any of the other practices that Postmoderns oppose are wrong.[94] Anyone that favors these practices is just as "correct" as anyone who opposes them under a Postmodern theory. As will be developed more thoroughly later in this study, the only way to say that any of these practices is wrong is to acknowledge that there is at least a skeletal universal morality.[95]

Another problem with moral relativism is that it is based on the limited observation of cultural diversity. What about the similarities among cultures? Any theory of morals must account for both the difference and similarities among societies.

A further problem with moral relativism is that postmoderns do not fully explore the implications of their ideas.[96] If all societies' moralities are equally valid, why not impose our values on everyone. In other words, why not nationalism, racism, and colonialism, rather than tolerance? Tolerance cannot be a universal moral principle if there are no universal moral principles. As Professors Benson and Strangroom ask, "[s]o epistemic relativism makes possible a world where bad arguments and no evidence are helped to win public discussions over justified arguments and good evidence. This is emancipatory?"[97]

The CLS critique that law and politics are not separate fails because there is an existing method of judging that judges generally respect. While politics may occasionally creep into judging, the constraints on judging that the school of Reasoned Elaboration[98] recognized are real constraints. Precedent, procedural requirements, due process requirements, the requirement of written opinions, etc., provide real constraints on judges that separate law from politics.

The CLS use of Trashing (or deconstruction) is just a game.[99] Anything can be trashed, even CLS and Postmodern writings. Noone can argue that our legal system is always determinant, objective, and neutral. However, it is determinant, objective, and neutral enough that we can consider it legitimate in the sense that it will usually produce the right, fair answer. That a car has to be taken into a mechanic a couple of times a year does not make that car unreliable.

CLS's rejection of the notion of rights is troubling. Without rights, the minority has no protection. We may be in the majority today, but someday we might be in the minority and need rights. As Patricia Williams, a member of the Critical Race Studies School, has stated: "It is very hard to watch the idealistic or symbolic importance of rights being diminished with reference to the disenfranchised, who experience and express their dispowerment as nothing more or less than denial of rights."[100]

CLS's attempts to eliminate hierarchy are unworkable. Hierarchy is an intrinsic part of organized society.[101] Or, to put it another way: Organization is hierarchy; there is a need for specialization in an organization. While it might be theoretically interesting to create a classroom without hierarchy,[102] a teacher is required that has knowledge of the subject to run the class. Similarly, a proposal by Duncan Kennedy to create a law school where all salaries are equal, including those of secretaries and janitors, where everyone spends a month doing a different job in the law school, such as professors becoming janitors, and where admissions to the law school are made by lottery with quotas,[103] is impractical. Janitors or secretaries would not be good at teaching law classes, and most law professors would fail as secretaries or janitors. In addition, no law student would want to attend a law school where some of the classes are taught by someone with no legal training. More realistically, no law professor would teach for a janitor's salary. Finally, a student does need a certain amount of intelligence and background to learn law. While the main purpose of Professor Kennedy's proposal may have been to provoke further thought, it still illustrates the impossibility of eliminating hierarchy.

Most of the constructive proposals of Postmodernism have been so vague as to be unworkable. While Enlightenment principles have not produced a perfect world, the Postmoderns have not shown that any other system would have done better. As Jay Moran has observed, "rather than unpacking the 'subjectivity' of law into a mass of principles that can be advantageously rebuilt, the true effect of a postmodern jurisprudence is to create an environment where Western law has been dismantled in an undesirable way."[104] He has added, "if there can be nothing beyond the linguistically and historically conditioned circumstances from which all legal systems are derived, any new ideology will be equally contaminated."[105]

Pragmatism is probably the best solution the Postmoderns have proposed.

However, it is not a totally satisfactory solution because, as Pragmatists admit, it is contingent. Who decides what is the pragmatic solution? If it is the judge, we are letting ourselves be ruled by one or the few. If it is the majority, then is the solution pragmatic or is it political? In addition, if it is the majority, who protects the minority? A pragmatic solution might generally protect minorities, but what if a particular pragmatic solution tramples on minority rights?

Moreover, as Professor Rorty has noted,[106] Pragmatism does not always preclude bad law. Maybe this is because of the vagueness of pragmatic method, which relies on concepts such as "edifying conversations" and "strategies through which a population . . . can seek a series of necessarily transient and provisional understandings."[107] Or, perhaps it is because the most "pragmatic" answer is not better than an answer that relies on pre-existing rules that have been worked out over many years.

Finally, there is the problem of the acceptance of the pragmatic solution. Is a losing party more likely to accept the explanation that the judge thinks the solution is better or that existing law dictates the solution? Fairness requires that there be some predictability in the law and that a person not be subjected to unknown, inconsistent, or ambiguous laws.[108] In addition, a justification like "Let's Try It"[109] is unlikely to convince someone who is adamantly opposed to a pragmatic proposal.

An approach that culture is contingent is also problematic. Professor Blumenson has pointed out that "cultural relativism's theory of 'local' truth cannot be applied without making the kind of objective, transcultural claims the theory rejects."[110] As he has noted, "for if we take all moral truths to have only *local* validity, the ethical focus necessarily shifts to the issue of *whose* truth we should privilege in practice, ours or theirs . . . ."[111] He has gone further: "If relativism cannot rely on the objectivity of relative justification, it follows that the relativist cannot distinguish someone's 'being right' from 'thinking he is right,' which is to say one cannot have any concept of truth at all, even local truth."[112]

In addition, if morality is local, what do we do with those who refuse to follow the local morality? Is it just to punish one for not following a culture's morality when morality itself is contingent? Perhaps, in the end, we can't do any better than a program like the one that Rorty proposed. However, this does not mean that we should not continue to try.[113]

II. Behavioral Biology and the Blank Slate

Behavioral biology, especially its rejection of the idea that the mind is a Blank Slate, demonstrates that one of the main foundations of Postmodern Legal Thought–that reality and thus law are purely social constructs–is fundamentally flawed. The Blank Slate (the Standard Social Science Model) is "the idea that the human mind has no inherent structure and can be inscribed at will by society and ourselves."[114] Stated differently, the human mind and thus subjects such as society, law, and culture are social constructs. As Professor Degler has noted, "[t]he main impetus came from the will to establish a social order in which innate and immutable forces of biology played no role in accounting for the behavior of social groups."[115] The Blank Slate has been the basis for much of the social sciences, humanities, politics, and law for over a century.[116] An example of the Blank Slate approach is contained in the once highly-influential but now discredited writings of B. F. Skinner (behaviorism), who argued "that harmful behavior is neither instinctive nor freely chosen but inadvertently conditioned."[117] Similarly, Margaret Mead declared, "[w]e are forced to conclude that human nature is almost unbelievably malleable, responding accurately and contrastingly to contrasting cultural conditions."[118]

Professors Cosmides and Tooby have alleged social scientists have purposely isolated themselves from scientific integration and methods.[119] They have also charged that the social sciences have been relatively unsuccessful as sciences because they have rejected the findings of the other sciences and because they have focused on the faulty standard social science model of behavior.[120] They have declared: "Those who jettison the epistemological standards of science are no longer in the position to use their intellectual product to make claims about what is true in the world or to dispute the others' claims about what is true."[121]

Behavioral biology has thoroughly debunked the notion that the human mind is a Blank Slate and that law is a social construct by showing that behavior derives from both heredity and environment.[122] As Professor Chen has asserted in 1995, "we stand on the brink of a century whose principal intellectual project may consist of overthrowing the Standard Social Science Model. . ."[123] Professors Jones and Goldsmith have similarly observed, "[t]he school of psychology known as behaviorism–the notion that all behavior of all importance results entirely from cultural learning–passed into history some time ago."[124] Likewise, Professor Pinker has declared: "In most cases the correct explanation will invoke a complex interaction between heredity and environment: culture is crucial, but culture could not exist without mental facilities that allow humans to create and learn culture to begin with."[125] Finally, Professor Kuklin has proclaimed: "The phenotype, the particular form and behavior of organisms, develops from its genotype responding to environmental factors."[126] In other words, "[a]lmost all behavior is mediated by many senses interacting with environmental input."[127]

Scientific studies like those discussed in Chapter Two more specifically destroy the Blank Slate. The Blank Slate started to disintegrate in 1966 when two scientists proved that equipotentiality–"the equal ability of any response to get hooked up to any stimulus"–was untrue.[128] The discovery of theory of mind and mirror neurons further weakened the edifice of the Blank Slate because they involved innate neural structures. Moreover, because the mind is modular with each module being adapted for a different evolutionary problem, the mind cannot be a Blank Slate.[129] Furthermore, fMRIs and similar devices have demonstrated how brains actually work. Finally, in contrast to many Postmodernists, behavioral biologists believe that brains can develop objective knowledge of reality, at last approximately.[130] In fact, it would be a strange survival machine that developed a distorted view of reality.

Most specifically, studies of twins have demonstrated that personality is largely genetic.[131] For example, in a study of twins concerning their views on religious fundamentalism, "[t]he correlation between the resulting scores for identical twins reared apart is 62 percent; for fraternal twins reared apart just 2 percent."[132] This does not mean that we should ignore other factors, but it is clear that heritability is vitally important in the human personality.

Based on the above, culture is not a social construct; rather, as behavioral biology has proven, it is significantly determined by the thought processes of the mind. Individuals are not passive recipients of culture; they cannot be socially engineered. You cannot change culture and thus change people. As Professor Pinker has concluded: "Culture, then, is a pool of technological and social innovations that people accumulate to help them live their lives, not a collection of arbitrary roles and symbols that happen to befall them."[133]

One wonders why the idea of law as a social construct became so embedded in contemporary thought considering the idea from a logical viewpoint is so baseless.[134]

How can the mind be a Blank Slate, considering that blank slates do nothing?[135] As Professor Pinker has noted, "[t]he inscriptions will sit there forever unless something notices patterns in them, combines them with patterns learned at other times, uses the combinations to scribble new thoughts onto the slate, and reads the results to guide behavior to goals."[136] In other words, at a minimum, the mind must contain mechanisms for learning, for seeing a world of objects, for understanding the content of a sentence, and for interpreting other individuals' behavior.[137]

The fact that law is not purely a social construct has enormous implications for Postmodern Legal Theory. For example, it significantly weakens its criticism of traditional legal thought. If our mental processes are innate, then law based on those mental processes is not purely contingent.[138] While our legal system has not consciously been based on the insights of behavioral biology, our legal system is based on our thought processes. For example, applying rules to facts is a natural part of human reasoning.[139] Similarly, following precedent involves a common type of human reasoning called case-based reasoning. Professor Leake has described case-based reasoning as: "A case-based problem-solver . . . solves new problems by retrieving traces of relevant prior problems from memory, establishing correspondences between those problems and the new situation, and adopting the prior solutions to fit the problem at hand."[140]

Similarly, behavioral biology has established that most categories are not just social constructs but part of how the mind processes information.[141] Our mind categorizes objects that are based on reality.[142] These categories come from two types of mental processes: "one of them notices clumps of entries in the mental spreadsheet and treats them as categories with fuzzy boundaries, prototypical members, and overlapping similarities, like members of the family" and "the other mental process looks for crisp rules and definitions and enters them into chains of reasoning."[143] Thus, the Postmodern rejection of categories is unfound. Similarly, strong rule scepticism is questionable, considering that the mind looks for clear rules and definitions.

Behavioral biology has also debunked the Postmodern view of the self as a social construct. The self is not just a Blank Slate that society writes upon, but an individual whose mind is significantly created by biology. This brings the Kantian notion of the autonomous self back into the picture,[144] which has enormous consequences for law. For one thing, as will be developed more fully throughout this study, if the self is autonomous instead of a social construct, then the unit of inquiry should be the individual, not the community.

The Postmodern attack on individualism is also unwarranted because the human mind does not work as Postmodernism thinks it does. As noted in Chapter Two and above, evolution works on the individual level, not the group level. A human group is not a living organism with a group consciousness, like the Borg on *Star Trek*. Instead, humans survived through selfish genes that led to cooperation. While benefitting the group incidently, that cooperation is self-interested cooperation that helps the individual survive. Self-fulfillment and self-discovery are not negative traits, but rather part of human nature that helped mankind survive. Individualism is essential to human nature. Humans are not ants who have communitarian societies centered around a queen because humans evolved in a different way.

As noted in Chapter 2, linguists, including Noah Chomsky, now believe that there is a universal grammar of language. If language is not socially constructed, then texts are not social constructs. If there is a universal moral grammar underlying all languages, then the fact that communities have different surface languages does not create different realities for those communities.

That texts are not social constructs is vitally important for law because cases, statutes, and administrative rules are texts. If texts are social constructs, as Postmodernists argue, then a reader is free to interpret them in any way that he or she might wish; there are no constraints on textual interpretation. This is also supported by the Postmodern concept that the self is purely a social construct. If there is no self behind the text, then it is not important what the writer intended, and the reader can freely interpret that text. However, if the writer is controlled by innate thought processes and there is a correspondence between language and reality, as is supported by behavior biology, then the reader is not free to make just any interpretation of the text.[145] The reader must interpret the text with an awareness of those thought processes. In other words, the reader cannot ignore conventions of language and grammar that make the text intelligible; there is a pre-existing "grid" for textual interpretation.[146] Furthermore, since there is a self behind the text, the writer becomes more important than the reader. The reader cannot ignore what the writer expressed in the text just because the reader would prefer a different interpretation.

To go further, the text under this theory is autonomous; the text is the only thing to be interpreted.[147] This is because "signs can only be used if they are separable from intent."[148] Because words are signs that are separable from intent, the reader must decipher those symbols, rather than trying to reconstruct the writer's intent.[149] In other word, the writer's intention can only be found by looking at the text, to discover the text's meaning. For example, a judge should use textualism[150] in interpreting a statute, instead of trying to go behind the text to discern the legislature's intention.

The above insights limit CLS's critique concerning textual indeterminancy. Every interpretation is not possible; rather, the choices are limited by the conventions of language established by our innate thought processes. If judges are limited to discovering the meaning in the statute's text, then their choices are limited by the rules of language. If a judge goes beyond the limits of statutory interpretation, then the judge has made an illegitimate choice, but that does not make the system of statutory interpretation illegitimate.

The above insights also limit CLS's use of trashing or deconstruction. Texts are not subject to the multiple interpretations that CLS claims because language is not a social construct. Many of the subjects that CLS trashes really do exist because they are part of our mental thought processes.

III. Neurocognitive Universals in the Law and Postmodern Moral Relativism

Behavioral biology's discovery of neurocognitive (innate) universals in mankind and human thought, as mentioned in Chapter Two, also weakens the basis of Postmodern Legal Thought, which rejects universals in general and in the law and believes that law and morality are relative. In addition to the universals discussed in Chapter Two, universals also exist in the law, including a concept of fairness, distinguishing right and wrong, inheritance rules, murder proscribed, normal distinguished from abnormal states, property, rape proscribed, reciprocal exchanges of labor, goods, or services (reciprocal altruism), redress of wrongs, and some forms of violence proscribed.[151] More specifically, the preliminary results of an extensive research program conducted under the direction of John Mikhail has shown that the prohibition of murder is universal and highly invariant and invariably contains a mental state element and that the particular justifications and excuses identified are remarkably similar and appear to consist of a relatively short list of familiar categories.[152]

Professors Jones and Goldsmith have gone further claiming that one can see the effects of the evolutionary process on the human brain in the architecture of legal systems.[153] They have asserted: "[A]ll legal systems, like the cultures of which they are a part, have been shaped to some degree by fundamental attributes of human brains that in turn are expressions of basic human goals and desires."[154] They have argued that all legal systems involve certain "Topics"–"sex, inheritance, family, status of children, reputation, property, and resources."[155] In addition, all legal systems contain social attitudes toward these Topics, which reflect the norms of the community.[156] The exact way that people care about these Topics they call "Content," which varies across cultures.[157] Although existing research has suggested that legal systems vary based on their culture, "[a]n evolutionary perspective should uniquely predict that the same general sets of motivational tools are central features of legal systems in virtually every human culture worldwide."[158]

Professor Strahlendorf has theorized that Darwinian algorithms ("the interaction between information in gene-determined structures and environmental information that occurs in the functioning of cognitive programs")[159] underlie our sense of justice.[160] He has explained: "It is the Darwinian algorithms that are [evolutionary] adaptions, the algorithms are solutions to problems, the solving of which must have resulted in greater reproductive success of individuals in the past."[161]

Finally, as mentioned in the Introduction, Professor Guttentag believes that there is a law instinct–that reliance on legal systems to organize social activity is an integral and universal part of human nature. . ."[162] He backs up his theory by looking at "(1) evidence that behavior is expressed early and predictably in individual development, (2) evidence that the underlying logic of the behavior is inaccessible to conscious reflection (dumbfounding), (3) evidence of specialized capabilities that are particularly well-suited to carrying out that behavior, (4) evidence that the behavior occurs in all societies (universality), and (5) evidence that the behavior could be the product of evolutionary processes."[163]

First, childhood developmental studies suggest that children have innate dispositions concerning law. These studies demonstrate that children reach normal developmental stages at about the same age.[164] Three- and four-year-old children understand fairness and appropriate behavior, and children can distinguish between moral rules and law-like rules.[165] Moreover, game playing is universal, and when children play games, they adopt two-tiered systems of law-like rules.[166]

Second, Guttentag thinks that "dumbfounding" (people have trouble explaining their intuitive judgments) shows that law is innate.[167] "Presumably, innate behaviors are less likely than other behaviors to be the product of conscious reflection."[168] For example, most individuals respond negatively to an incestuous relationship, but they cannot explain why they reacted this way.[169] Guttentag posits that this is a product of natural selection (and thus) innate "because of the potential harm from incestuous mating."[170] Concerning law, he believes that psychological experiments, such as the ultimatum game, establishes dumbfounding in legal intuitions.[171] He also thinks that there is evidence of dumbfounding in shared practice of rule following. Again, psychological experiments show the probable universality of rule following.[172] In addition, "[p]eople tend to be quite facile at and have strong intuitions about participation in a legal system, even though such participation engages a complex and nuanced suite of behaviors. At the same time, few people are capable of explaining in a coherent manner the logic underlying the basis for their participation in a legal system."[173] This dumbfounding even applies to lawyers.[174]

Third, Guttentag argues that the fact that the human mind seems particularly well-tailored to execute legal behavior indicates that legal behavior is innate.[175] "The existence of specialized anatomical features often suggests that a behavior is innate."[176] First, the theory of mind discussed in the second chapter of this book, "the ability to evaluate the mental states of others, the ability to reason about the mental states of others, and the ability to experience emotional empathy" through mirror neurons, is vital to legal reasoning.[177] Guttentag declares, "[t]he existence of a specialized neuroanatomy for dealing with social behavior is consistent with the claim that reliance on a legal system to order social behavior draws directly upon innate foundations."[178] Second, while there have been no conclusive fMRI studies concerning legal decision-making, the fMRI studies on morality mentioned throughout this book support that legal judgment is at least partially innate.[179] Finally, psychological studies show that individuals are generally "better able to detect the violation of a logical rule when the rule is set in the context of a social contract."[180]

Fourth, as this author argued above, Guttentag feels that essential aspects of the law are universal based on anthropological research, the historical record, and psychology experiments.[181] For example, "[e]very society for which there is a written record appears to have had a social rule system" with the attributes that Guttentag believes are required for a two-tiered legal system.[182] Likewise, similar results appear in psychological game experiments conducted throughout the world.[183]

Finally, "ethological research into related behavior in other species and a consideration of modeling through natural selection of a law instinct support the claim that a law instinct could have been provided by evolutionary processes."[184] Ethological studies show that other species have precursor behaviors to participation in a legal system, such as the use of normative rules by capuchin monkeys or systems of social rules, such as dominance hierarchies, in social species.[185] Finally, Guttentag uses modeling to establish that "the evolutionary viability of a law instinct is as plausible as the models that are generally accepted as providing an evolutionary viable model of the language instinct or a moral instinct."[186] "Just as the perspective of the selfish gene can explain a willingness to abide by moral commitments, so too can it explain the willingness to abide by legal commitments."[187]

Behavioral biology's discovery of neurocognitive universals establishes the fallacy of postmodern moral relativism.[188] As demonstrated above, Truth is not relative; Truth, to a significant extent, is universal. Similarly, morality and culture are not relative; they are, also to a significant extent, universals. Unlike earlier conceptions of truth, truth does not exist externally or come from a god. It comes from within our minds; how the human mind developed in light of survival considerations. Professor Haidt calls such truths "anthropocentic" truths in contrast to "nonanthropocentic" truths, which are the truths of physical nature and mathematics.[189] Professor Haidt and Bjorklund have declared, "[i]f moral truths are anthropocentric truths, then moral systems can be judged on the degree to which they violate important moral truths held by members of that society."[190]

Anthropocentric truths do not have an external or metaphysical source for their validity.[191] They are only valid within the human species. If another intelligent species evolved on Earth or elsewhere, they would probably have different truths, morality, and cultures. However, human truths are constraining for human beings because human beings developed this way. Humans are not Martians or ants or chimpanzees.

As noted in Chapter Two, culture builds on innate human behavior so there are some differences among cultures. However, this does not restore moral relativism. The basics of all cultures are the same, but the details differ. The above has shown the myriad of universals, including in law, that cultures universally share. These serve as limits on what humans can do and thus on morality. In addition, the anatomy of the brain and how humans communicate and learn place limitations on human behavior.

V. Behavioral Biology and The Postmodern Political Agenda

With a theory that much of a human's essence is innate in our psychology and that the mind is not a Blank Slate, much of the Postmodern political agenda crumbles. As Professor Pinker has pointed out: "Postmodernists and other relativists attack truth and objectivity not so much because they are interested in philosophical problems of ontology and epistemology but because they feel it is the best way to pull the rug out from under racists, sexists, and homophobes."[192] Destabilizing power and dismantling hierarchy becomes much more difficult when much of our political structure derives from our thought processes. It is a much more difficult struggle to overcome human nature than a social construct.

Similarly, behavioral biology also limits the Postmodern notion of radical change. If there are innate mechanisms within individuals that affect how we think and how we control our emotions, there is not as much possibility for change as the Postmoderns have posited. In addition, that change is more likely to occur incrementally rather than suddenly. For example, paradigm shifts in twentieth-century American legal history were incremental, not total.[193] Consequently, the postmodern notion of utopia though social engineering (child rearing and education) is unattainable because it goes against human nature.[194]

The above does not mean that we have to return to the politics of an earlier time.[195] For example, a view of human nature as being significantly innate and other insights of behavioral biology can support a fight against racism. First, evolutionary scholars have shown that race does not explain the differences between cultures.[196] Cultures developed as better and worse ways of doing things from the standpoint of the people themselves, and they depended on variations in geography and ecology.[197] Because innovations, such as those in agriculture tended to spread along lines of similar climate, such innovations moved more easily in Eurasia because Eurasia runs from east to west in contrast to Africa and the Americas, which run north to south.[198] Similarly, in early cultures, transportation of large goods occurred over water, requiring natural

harbors and navigable rivers, which Europe and parts of Asia had but Africa and
Australia did not, allowing innovations to spread over large distances in Eurasia.[199]
Thus, "Eurasia conquered the world not because Eurasians were smarter but because
they could best take advantage of the principle that many heads are better than one."[200]

Significantly, an innate concept of human nature provides more protection for
people, including protection from racism, than moral relativism does. Professor
Chomsky has declared:

> But a deeper look will show that the concept of the "empty organism,"
> plastic and unconstructed, apart from being false, also serves naturally
> as support for the most reactionary social doctrines. If people are, in
> fact, malleable and plastic beings with no essential psychological
> nature, then why should they not be controlled and coerced by those
> who claim authority, special knowledge, and a unique insight into what
> is best for those less enlightened.[201]

In other words, "The principle that human nature, in its psychological aspects, is nothing
more than a product of history and given social relations removes all barriers to coercion
and manipulation by the powerful."[202] Or, as Professor Pinker has remarked, "the
conviction that humanity could be shaped by massive social engineering projects led to
some of the greatest atrocities in history."[203] For example, Professor Pinker has noted
that Mao Zedong justified "his radical social engineering by saying, 'It is on a blank page
that the most beautiful poems are written.'"[204]

These principles apply to racism; individuals are not protected from racism by
a relativistic approach to human nature.[205] As Professor Bracken has argued, "racism is
easily and readably stateable if one thinks of the person in accordance with empiricist
teaching because the essence of the person may be deemed his color, language, religion,
etc., while the Cartesian dualist model provided . . . a modest conceptual brake to the
articulation of racial degradation and slavery."[206] In other words, society should protect
against racism not because there is no truth and no position is privileged as the
Postmoderns think, but because all individuals are human beings.

As noted in Chapter Two, in opposition to moral relativism, behavioral biologists
believe that there is a universal morality hardwired into our brains, which aided

mankind's survival.[207]   The fundamentals of morality derived from how our brains evolved with the details of morality arising from how an individual culture reacted to how differing geography, ecology, and social conditions affected survival. This innate morality provides protection from racism, while moral relativism cannot.

Under behavioral biology, all humans are moral equals. Because there is a vast number of genetic combinations, each person is unique. Thus, society should treat each person as an individual, not as a member of a group with its stereotypes.[208]

Part of our moral sense is that human beings can identify suffering in others through mirror neurons. "Individuals recognize actions made by others because the pattern of firing neurons [mirror neurons] made when observing an action is similar to the pattern produced to generate that action."[209] In other words, empathy and sympathy are innate. When we feel someone else's suffering, we want to reduce that other person's suffering.[210] Accordingly, individuals identify with suffering caused by racism, and they have an innate sense that they should reduce that suffering.

As mentioned in Chapter Two, behavioral biologists also believe that mankind has an innate sense of fairness, which is similar to the golden rule (Do unto others as you would have them do unto you.).[211] For example, slavery is against our innate sene of fairness because slavery contradicts man's moral sense not to be exploited.[212] It also interferes with the autonomy of the individual and the individual's right not to be treated as a means to an end. The same principles apply to other types of racism.

Racism is also a type of cheating as discussed in Chapter Two. As with other types of cheating, societies need to punish racism in order to preserve the social contract. Laws against racism have an ameliorative effect because, as with all forms of punishment, individuals do a cost-benefit analysis of the consequences of their actions.[213]

Most importantly, behavioral biology has shown that from a genetic standpoint racism is unfounded. There hasn't been enough time in the human evolutionary process for significant differences to occur among localized populations.[214] Professor Pinker has noted that "people are qualitatively the same but may differ quantitatively. The quantitative differences are small in biological terms, and they are found to a much greater extent among the individual members of an ethnic group or race than between ethnic groups or races."[215] Likewise, Professor Goldsmith has declared: "Even when different members of different human populations look different and where there are demonstrable differences in gene frequencies underlying physical characteristics, the presumption remains that cultural differences reflect alternative phenotypic expressions of a common genetic heritage."[216]

Finally, some scientist believe that racism is based on coalition recognition.[217] Coalitions are often delineated by arbitrary clues, such as skin color or manner of dress.[218] When scientists created a social context in which alliances were not based on race, but on something else such as shirt color, the subjects quickly no longer noticed race.[219] As Professor Ridley has observed "the more people of different races seem to act or be treated as members of a rival coalition, the more racist instincts they risk invoking."[220] In sum, when one shows that the mind is the same in all humans, then unimportant biological aspects like skin color become irrelevant, and the reasons for prejudice should vanish.

The universality of dominance in all societies requires that we reject the Postmodern notion that crime is the result of the environment and that the primary reason for prison is rehabilitation.[221] Violence is one of the human traits that are the result of evolutionary factors that are no longer desirable in modern society.[222] On the other hand, this means that environmental determinism has been vastly overstated (especially based on the twin studies mentioned above); "[a] disadvantaged childhood does not condemn a person to a certain personality."[223]

Under behavioral biology, there is a need for both deterrence and retribution. As noted in Chapter Two, punishment is necessary to deter cheaters; the facts that cheaters are punished helps hold society together because punishment lowers a person's survival chances so a potential cheater will often do a cost-benefit analysis before cheating.[224] Thus, we need to continue deterrence disincentives for crime, such as incarceration. Such disincentives can work because "if the brain is equipped with strategies for violence, they are *contingent* strategies, connected to complicated circuitry that computes when and where they should be deployed."[225] In other words, through punishment "the law gives us selfish reasons to act unselfishly."[226]

Behavioral biology also demonstrates the need for retribution. Professors Hoffman & Goldsmith have conjectured that retribution should be the basis for punishment.[227] Because our evolved behaviors include an urge for civilization, "our urge to punish individuals who break the social contract appeared as an important stabilizing feature."[228] In other words, society is punishing the "free-rider," whose actions violate our intrinsic sense of fairness.[229] They have explained that the urge of punishment has evolutionary advantages: "Without such an urge, nothing would restrain unbounded selfishness, and social groups would have fallen apart in anarchy, to the reproductive detriment of their individual members."[230] They believe that only retribution satisfies the above criteria.[231] Not a retribution based on a social aggregate of vengeance, but one based on punishing the free-rider, which "is the crux of free living."[232]

In addition, deterrence and retribution approaches provide limitations on punishment. An individual should be punished no more than is necessary to deter the cheating and repair the injury to society.

A group of scholars have demonstrated that, based on empirical studies, there are shared intuitions of justice "that serious wrongdoing should be punished" and that people "share intuitions about the relative blameworthiness of different transgressions."[233] These scholars think that shared intuitions of justice are more likely due to evolution, than a universal social learning explanation.[234] Once individuals have an intuition about when they have been wronged (through mirror neurons), they can sense when others have been wronged.[235] Groups that punish gain survival benefits over those that do not because punishment cuts down on cheating.[236]

Finally, understanding human morality and the limits of human morality suggest the kinds of things that should not be criminalized. We should not illegalize anything that is based on taboo mentality or that is based on a confusion with conformity, rank, cleanliness, and beauty.[237] For example, since homosexuality is probably the result of biology[238] and laws against it derive from taboo mentality, laws should not forbid homosexuality, explicitly or implicitly.

Behavioral biology can also help determine the political system that is best for mankind, based on human nature. Behavioral biology supports a Kantian-like approach to rights[239] and a modified Libertarian approach to government, both of which are antithetical to the Postmodern political agenda.

Rights have traditionally been based on either a Kantian approach (individual rights) or a utilitarian one.[240] Kantianism "is the view that the rational choice in ethics is always the choice that respects the rights of autonomous persons freely to determine their own destinies, even if this respect is bought at the cost of loss of happiness or well-being."[241] Kant believed that human beings are morally special because they have the capacity for rational choice and that the freedom of rational beings should be respected.[242] Thus, individuals cannot be used as a means to an ends.[243] In contrast, utilitarianism evaluates human actions and practices "in terms of their general tendencies to advance the human welfare or social good. . ."[244] Utilitarianism looks to produce the greatest happiness for the greatest number.[245] This approach is based on the theory that something is moral if the majority is benefitted.[246]

Behavioral biology supports an individual rights approach (which is antithetical to Postmodernism because of its emphasis on the individual), and it casts doubt on utilitarianism.[247] That an individual is mainly determined by the inner workings of his or her mind backs up Kant's notion that humans should be respected because they can make rational choices. Since individuals are not social constructs but rather autonomous beings, using a person as a means to an end, as utilitarianism might do, is abhorrent. What is best for most should not supercede the basic rights of autonomous individuals, who evolved through selfish genes. Moreover, utilitarianism works well only in a small, homogeneous societies, not a diverse one like we presently live in. As Professor Goldsmith has pointed out, "[t]he concept of morality's producing the greatest good for the greatest number is consistent with evolutionary principles only when the interests of individuals are very similar."[248]

Only an individual rights approach can be used to justify eliminating such repugnant practices as slavery, racism, female circumcision, and discrimination.[249] Slavery is wrong, under an individual rights theory, because it fails to respect the basic dignity of a human being who in essential ways is just like any other human being. It interferes with human freedom, and it treats an individual like a means to an end. On the other hand, utilitarianism would allow slavery if it produced the greatest happiness for the greatest number. Under utilitarianism, the unhappiness of the few cannot outweigh the benefit to the many.

Some would argue that the above presents a simplistic view of utilitarianism–that not only can utilitarianism "condemn scapegoating and victimizing but [it can] defend the claim that persons have a right not to be victimized."[250] Professor Murphy and Coleman have written:

> We might, as utilitarians, approve of certain general rules or practices
> that assign certain rights to persons–e.g., the right not to be
> experimented upon without one's consent. . . . The reason we adopt this
> rule or practice, however, is because of our belief that the majority of

people will be happier in the long run living in a society having a rule (or conferring a right) of this nature. For if citizens had no protection against simply being used by the state whenever the state believed that the general welfare could be promoted by such use, then they would never be secure, would never be able to live lives of stability and predictability, and thus could not be happy.[251]

Nevertheless, what about the question of slavery? The happiness of 75% of the population would be improved if 25% of the population were enslaved. But what of the unhappiness created in the free 75% by the possibility that they might be enslaved at a later time? Such unhappiness, however, could be avoided if slavery were limited to a certain race or foreign-born peoples. Thus, in the long run, the only notion of rights that prevents slavery and similar inhumanities is one that respects the individual as an individual, not one that balances benefits and burdens.

Despite the above, our laws do not have to rely exclusively on individual rights; individual rights should prevail when the right involves something basic to the autonomous individual, such as the right not be used, and utilitarian rights can be employed when the matter does not involve such a basic right. In fact, there is a need for policy-based decisions in a society. Behavioral biology has demonstrated that mankind has "evolved a pattern of behavior that is sufficiently flexible to deal with a spectrum of contingencies."[252] Thus, policy is often needed to choose between contingencies. As Professor Goldsmith has noted, "[i]f particular social conditions can be counted on to produce behavior that consensus deems undesirable, a reasonable strategy is to change the conditions."[253] Thus, the legislature can consider policy when drafting most laws since most laws do not affect the basic rights of the individual. For example, land use can be determined by what does the greatest good for the greatest number (such as a football stadium), even if some individuals in the community would prefer a different use (a riding stables). However, a legislature cannot take a person's land for that football stadium without just compensation because the community cannot use an individual for the greater good.

The above suggests a theory of judging that places significant constraints on judges.[254] The legislature can consider both individual rights (principle) and utilitarian rights (policy) in making its decisions. A judge can use individual rights (as embedded in our Constitution; see below) to overrule a legislative decision. However, a judge should not be able to use policy considerations to overrule the legislature. Only a democratic institution like a legislature can make a utilitarian decision because such a decision requires that the majority (or at least the majority's representatives) prevail. Not only is a judge less likely to be able to determine the will of the majority, the judge is likely to substitute the judge's views of what is best for the view of the majority. It is okay when a judge overrules the majority when individual rights are involved because the majority cannot overcome the basic rights of the individual, but it is another matter when the judge substitutes his or her policy preference for that of the majority.

The above leaves open a question that is also basic to natural law theories: Should a judge be able to base a decision on a concept of individual rights when those rights have not been reduced to positive law? The preliminary answer to that question should be no. Behavioral biology has not gotten to the point where we can agree precisely what the basic rights of humans are. Thus, allowing a judge to determine what individual rights are can lead to a judge creating his or her own notion of rights, instead of the rights that are within us.

For now at least, our Constitution can serve as a source of basic rights like it has served as a source of basic rights for the last two hundred years. Professor McGinnis has argued that the framers of our Constitution and Bill of Rights based these documents on an accurate view of human nature.[255] He has declared: "As the classical philosopher Democritus conceived an atomic theory two thousand years before the mechanisms of such theory were understood, the Framers developed a generally accurate theory of the psychology of man and distribution of talents two centuries before modern evolutionary biology largely confirmed that theory."[256] For example, they saw that man was self-interested, and they encouraged that self-interest in the private sphere by limiting government interference in this sphere in order to benefit society through individual commerce and enterprise.[257] On the other hand, they recognized the problems of selfishness in the public sphere, so they created such mechanisms as federalism, separation of powers, and bicameralism.[258]

The fact that mankind's nature is mainly innate, rather than being socially constructed, suggests a modified Libertarian approach to government.[259] This avoids the problem of lack of cooperation that often dooms communitarian structures, often supported by Postmodernists. As Professor McGinnis has noted, "[s]ocial structures that are premised on unrelated individuals interacting with the degree of altruism and sacrifice that family members display are unlikely to succeed."[260] Noam Chomsky has also supported Libertarianism,[261] and he has written, "[l]ike many others who have tried to develop a humanistic conception of man, with due respect for man's intrinsic nature and the admirable form it might achieve, [Bertrand] Russell inclined toward libertarian conceptions of education and social organization."[262] A Libertarian approach to government would also accord with Kant's notion that morality is grounded in freedom.[263]

In a Libertarian system, government interferes with the liberty of an individual only when that individual is interfering with the liberty of another.[264] As long as an individual's conduct does not harm another, then the government should not regulate that conduct.[265] For example, since sex between two adult men in private does not harm anyone, then the state should not regulate it. The fact that such an act is repugnant to some people is irrelevant; a self-serving bias or a morality taboo should not be able to trump an intrinsic human right to be left alone when not harming another. Utilitarian preferences no matter how strong should not trump individual rights. Finally, the government leaves this conduct alone because of the right to liberty, not because there are many truths and moralities and one position should not be privileged as the Postmoderns would argue.

On the other hand, the government should be able to step in when someone's exercise of liberty does harm others. In that case, the other person's basic rights are at stake. As noted in Chapter Two, humans can be selfish, violent, and biased. Therefore, the government can interfere when a person harms someone else. For example, the government can interfere when a man has sex with a young boy because it is assumed that the boy cannot consent to sex and is harmed. Similarly, a government can punish murder, theft, rape, and other violent crimes because an individual (or individuals) has been harmed.

The above suggests that government should not regulate community morality, but it should sometimes regulate the economy. As was demonstrated earlier, conduct that violates community morality, like homosexuality, does no real harm to others. However, economic activities contain the potential for great harm to individuals so the government should be able to pass laws concerning antitrust, security regulation, etc.[266] As mentioned previously, people can be selfish and biased so the government needs to protect individuals in both economic and criminal spheres and punish cheaters.

Conclusion

Behavioral biology demonstrates that Postmodern Legal Thought is nonsense–that it is a type of fiction. While fiction is an entertaining genre in literature, it is destructive as a basis of law. Law must be based on human behavior and use rigor of thought, not unprincipled ideology or wishful thinking. Thought experiments without thorough testing are useless. To properly regulate behavior, institutions need to understand behavior, and, as demonstrated above, Postmodern Legal Thought lacks an accurate picture of behavior. It is a religion that is based on faith, not facts. As Professor Pinker has observed: "It blinds us to our cognitive and moral shortcomings. . . It has elevated sappy dogmas above the search for workable solutions."[267]

Notes

1. Leda Cosmides & John Tooby, *Evolutionary Psychology, Moral Heuristics, and the Law, in* HEURISTICS AND THE LAW 182 (Gerd Gigerenzer & Christoph Enge eds., 2006).

2. Larry Solum, Legal Theory Blog, *Most Cited Authors in the Humanities in 2007 (with some law comparisons)*, http://lsolum.typepad.com/legaltheory/2010/04/most-cited-authors-in-the-humanities-in-2007. html (April 6, 2010).

3. DOUGLAS E. LITOWITZ, POSTMODERN PHILOSOPHY AND LAW 10 (1997) (Postmodernists "deny the existence of a neutral and objective faculty of reason which can be used to generate first principles of morality and law."); Eric Blumenson, *Mapping the Limits of Skepticism in Law and Morals*, 74 TEX. L. REV. 523, 527-28 (1996) ("On this view, all judgements are contingent cultural products that cannot be objectively true."); Allan C. Hutchinson, *Identity Crisis the Politics of Interpretation*, 26 NEW ENG. L. REV. 1173, 1184 (1992); Peter C. Schanck, *Understanding Postmodern Thought and Its Implications*, 65 S. CAL. L. REV. 2505, 2508 (1992); *see also* JEAN FRANÇOIS LYOTARD, THE POSTMODERN CONDITION: A REPORT ON KNOWLEDGE xxiv (1984). Professor Litowitz has pointed out that "postmodern legal theory does not revolve around a particular work functioning as a kind of manifesto, nor is there a key postmodern thinker." LITOWITZ, *supra*, at 3. Professor Litowitz identifies the major Postmodern philosophers as Jacques Derrida, Michael Foucault, Jean-Louis Lyotard, Jacques Lacan, Fredric Jameson, and Richard Rorty and the major Postmodern legal theorists as Stanley Fish, Pierre Schlag, Peter Goodrich, J. M. Balkin, Richard Delgado, Drucilla Cornell, Duncan Kennedy, and Allan Hutchinson. *Id.* at 1.

4. Hutchinson, *supra*, at 1184; *see also* Calvin Massey, *The Constitution in a Postmodern Age*, 64 WASH. & LEE L. Rev. 169, 169 (2007) ("In the postmodern world nothing can be known for certain, including that assertion.").

5. Schanck, *supra*, at 2508.

6. *Id.*; *see also* Catherine A. MacKinnon, *Points Against Postmodernism*, 75 CHICAGO-KENT L. REV. 687, 693 (2000) ("Its main target is, precisely, reality.").

7. ANDREW ROSS, STRANGE WEATHER: CULTURE, SCIENCE, AND TECHNOLOGY IN THE AGE OF LIMITS 60 (1991).

8. GARY MINDA, POSTMODERN LEGAL MOVEMENTS: LAW AND JURISPRUDENCE AT CENTURY'S END 248 (1995).

9. STEVEN LUKES, MORAL RELATIVISM 23, 129 (2008) ("The journey down the road to moral relativism begins from the observation of the facts of diversity." *Id.* at 129.).

10. *Id.* at 23-24.

11. *Id.* at 18; Hutchinson, *supra*, at 1185, 1188-91; Joan C. Williams, *Culture and Certainty: Legal History and the Reconstructive Project*," 76 VA. L. REV. 713, 714, 735-36 (1990); Martha Minow and Elizabeth Spelman, *In Context*, 63 S. CAL. L. REV. 1597 (1990). Professor Lukes defines norms as, "rules that indicate which actions are required, prohibited, permitted, discouraged, and encouraged." LUKES, *supra*, at 18.

12. Williams, *supra*, at 745.

13. Minow & Spelman, *supra*, at 1601.

14. Susan H. Williams, *Symposium: An Ocean Apart? Freedom of Expression in Europe and the United States: Feminist Theory and Freedom of Speech*, 84 IND. L.J. 999, 1007 (2009).

15. LITOWITZ, *supra*, at 38; *see also* LUKES, *supra*, at 3.

16. LUKES, *supra*, at 38-39. Professor Lukes notes that such views discourage criticism and self-criticism. *Id.* at 133.

17. Massey, *supra*, at 168; LITOWITZ, *supra*, at 11-14; Hutchinson, *supra*, at 1192; Schanck, *supra*, at 2508; Peter Schlag, *The Problem of Subject*, 69 TEXAS L. REV. 1627, 1697 (1991) [hereinafter Schlag, *Problem*].

18. Massey, *supra*, at 174.

19. Schanck, *supra*, at 2508.

20. Hutchinson, *supra*, at 1184-85.

21. Schlag, *Problem*, *supra*, at 1697.

22. Peter Schlag, *The Aesthetics of American Law*, 115 HARV. L. REV. 1047, 1084 (2002).

23. Massey, *supra*, at 174-82.

24. *Id.* at 174-75.

25. *Id.* at 176

26. Id. at 168; LITOWITZ, *supra*, at 10-11; Schanck, *supra*, at 2508-09.

27. LITOWITZ, *supra*, at 10-11.

28. DANIEL A. FARBER & SUZANNA SHERRY, BEYOND ALL REASON: THE RADICAL ASSAULT ON TRUTH IN AMERICAN LAW 5 (1997).

29. Schanck, *supra*, at 2508-09.

30. LUKES, *supra*, at 7.

31. Massey, *supra*, at 167.

32. LUKES, *supra*, at 10.

33. Schanck, *supra*, at 2593; Williams, *supra*, at 735-46.

34. Williams, *supra*, at 735.

35. Blumenson, *supra*, at 548.

36. FARBER & SHERRY, *supra*, at 5.

37. LITOWITZ, *supra*, at 10; *see also* SAM HARRIS, THE MORAL LANDSCAPE: HOW SCIENCE CAN DETERMINE HUMAN VALUES 45 (2010) ("Moral relativism is clearly an attempt to pay intellectual reparations for the crimes of Western colonialism, ethnocentrism, and racism.").

38. Hutchinson, *supra*, at 1185.

39. Minow & Spelman, *supra*, at 1606.

40. Massey, *supra*, at 167.

41. Anthony E. Cook, *Reflections on Postmodernism*, 26 NEW ENG. L. REV. 751, 754 (1992).

42. LITOWITZ, *supra*, at 14.

43. STEVEN PINKER, THE BLANK SLATE: THE MODERN DENIAL OF HUMAN NATURE 198 (2002).

44. Carrie Menkel-Meadow, *The Trouble with the Adversary System in a Postmodern Multicultural World*, 38 WILLIAM & MARY L. REV. 5 (1996).

45. *Id.* at 6.

46. *Id.*

47. *Id.* at 23-24.

48. Jay Moran has stated that "CLS has offered perhaps the most unified attempt to craft postmodern ideology into the doctrine of legal study." Jay Moran, *Postmodern's Misguided Place in Legal Scholarship: Chaos Theory, Deconstruction, and Some Insight from Thomas Pynchon's Theory*, 6 S. CAL. INTERDISCIPLINARY J. 155, 157 (1997). Important exponents of Critical Legal Thought include Duncan Kennedy, Morton Horwitz, Roberto Unger, Mark Tushnet, David Trubek, Karl Klare, Peter Gabel, and Mark Kellman. Although CLS reached its apex in the mid80s, many of its adherents are still active today. *E.g.*, DUNCAN KENNEDY, A CRITIQUE OF ADJUDICATION (1998).

49. Roberto Mangabeira Unger, *The Critical Legal Studies Movement*, 96 HARV. L. REV. 561 (1983).

50. Mark Tushnet, *Critical Legal Studies: An Introduction to Its Origins and Underpinnings*, 36 J. LEG. EDUC. 505, 509 (1986) [hereinafter Tushnet, Critical Legal Studies].

51. *Id.* at 505-06; *see also* MORTON J. HORWITZ, THE TRANSFORMATION OF AMERICAN LAW (1860-1970): THE CRISIS OF LEGAL ORTHODOXY 269-72 (1992).

52. *See* Moran, *supra*, at 168; MARK KELLMAN, A GUIDE TO CRITICAL LEGAL STUDIES 1-14 (1987); *Peter Gabel, The Phenomenology of Rights-Consciousness and the Pact of the Withdrawn Self*, 62 TEX. L. REV. 1563 (1984).

53. HORWITZ, *supra*, at 27-71.

54. G. Edward White, *The Inevitability of Critical Legal Studies*, *in* INTERVENTION AND DETACHMENT: ESSAYS IN LEGAL HISTORY AND JURISPRUDENCE 257 (1994) [hereinafter White, *Critical Legal Studies*].

55. Joseph William Singer, *The Player and the Cards: Nihilism and Legal Theory*, 94 Yale L.J. 1 (1984); *see also* Moran, *supra*, at 158. CLS also sometimes gives these terms different definitions than they normally have. For example, Professor Unger defines formalism as: "[A] commitment to, and therefore also a belief in the possibility of, a method of legal justification that can be clearly contrasted to open-ended disputes

about the basic terms of social life, disputes that people call ideological, philosophical, or visionary." Unger, *supra*, at 564.

56. Moran, *supra*, at 169; Tushnet, *Critical Legal Studies*, *supra*, at 506-07; Owen M. Fiss, *The Death of the Law*, 72 CORNELL L. REV. 1, 9 (1986) ("Law is not what it seems–objective and capable of yielding right answers–but simply politics in another guise."); Duncan Kennedy, *Legal Education and the Reproduction of Hierarchy*, 32 J. LEGAL EDUC. 591, 596 (1982) [hereinafter Kennedy, *Hierarchy*]. Concerning Postmodernism in general, Benson and Strangroom write, "epistemology is a matter of choice, and thus of fashion and convention, and of politics and commitment, as opposed to being a matter of truth or falsehood, warrant, or lack of it." OPHELIA BENSON & JEREMY STANGROOM, WHY TRUTH MATTERS 46 (2007).

57. Mark Tushnet, Critical *Legal Studies: A Political History*, 100 Yale L.J. 1515, 1517 (1991).

58. Singer, *supra*, at 6.

59. Fiss, *supra*, at 9.

60. HORWITZ, *supra*, at 272.

61. *Id.*

62. *See generally* Alan Freeman & Elizabeth Mensch, *The Public-Private Distinction in American Law and Life*, 36 BUFF. L. REV. 237 (1987).

63. *Id.* at 238.

64. *Id.*

65. *See generally* Mark G. Kellman, *Trashing*, 36 STAN. L. REV. 293 (1984) [hereinafter Kellman, *Trashing*].

66. *Id.* at 293.

67. *Id.* at 321; Kennedy, *Hierarchy*, *supra*, at 603 ("Hierarchical behavior will come to express and realize the hierarchical selves of people who were initially only wearers of masks.").

68. Kellman, *Trashing*, *supra*, at 327.

69. Kennedy, *Hierarchy*, *supra*, at 598.

70. *Id.*

71. Gabel, *supra*, at 1563; Kennedy, *Hierarchy*, *supra*, at 598.

72. Kennedy, *Hierarchy*, *supra*, at 598.

73. *Id.*

74. Gabel, *supra*, at 1576.

75. Freeman & Mensch, *supra*, at 256-57.

76. Rorty produced only four short articles on law: Richard Rorty, *Pragmatism and Law: A Response to David Luban*, 18 CARDOZO L. REV. 75 (1996) [hereinafter Rorty, *Pragmatism and Law*]; *Richard* Rorty, *What Can You Expect from Anti-Foundationalist Philosophers: A Reply to Lynn Baker*, 78 VA. L. REV. 719 (1992) [hereinafter Rorty, *Anti-Foundationalist Philosophers*]; Richard Rorty, *The Banality of Pragmatism and the Poetry of Justice*, 63 SO. CAL. L. REV. 1811 (1990) [hereinafter Rorty, *Poetry of Justice*]; Richard Rorty, *Unger, Castoriadis, and the Romance of a National Future*, 82 N.U. L. REV. 335 (1980) [hereinafter Rorty, *Unger*]. Other of Rorty's important philosophical works include RICHARD RORTY, CONTINGENCY, IRONY, AND SOLIDARITY (1989); Richard Rorty, *The Priority of Democracy to Philosophy*, in 1 OBJECTIVITY,

RELATIVISM, AND TRUTH: PHILOSOPHICAL PAPERS (1989); Richard Rorty, *Postmodern Bourgeois Liberalism*, in 1 OBJECTIVITY, RELATIVISM, AND TRUTH: PHILOSOPHICAL PAPERS (1991) [hereinafter Rorty, *Postmodern Bourgeois Liberalism*].

77. LITOWITZ, *supra*, at 136-37.

78. *Id.* at 137.

79. *Id.* at 138-39. For a similar view from a legal scholar see RICHARD POSNER, THE PROBLEMATICS OF MODERN MORAL THEORY 8 (1999) ("I believe that the criteria for pronouncing a moral claim valid are given by the culture in which the claim is advanced rather than by some transcultural ('universal') source of moral values, so that we cannot, except for polemical effect, call another culture immoral. . .").

80. LITOWITZ, *supra*, at 141.

81. Rorty, *Postmodern Bourgeois Liberalism*, *supra*, at 199.

82. LITOWITZ, *supra*, at 139-40.

83. *Id.* at 140.

84. Rorty, *Anti-Foundamentalist Philosophers*, *supra*, at 719.

85. *Id.* at 721.

86. Rorty, *Unger*, *supra*, at 347.

87. Rorty, *Pragmatism and Law*, *supra*, at 82.

88. Rorty, *Anti-Foundaltionalist Philosophers*, *supra*, at 719-20.

89. Rorty, *Poetry of Justice*, *supra*, at 1819.

90. *Id.* at 1817.

91. LITOWITZ, *supra*, at 20-25. For a devastating attack on Postmodernism by a philosopher, see PAUL BOGHOSSIAN, FEAR OF KNOWLEDGE: AGAINST RELATIVISM AND CONSTRUCTIONISM (2006).

92. MINDA, *supra*, at 255.

93. Postmodern relativism differs significantly from modern relativism. Professor Gertrude Himmelfarb has noted:

> Where modernism tolerates relativism, postmodernism celebrates it. Where modernism, aware of the obstacles in the way of objectivity, regards this as a challenge, and makes a strenuous effort to attain as much objectivity and unbiased truth as possible, postmodernism takes the rejection of absolute truth as a deliverance from all truth and from the obligation to maintain any degree of objectivity.

Gertude Himmelfarb, *Postmodernist History, in* ON LOOKING INTO THE ABYSS 137 (1994).

94. Professor Rorty has acknowledged: "When the secret police come, when the torturers violate the innocent, there is nothing to be said to them of the form 'There is something within you that you are betraying. Though you embody the practices of a totalitarian society, which will endure forever, there is something beyond those practices which condemns you.'" RICHARD RORTY, CONSEQUENCES OF PRAGMATISM xlii (1982). Similarly, Catherine MacKinnon has written, "according to postmodernism there are no facts; everything is a reading so there can be no lies. Apparently it cannot be known whether the Holocaust is a hoax, whether women love to be raped, whether Black people are getting genetically inferior to white people, whether homosexuals are child molesters." MacKinnon, *supra*, at 703.

95. As Professors Farber and Sherry have declared: "With no possibility of appeal to a standard of truth independent of politics, there is no way to mediate among truth claims except by recourse to authoritarian fiat." SHERRY & FARBER, *supra*, at 117.

96. *See* LUKES, *supra*, at 38-40.

97. BENSON & STANGROOM, *supra*, at 172.

98. After World War II, Legal Realism was replaced by process-oriented "Reasoned Elaboration," which was characterized by (1) an emphasis on the existence of institutional constraints, (2) a call for full articulation of the reasoning behind judicial opinions, and (3) the use of "neutral principles" in deciding constitutional issues, which "meant that judges should subordinate their personal predilections to the competing values cases presented." G. Edward White, *The Evolution of Reasoned Elaboration: Jurisprudential Criticism and Social Change*, *in* PATTERNS OF AMERICAN LEGAL THOUGHT 143-50 (1978); *see also* HORWITZ, *supra*, at 253 ("The single dominant theory in post-war American academic legal thought is the effort to find a 'morality of process' independent of results.").

99. Professor Himmelfarb has observed concerning deconstruction: "The result is a kind of free-floating verbal association, in which any word or idea can suggest any other (including, or especially, its opposite), and any text can be related in any fashion to another." Gertrude Himmelfarb, *On Looking Into the Abyss*, *in* ON LOOKING INTO THE ABYSS 9 (1994). "Jay Moran has asserted that CLS "[f]ocus[es] on interpretation not so much to enhance our understanding of the law in a positive sense, but rather to subvert liberalism altogether." Moran, *supra*, at 169.

100. Patricia J. Williams, *Alchemical Notes: Reconstructing Ideals from Deconstructed Rights*, 22 HARV. C.R.-C.L. L. REV. 401, 405 (1987).

101. Professors Grady and McGuire have written that "[h]umans use exchange and hierarchy as alternative structures for their cooperative dealings." Mark F. Grady & Michael T. McGuire, *A Theory of the Origin of Natural Law*, 8 J. CONTEMP. LEGAL ISSUES 87 (1997). They have continued: "Economic theory posits that institutions result from individual human decisions to maximize individual welfare." *Id.* at 88.

102. *See* Kennedy, *Hierarchy*, *supra*, at 591.

103. Duncan Kennedy, *Utopian Proposal or Law School as a Counter-Hegemonic Enclave*, (unpublished 1980), *quoted in*, White, *Critical Legal Studies*, *supra*, at 261.

104. Moran, *supra*, at 159.

105. *Id.*

106. Rorty, *The Poetry of Justice*, *supra*, at 1819.

107. Williams, *supra*, at 735.

108. As Professor Dworkin has observed, "Hercules [the ideal judge] is prevented from achieving integrity viewed from the standpoint of justice alone–coherence in the substantive principle of justice that flows throughout his account of what the law now is–because he has been seeking a wider integrity that gives effect to principles of fairness and procedural due process as well." RONALD DWORKIN, LAW'S EMPIRE 404 (1986) [hereinafter DWORKIN, LAW'S EMPIRE]; *see also* Antonin Scalia, *The Rule of Law as a Law of Rules*, 56 U. CHI. L. REV. 1175, 1178-79 (1989); LON L. FULLER, THE MORALITY OF THE LAW 39-40 (1964).

109. Rorty, *Anti-Foundamentalist Philosophers*, *supra*, at 719.

110. Blumenson, *supra*, at 534.

111. *Id.* at 543-44.

112. *Id.* at 552.

113. Maybe part of the problem is that many scholars have vested their careers in Postmodern theories. As Professor Harris has remarked: "There are academics who have built entire careers on the allegation that the foundations of science are rotten with bias–sexist, racist, imperialist, Northern, etc." HARRIS, *supra*, at 47.

114. PINKER, *supra*, at 2; *see generally* PINKER, *supra*.

115. C. N. DEGLER, IN SEARCH OF HUMAN NATURE: THE DECLINE AND REVIVAL OF DARWINISM IN AMERICAN SOCIAL THOUGHT viii (1991).

116. PINKER, *supra*, at 6.

117. *Id.* at 20. Other advocates of the Blank Slate included psychologist John B. Watson, anthropologist Franz Boa, Freud, and sociologist Émile Durkheim. MATT RIDLEY, THE AGILE GENE 40 (2003) [hereinafter RIDLEY, AGILE GENE]. Professor Ridley has called Skinner: "The high priest of nothing buttery. . ." *Id.* at 189. Concerning Boas, Benson and Strangroom have written that Boas was a cultural determinist–"that social conditioning shaped all human thought and behavior." BENSON & STRANGROOM, *supra*, at 11.

118. MARGARET MEAD, SEX AND TEMPERAMENT IN PRIMITIVE SOCIETIES 280 (1935/1963). Ridley relates that Mead was fooled by a practical joke: "it is now known that she had been duped by a handful of prank-playing young woman during her all too brief visit to the island, and that Samoa in the 1920s was if anything slightly more censorious about sex than America." RIDLEY, AGILE GENE, *supra*, at 204; *see also* PINKER, *supra*, at 56.

119. John Tooby & Leda Cosmides, *The Psychological Foundations of Culture, in* THE ADAPTED MIND: EVOLUTIONARY PSYCHOLOGY AND THE GENERATION OF CULTURE 21-23 (Jerome H. Barkow, Leda Cosmides, & John Tooby eds., 1992); *see also* , RIDLEY, AGILE GENE, *supra*, at 14 ("[A]nthropologists and sociologists were trained to ignore animal findings as irrelevant.").

120. Tooby & Cosmides, *supra*, at 22-23.

121. *Id.* at 22.

122. Jonathan Haidt & Fredrik Bjorklund, *Social Intuitionists Reason, in Conversation, in* 2 MORAL PSYCHOLOGY 245 (W. Sinnott-Armstrong ed., 2006) ("As we read the literature from neuroanatomy and behavioral genetics blank-slate models of the brain are no longer tenable."); PINKER, *supra*, at vii-ix; *see also generally* Owen D. Jones & Timothy H. Goldsmith, *Law and Behavioral Biology*, 105 COLUM. L. REV. 405 (2005); PINKER, *supra*. For example, although incomplete, babies have a "fundamental understanding of what objects are and how they act. . ." PAUL BLOOM, HOW THE SCIENCE OF CHILD DEVELOPMENT EXPLAINS WHAT MAKES US HUMAN 13 (2004).

123. Jim Chen, *Law as A Species of Language Acquisition*, 73 WASH. U. L.J. 1263, 1272 (1995).

124. Jones & Goldsmith, *supra*, at 424.

125. PINKER, *supra*, at viii-ix; *see also* TIMOTHY H. GOLDSMITH, THE BIOLOGICAL BASIS OF HUMAN NATURE: FORGING LINKS BETWEEN EVOLUTION AND BEHAVIOR 73-75 (1991). Professor Goldsmith has noted that if a songbird is raised in isolation, its adult vocalization is not completely normal. *Id.* at 74. He has written: "It is as though birds possess some kind of internal representation of their species' song against which they compare and refine their own vocalization." *Id.*

126. Bailey Kuklin, *Evolution, Politics and Law*, 38 VAL. U.L. REV. 1129, 1135-36 (2004).

127. ANTHONY WALSH, BIOSOCIOLOGY: AN EMERGING PARADIGM 32 (1995).

128. Jonathan Haidt & Fredrik Bjorklund, *Social Intuitionists Answer Six Questions About Moral Psychology*, in 2 MORAL PSYCHOLOGY 183 (W. Sinnott-Armstrong ed., 2006) [hereinafter Haidt & Bjorklund, *Social Intuitionists*].

129. Cosmides & Tooby, *supra*, at 185.

130. PAUL THAGARD, THE BRAIN AND THE MEANING OF LIFE 67, 69 (2010).

131. RIDLEY, AGILE GENE, *supra*, at 79-87 ("The twin studies have caused a genuine evolution in the understanding of personality." *Id.* at 82).

132. *Id.* at 79.

133. PINKER, *supra*, at 65.

134. Professor Goldsmith, has asserted, "that social scientists, as a group, have limited understanding of the rich fabric of evolutionary theory." GOLDSMITH, *supra*, at ix. The same is true of legal scholars: There has been "a near-total absence of recognition in legal thinking that all behavior, and all brain activity that perceives and directs it, are fundamentally biological phenomena, rendering the study of behavioral biology manifestly relevant to any deep and current understanding of how and why humans behave in ways important to law." Jones & Goldsmith, *supra*, at 419.

135. PINKER, *supra*, at 34.

136. *Id.*

137. Jones & Goldsmith, *supra*, at 125; PINKER, *supra*, at 34-35.

138. Professor Thagard has written, "concepts and other mental representations are patterns of neural activity." THAGARD, *supra*, at 78.

139. *Id.* at 56 ("Much of human knowledge is naturally described in terms of rules, and many kinds of thinking such as planning can be modeled by rule-base systems."); *see also* Sebastien Heilie et. al., *Evidence for Cortical Automaticity in Rule-Based Categorization*, 30 J. NEUROSCI. 14225 (2010) (There is evidence that rule-based category learning is supported by a broad neural network that includes the prefrontal cortex, the anterior cingulate cortex, the head of the caudate nucleus, and medial temporal lobe structures.).

140. David B. Leake, *Case-Based Reasoning*, in A COMPANION TO COGNITIVE SCIENCE 465 (William Bechtel & George Graham eds., 1998).

141. BLOOM, *supra*, at 40 ("We lump the world into categories so we can learn."); PINKER, *supra*, at 201-207; CAROLYN P. SOBEL, THE COGNITIVE SCIENCES: AN INTERDISCIPLINARY APPROACH 33 (2001) ("Categorization is a function so fundamental that we cannot think without engaging in it.").

142. BLOOM, *supra*, at 42 ("Such categories exist in the first place because objects are not randomly distributed in the universe with regard to the properties they possess."); PINKER, *supra*, at 202-03.

143. PINKER, *supra*, at 203; *see also* BLOOM, *supra*, at 39.

144. Professor Noam Chomsky also has stated that Kant and Descartes may be right and radical empiricism wrong. NOAM CHOMSKY, PROBLEMS OF KNOWLEDGE AND FREEDOM: THE RUSSELL LECTURES 13 (1971) [hereinafter CHOMSKY, PROBLEMS].

145. Professor Chen has declared, "law is 'sharply limited' by the biological constraints of universal grammar." Chen, *supra*, at 1278-79.

146. Professor Fodor has posited that there is an internal private language within the mind that other parts of the mind translate. JERRY A, FODOR, THE LANGUAGE OF THOUGHT 55-97 (1975). He has observed: "Communication is successful only when the hearer infers the speaker's intentions from the character of the utterance he produced." *Id.* at 103.

147. *See* Scott Fruehwald, *Pragmatic Textualism and the Limits of Statutory Interpretation:* Dale v. Boy Scouts of America, 35 WAKE FOREST L. REV. 973, 999-1000 (2000).

148. George E. Taylor, *Structural Textualism*, 75 B.U. L. REV. 321, 337 (1975).

149. Fruehwald, *Pragmatic Textualism, supra*, at 999-1000.

150. "Textualists attempt to determine what the words mean, rather than trying to establish what the legislature intended." Fruehwald, *Pragmatic Textualism, supra*, at 974-75.

151. DONALD E. BROWN, HUMAN UNIVERSALS (1991), *summarized in* PINKER, *supra*, at 435-39.

152. John Mikhail, Is the Prohibition of Homicide Universal? Evidence from Comparative Criminal Law, 75 Brook. L. Rev. 497 (2009).

153. Jones & Goldsmith, *supra*, at 466.

154. *Id.*

155. *Id.*

156. *Id.* at 466-67.

157. *Id.* at 467-69.

158. *Id.* at 471.

159. Peter Strahlendorf, *Legal Concepts from an Evolutionary Perspective, in* THE SENSE OF JUSTICE: BIOLOGICAL FOUNDATIONS OF LAW 142 (Roger D. Masters & Margaret Gruter eds., 1991).

160. *Id.* at 148-49.

161. *Id.* at 149.

162. Michael D. Guttentag, *Is There a Law Instinct?*, 87 WASH. U.L. REV. 269, 269 (2009).

163. *Id.* at 273-74.

164. *Id.* at 286.

165. *Id.* at 287.

166. *Id.* at 287, 291. Two-tired systems consist of primary rules and secondary rules that govern how to change, apply, and adjudicate primary rules.

167. *Id.* at 292-305. Guttentag has derived the notion of dumbfounding from Jonathan Haidt, *The Emotional Dog and Its Rational Tail: A Social Intuitionist Approach to Moral Judgment*, 108 PSYCHOL. REV. 814 (2001) [hereinafter Haidt, *Emotional Dog*].

168. Guttentag, *supra*, at 292.

169. *Id.*

170. *Id.*

171. *Id.* at 294-301. I will discuss the ultimatum game in depth in Chapter Five.

172. *Id.*

173. *Id.* at 304.

174. *Id.*

175. *Id.* at 305-314.

176. *Id.* at 306.

177. *Id.* at 307-08.

178. *Id.* at 308.

179. *Id.* at 307-10.

180. *Id.* at 312.

181. *Id.* at 313-321.

182. *Id.* at 317.

183. *Id.* at 320-21.

184. *Id.* at 327.

185. *Id.* at 324.

186. *Id.* at 327.

187. *Id.*

188. Brown, *supra*, at vii ("[W]hat we know about universals places clear limits on cultural relativism that anthropologists have developed and disseminated widely."). Cosmides and Tooby have asserted: "The relativity of human behavior, far from being the critical discovery of anthropology, is something imposed *a priori* on the field by the assumptions of the SSSM, because it premises define a program that is incapable of finding anything else." Cosmides & Tooby, *supra*, at 42.

189. Jonathan Haidt, *Invisible Fences of the Moral Domain*, 28 BEHAV. & BRAIN SCI. 552, 552-53 (2005) [hereinafter Haidt, *Invisible Fences*]; *see also* Haidt & Bjorklund, *Social Intuitionalists*, *supra*, at 213-14.

190. Haidt & Bjorklund, *Social Intuitionalists*, *supra*, at 215.

191. Haidt, *Invisible Fences*, *supra*, at 552-53.

192. PINKER, *supra*, at 202.

193. White, *Critical Legal Studies*, *supra*, at 259-60.

194. Professors Haidt and Bjorklund have observed, "[s]ocializing the reverse preferences would be difficult or impossible. The resistence of children to arbitrary or unusual socialization has been the downfall of many utopian efforts." Haidt & Bjorklund, *Social Intuitionalists*, *supra*, at 201. This author believes that social engineering is just as repugnant as eugenics.

195. As Professor Pinker has written, "Nor does acknowledging human nature have the political implications so many fear. It does not, for example, require one to abandon feminism, or to accept current levels of inequality or violence, or to treat morality as a fiction." PINKER, *supra*, at ix.

196. *Id.* at 65-69.

197. *Id.* at 68; Thomas SOWELL, MIGRATIONS AND CULTURES: A WORLD VIEW 376-77 (1996); TIMOTHY H. GOLDSMITH, THE BIOLOGICAL BASIS OF HUMAN NATURE: FORGING LINKS BETWEEN EVOLUTION AND BEHAVIOR 128 (1991) ("Many cultural choices represent options that, like adaptions, enhance reproductive success and survival."); Lionel Tiger, *The Evolution of Cultural Norms*, *in* THE SENSE OF JUSTICE: BIOLOGICAL FOUNDATIONS OF THE LAW 282 (Roger D. Masters & Margaret Gruter eds., 1991); *see generally* JARED DIAMOND, GUNS, GERMS, AND STEEL (1997) . Professor Tiger has continued: "By displaying this situational flexibility [humans] can maintain basic hominid patterns such as group formation and sociality,

reproductive access and assortment, management of space and resources, protection and socialization of the young, and so on. *Humans generate cultural variation in order to maintain their basic behavioral social biology.*" Tiger, *supra*, at 282.

198. PINKER, *supra*, at 68.

199. SOWELL, *supra*, at 377; PINKER, *supra*, at 68.

200. PINKER, *supra*, at 68.

201. NOAM CHOMSKY, REFLECTIONS ON LANGUAGE 132 (1975) [hereinafter, CHOMSKY, REFLECTIONS].

202. *Id.*

203. PINKER, *supra*, at xi.

204. *Id.* at 11.

205. Behavioral biologists reject strong moral relativism. For example, two scholars have declared, "From an evolutionary perspective, the survival of the animal depends on its maintaining its inner milieu within a very narrow range of values." William D. Casebeer & Patricia S. Churchland, *The Neural Mechanisms of Moral Cognition: A Multiple Aspect Approach to Moral Judgment and Decision-Making*, 18 BIOLOGY & PHIL. 169, 175 (2003); *see also* Morris B. Hoffman, *The Neuroeconomic Path of the Law*, 359 PHIL. TRANS. R. SOC. LOND. B. 1667, 1669 (2004) ("[T]here is indeed a relatively fixed and immutable set of right and wrong human behaviors.").

206. Harry M. Bracken, *Essence, Accident, and Race*, 116 HERMATHENA 81 (1973); *see also* CHOMSKY, REFLECTIONS, *supra*, at 130-32.

207. MICHAEL S. GAZZANIGA, HUMAN: THE SCIENCE BEHIND WHAT MAKES US UNIQUE 115-18 (2008); Sharon Street, *A Darwinian Dilemma for Realist Theories of Value*, 127 PHIL. STUD. 109, 113-114 (2006); PINKER, *supra*, at 187-88, 193.

208. Ayn Rand has called racism "the lowest, most crudely primitive form of collectivism." AYN RAND, THE VIRTUE OF SELFISHNESS 147 (1963).

209. GAZZANIGA, *supra*, at 63; *see also* MARCO IACOBONI, MIRRORING PEOPLE: THE NEW SCIENCE OF HOW WE CONNECT WITH OTHERS 4 (2008).

210. Jonathan Haidt, *Emotional Dog*, *supra*, at 824.

211. DONALD W. PFAFF, THE NEUROSCIENCE OF FAIR PLAY: WHY WE USUALLY FOLLOW THE GOLDEN RULE 410-12 (2007).

212. LARRY ARNHART, DARWINIAN NATURAL RIGHT: THE BIOLOGICAL ETHICS OF HUMAN NATURE 163-69 (1998).

213. MATT RIDLEY, THE RED QUEEN: SEX AND THE EVOLUTION OF HUMAN NATURE 8 (1993) [hereinafter RIDLEY, RED QUEEN].

214. Jones & Goldsmith, *supra*, at 477; *see also* RIDLEY, RED QUEEN, *supra*, at 13.

215. PINKER, *supra*, at 143; *see also* Jones & Goldsmith, *supra*, at 497.

216. GOLDSMITH, *supra*, at 125.

217. GAZZANIGA, *supra*, at 136.

218. *Id.*

219. *Id.*

220. RIDLEY, AGILE GENE, *supra*, at 266.

221. Professors Hoffman and Goldsmith have stated, "[a]ccording to rehabilitationists, in a perfect world there can be no punishment at all, because there are no intentional wrongs, only a spasmodic confluence of other causes (our schools, our diet, our friends, our mothers, our atoms). This could be only true if we came into the world as soft, amorphous balls of clay. . . But of course this view is not at all consistent with what we know about human evolution and development." Morris B. Hoffman & Timothy H. Goldsmith, *The Biological Roots of Punishment*, 1 OHIO ST. J. CRIM. L. 627, 639 (2004).

222. *See* PINKER, *supra*, at 55-56; GOLDSMITH, *supra*, at 67.

223. RIDLEY, AGILE GENE, *supra*, at 86.

224. Robinson et. al., *The Origins of Shared Intuitions of Justice*, 60 VAND. L. REV. 1653 (2007).

225. PINKER, *supra*, at 315. Professor Kulkin has written: "Instead of channeling behavior by affecting the genetic component of natural tendencies in the population through positive or negative eugenics, society realistically is limited to creating an environment in which individual character is refined to the point where it can overcome, as much as possible, personal temperament that is individually injurious or socially detrimental." Kulkin, *supra*, at 1196.

226. E. Donald Elliot, *Law and Biology: The New Synthesis*, 41 ST. LOUIS L.J. 595, 610 (1997).

227. Hoffman & Goldsmith, *supra*. Some scientists believe that proportional retribution is universal. LUKES, *supra*, at 141-42.

228. Hoffman & Goldsmith, *supra*, at 633. They have further declared: "Punishing wrongdoers is a critical part of the glue that holds people together in groups, and ultimately as a defining character of all civilizations." *Id.*

229. *Id.* at 634.

230. *Id.*

231. *Id.* at 640.

232. *Id.* at 640-41.

233. Robinson et. al., *supra*, at 1633.

234. *Id.* at 1638-39. The evidence the authors present comprises fMRI studies, including some of the studies discussed in Chapter Two, the fact that young children believe that immoral acts are wrong, even in the absence of rules, dumbfounding in connection with institutions of justice, etc. They add that "the spontaneous social learning explanation for agreement on views of justice is inconsistent with what is known about the limits of human calculation, including the sharp limits on the human cognitive capacity for deduction, the common human tendency to rely on simplifying heuristics, and other limitations on cognitive." *Id.* at 1681.

235. *Id.* at 1649.

236. *Id.* at 1649-52.

237. Professor Pinker has written that "the design of the moral sense leaves people in all cultures vulnerable to confusing defensible moral judgements with irrelevant passions and prejudices." PINKER, *supra*, at 272.

238. Professor Posner has stated "there is compelling scientific evidence that homosexual preference is genetic or at least congenital, and not acquired . . ." RICHARD POSNER, THE PROBLEMATICS OF MODERN

MORAL THEORY 175 (1999). Under behavioral biology "good" is not always normal or the majority practice.

239. I will deal with rights in greater depth in Chapter Five. In this chapter, I am contrasting individual rights with utilitarian rights favored by many Postmodernists.

240. JEFFRIE G. MURPHY & JULES L. COLEMAN, PHILOSOPHY OF LAW: AN INTRODUCTION TO JURISPRUDENCE 70-82 (rev. ed 1990). While this author agrees with this part of Kant's theory, much of Kant's philosophy is inconsistent with behavioral biology. Of course, Kant is not the only philosopher to have advocated the notion of human autonomy. For example, although Ayn Rand disagreed strongly with Kant's philosophical method, she came to the same conclusion as Kant concerning individual rights. E.g., RAND, *supra*, at 30, 108-117 ("[S]o every living human being is an end in himself, not the means to the ends or the welfare of others. . ." *Id.* at 30).

241. MURPHY & COLEMAN, *supra*, at 71.

242. *Id.* at 77-79.

243. *Id.* at 79.

244. *Id.* at 72.

245. *Id.* at 72-73.

246. *Id.* at 72.

247. Professor Kuklin believes that sociobiology supports Lockean conservatism, where "the individual is said to be prior to the state and thus has superior claims against the community." Kuklin, *supra*, at 1206. He also believes that it coincides with the Smithian view of human nature in which the Smithians "stress the 'invisible hand' approach to political economy." *Id.* at 1205-06, 1212-16. He noted, "[f]or both Smithians and sociobiologists, the individual's selfish interest is the salient, controlling ingredient." *Id.* at 1213. In contrast, sociobiology does not strongly support the Burkean conservative approach, which "see[s] the social contract as producing an obligation to one's ancestors, fellow citizens, and descendants to maintain the traditions of society, because Burkeans do not center their criterion on the individual and work bottom up." *Id.* at 1216-19. Finally, sociobiology does not support communitarian liberalism, the political position of many Postmodern thinkers. *Id.* at 1216-19. Liberals have greater "other-regardedness" than Lockean or Smithian conservatives in that in the tradeoff between liberty and equality, they value equality more and their primary center of value is the community." *Id.* at 1222-24.

248. GOLDSMITH, *supra*, at 123.

249. Professor Pinker has noted: "It is ironic that a philosophy that prides itself on deconstructing the accouterments of power should embrace a relativism that makes challenges to power impossible, because it denies that there are objective benchmarks against which the deceptions of the powerful can be evaluated." PINKER, *supra*, at 426.

250. MURPHY & COLEMAN, *supra*, at 73.

251. *Id.* at 74.

252. GOLDSMITH, *supra*, at 123.

253. *Id.* at 435-36.

254. One might notice a resemblance to some of Ronald Dworkin's theories. *See* RONALD DWORKIN, TAKING RIGHTS SERIOUSLY 82-86, 115 (1986); *see also* DWORKIN, LAW'S EMPIRE, *supra*, at 244 ("Judges must make their common-law decisions on grounds of principle, not policy; they must deploy arguments why

the parties actually had the 'novel' legal rights and duties they enforce at the time the parties actually acted or at some other pertinent time in the past.").

255. John O. McGinnis, *The Original Constitution and Our Origins*, 19 HARV. J.L. & PUB. POL. 251, 251-52 (1996) [hereinafter McGinnis, *Original Constitution*]. Professor Strahlendorf has written: "Natural-law philosophers have stated that there are a set of basic human values that are 'self-evident.' This means that humans sense that these values are good. . . . The point here . . . is . . . to suggest that there must be sets of biological mechanisms (epigenetic rules and Darwinian algorithms) that make things 'self-evidently' good." Strahlendorf, *supra*, at 154.

256. McGinnis, *The Original Constitution, supra*, at 252.

257. *Id.* at 252-53.

258. *Id.* at 253.

259. The classic statement of Libertarianism comes from J. Stuart Mill: "[T]he sole end for which mankind are warranted, individually or collectively, in interfering with the liberty of action of any of their number, is self-protection. That the only purpose for which power can be exercised over any member of a civilized community, against his will, is to prevent harm to others." JOHN STUART MILL, ON LIBERTY 68 (1910).

260. John O. McGinnis, *The Human Constitution and Constitutive Law: A Prolegomenon*, 8 J. CONTEMP. LEGAL ISSUES 222 (1997); McGinnis, *The Human Constitution, supra*, at 216.

261. CHOMSKY, REFLECTIONS ON LANGUAGE, *supra*, at 133-34.

262. CHOMSKY, PROBLEMS, *supra*, at 54.

263. LLOYD L. WEINREB, NATURAL LAW AND JUSTICE 90-92 (1987).

264. MURPHY & COLEMAN, *supra*, at 165.

265. Professor Kuklin has noted that Libertarians think that "it is costly in many ways to counter human disposition." Kuklin, *supra*, at 1211. Professor Lukes has observed:

> Within that framework, we focus on actions that are universally wrong rather than universally right. The later concern seems moralistic rather than moral; we proscribe, say, torture and rape but we are reluctant to prescribe how people ought to act and live their lives.

LUKES, *supra*, at 154.

266. As Professor Ridley has observed: "Even the most libertarian politician today believes in the need to regulate, oversee, and tax the efforts of ambitious individuals so as to ensure that they do not satisfy their ambitions entirely at the expense of others." RIDLEY, RED QUEEN, *supra*, at 91.

267. PINKER, *supra*, at 421.

Chapter Four

Reciprocal Altruism as the Basis for Contract

Ideologies come and go, but human nature is here to stay.

Frans De Waal[1]

Behavioral biology illuminates the basis of contract. As mentioned in Chapter Two, behavioral biologists believe that genes are selfish; they are only interested in their survival. However, reciprocal altruism–"I'll scratch your back if you scratch mine"–provides a basis for cooperation among humans that promotes survival. If two humans cooperate in obtaining and allocating resources, they will have greater resources and a greater chance to survive and reproduce, thus continuing their genes. Contract law reflects and reinforces this reciprocal altruism from our evolutionary past.

Connected with reciprocal altruism is a human instinct for equity in reciprocal exchanges. As mentioned in Chapter Two, mirror neurons allow humans to sense the emotions and intentions of others. Consequently, humans can detect unfair situations and rectify them. Evolutionary fairness is reflected in the contract rules of frustration, unconscionability, and mistake, as well as in the good faith duty in performance and unconscionability. Also connected with reciprocal altruism is the need to deter cheaters. In contract law, cheaters–those who breach the contract–are deterred through contract remedies.

Part I of this chapter will discuss traditional theories of contract law, including the objective theory of contract formation, deontological and consequentialist approaches, redistributive theories, and more recent theories by Professor Solan (contract as agreement) and Professor Markovits (contract as collaboration). Part II will then analyze the relationship between reciprocal altruism and contract law. It will argue that reciprocal altruism is the best explanation for the formation of contracts, compare reciprocal altruism as the basis of contract to the theories discussed in Part I, examine the other necessary element for contract validity–consideration–under reciprocal altruism, and give a justification for courts to enforce contracts under reciprocal altruism. Part III will demonstrate that contract damages are the glue for reciprocal altruism and that expectation damages are the proper measure of damages under this approach. Finally, Part IV will deal with reciprocal altruism and other contract issues–gap filling, unallocated risks, good faith in performance, and unconscionability.[2]

I. Theories of Contract Law

Traditional contract theory views the formation of contracts as objective with actual intent being irrelevant.[3] As Professor Gilmore has noted, "Holmes and his successors substituted an 'objectivist' approach to the theory of contract for the 'subjectivist' approach which the courts had–*almost instinctively, it would seem, and without giving any thought to the matter*–been following."[4] Under this theory, the promisor's actual intent is irrelevant as long as a reasonable person would think that a promise has been given.[5]

The classic case of *Lucy v. Zehmer*[6] employed the objective theory of contract formation. Lucy and Zehmer had entered into a written contract for Lucy to buy Zehmer's farm for $50,000. Zehmer stated that at the time he had executed the contract both parties had been drinking, and he had thought that Lucy had made the offer in jest. Lucy had written up an agreement, and Zehmer had rewritten it before he and his wife signed it. The next day Lucy sold a half interest in the property to his brother.

  The court held that an enforceable contract had been made.[7] The court declared: "If it be assumed, contrary to what we think the evidence shows, that Zehmer was jesting about selling his farm to Lucy and that the transaction was intended by him to be a joke, nevertheless the evidence shows that Lucy did not so understand it but considered it to be a serious business transaction and the contract to be binding on the Zehmers as well as on himself."[8] In upholding the contract, the court wrote, "[i]n the field of contracts, as generally elsewhere, we must look to the outward expression of a person as manifesting his intention rather than to his secret and unexpressed intention. The law imputes to a person an intention corresponding to the reasonable meaning of his words and acts."[9] The court continued: "The mental assent of the parties is not requisite for the formation of a contract. If the words or other acts of one of the parties have but one reasonable meaning, his undisclosed intention is immaterial except when an unreasonable meaning which he attaches to his manifestations is known to the other party."[10] The court concluded: "An agreement or mutual assent is of course essential to a valid contract but the law imputes to a person an intention corresponding to the reasonable meaning of his words and acts. If his words and acts, judged by a reasonable standard, manifest an intention to agree, it is immaterial what may be the real but unexpressed state of his mind."[11]

  Professor Solan has attacked the objective theory of contract formation as being too narrow.[12] He has asserted that the objective account

> ignores certain situations in which it would not be reasonable to construe a statement as a promise, and it fails to take into account the understanding of the promisee, which is an important variable in determining contractual liability. Most problematic for the objective account is that when both parties agree that a commitment has been made, the promisor is bound, and when neither believes that a promise has been made, the promisor is not bound.[13]

Solan wrote that, when one rejects the objective theory of contract, contract doctrines fit together better.[14]

  Instead of an objective theory, he thought that agreement (mutual intent) is fundamental in contract formation: "Promises are enforced when the parties have reached an agreement, unless the promisee actually and reasonably believes that a promise was made even though none was intended."[15] He declared: "Right from the beginning, it is possible to tell students that the law of contracts is about mutual assent, and favors objective evidence of that assent in various ways that will come out as they learn the various doctrines."[16]

The following table of when a contract is binding illustrates his theory:[17]

	Reasonable Inference	Promisor's Intent	Promisee's Understanding	Promisor Bound?
1	Yes	Yes	Yes	Yes
2	Yes	Yes	No	No
3	Yes	No	Yes	Yes
4	Yes	No	No	No
5	No	Yes	Yes	Yes
6	No	Yes	No	No
7	No	No	Yes	No
8	No	No	No	No

Some of these examples contradict the objective theory of contract formation. Notably, a contract can exist when there is no reasonable inference, but the parties have reached an agreement (scenario 5). Similarly, where there is a reasonable inference, but the promisee doesn't understand that a promise has been made, there is no contract (scenarios 2 & 4). Solan quoted Judge Linde, who averred, "The staunchest objectivist would not let a jury hold two parties to an apparently manifested agreement if neither thought the other meant to assent."[18] Professor Solan remarked that

these facts are highly consistent with a theory of contract law based on notions of personal autonomy. But it is not the autonomy of the promisor alone that predicts judicial outcomes in a wide range of cases.

Rather, courts are concerned with protecting the autonomy of both parties.[19]

He added: "Intent must be mutual to be effective; unilateral intent does not count."[20] He concluded that

> the standard objective approach to contract formation is off base. The very same facts concerning what does and does not count as contract can be better handled by a theory based on the parties' actual agreement, with a special rule carved out to bind those who give the impression that they have made a promise, if the hearer actually takes it as such. This misconceptionalization of contract law has lasted as long as it has in large part because the crucial cases that display its weakness do not occur very often.[21]

Professor Solan also noted other problems with the objective approach to contract formation. He pointed out that courts interpret contacts based on the parties' intent.[22] Actual (subjective) intent overcomes ordinary meaning (objective) contract interpretation, thus creating an inconsistency between the theory behind contact formation (objective) and interpretation (subjective).[23] He also observed that courts' notions of consideration are intentionalist: "Contract law rests on obligations imposed by bargain."[24] Similarly, "[c]ourts fill gaps in contract to effectuate the intent of the parties when they failed to state all of the contract's details in advance."[25] "Gap filling . . . [is] 'interpretative' in the sense that [it is an effort] to determine how the parties would have resolved the issue that has arisen had they foreseen it when they negotiated their contract."[26]

Professor Markovits has also rejected traditional contract theories and proposed a forward-looking theory based on collaboration.[27] He has claimed that "promises generally, and contracts in particular, establish a relation of recognition and respect–and indeed a kind of community–among those who participate in them. . ."[28] He has stated that "[t]he centerpiece of my approach to morality of contract is an argument that finds the value of community directly in the form of the contract relation rather than the substantive ends that the parties to contracts pursue."[29]

Professor Markovits began by contrasting truth-telling and lying: "When a person tells the truth, she promotes a kind of community between herself and her listeners. . . Lying, by contrast, places a speaker actively out of community with her listeners."[30] Next, he tied this in with the Kantian "Formula of the End in Itself": "[f]irst, that one should never use persons merely as means; second that one should always treat them as ends in themselves."[31] This relates to Markovits's idea of community:

> First, the basis of respectful community must be free: Persons must join the community willingly, and one of the basic forms of estrangement arises when one person manipulates another through deception (or coercion). Second, the basis of respectful community must be shared: Persons must enter into community with each other through the pursuit of ends that they adopt together . . ., and a second form of estrangement arises when one person adopts pursuits in which another, who is implicated in them, cannot participate.[32]

He concluded: "Promises therefore render persons practically open to one and other. Without promises, their wills would remain isolated (just as their minds would remain isolated without truthful communications)."[33]

Professor Markovits argued that "[t]he value of a certain communal relation underwrites a powerful and broad-reaching moral theory of promise. In order to enter into this relation, persons must (negatively) refrain from treating one another merely as means by refraining from acting under principles that others could not accept, and also (positively) treat one another as ends by pursuing ends others share."[34] He elaborated: "The reason for making honest promises is that the intentions they involve enable persons to cease to be strangers by sharing in the ends of the promises; and the reason for keeping honest promises is that breaches betray these shared ends in favor of others that cannot be shared, and in this way estrange the parties from each other."[35] "Contract is a mechanism through which persons may cease to be strangers and enter into a community."[36] In addition, courts should enforce contractual promises because "contractual promisors intend to give their promisees not just moral authority but also legal capacity to compel them to pursue the ends that contract specifies."[37] Markovits then applied his view of contract as collaboration to consideration and expectation damages.[38]

Theories of contract law can also be deontological or consequentialist.[39]   A deontological system "is any system which does not appeal to the consequences of our actions, but which appeals to conformity with certain rules of duty."[40] A deontological approach emphasizes the litigants' preexisting rights, and it downplays society's interest in the outcome.   It is frequently associated with Kantianism–"the view that rational choice . . . is always the choice that respects the rights of autonomous persons freely to determine their own destinies, even if this respect is bought at the cost of a loss of happiness or well-being."[41] On the other hand, in a consequentialist system, "alternative courses of action are evaluated according to the desirability of their consequences."[42] Consequentialism focuses on policy and social goals.[43] In other words, it looks to see which contract rule produces the better result for society at large.

Professor Fried's view of contract as promise presents an example of a deontological approach to contact, as well as another instance of the will theory of contract.[44]   Fried argued that "[a]n individual is morally bound to keep his promises because he has intentionally invoked a convention whose function it is to give grounds–moral grounds–for another to expect the promised performance."[45]   He contended that "[t]he obligation to keep a promise is grounded not in arguments of utility but in respect for individual autonomy and in trust."[46] He declared, "so long as we see contractual obligation as based on promise, on obligations that the parties themselves assumed, the focus of the inquiry is on the will of the parties."[47] He added that "[t]he need for acceptance shows the moral relation of promising to be voluntary on both sides."[48] He asserted: "unless one assumes the continuity of the self and the possibility of maintaining complex projects over time, not only the morality of promising but also any coherent picture of the person becomes impossible."[49] Therefore, under Fried's theory, "[b]ecause the law ought to do what is morally required, the state has a legitimate interest in enforcing the terms of private agreements."[50]

Professor Fried attacked those who regard contracts as imposing the community's will or as a way to do justice (consequentialist approaches).[51] In Fried's view, "courts are not entitled to use a dispute that arises in contract to promote an independent ideal of *justice* by refusing to enforce bad or hard deals, or to further the economic or other aims of society as a whole."[52] He also rejected the view of contract as tort–those theories that focus "on an injury suffered by the plaintiff and asks if the defendant is somehow sufficiently responsible for that injury that he should be made to pay compensation."[53]

The law and economics approach to contracts is consequentialist in that it intends contract rules to change behavior to the most efficient behavior. Proponents of law and economics believe that man is a rational actor–"that man is a rational maximizer of his ends in life."[54] They also think that man responds to incentive–"that if a person's surroundings change in such a way that he could increase his satisfactions by altering his behavior, he will do so."[55] Thus, "rule formulation seeks to maximize or minimize some specific goal of allocative efficiency."[56] Law and economic proponents believe that "[i]f voluntarily exchanged, resources are shifted to those uses in which the value to the consumer, as measured by the consumer's willingness to pay, is highest. Where resources are being used where their value is greatest they are being employed efficiently; they produce the largest possible output; therefore, courts should formulate contract rules that produce the most efficient allocation of resources."[57]

Other consequentialist approaches view contact law as positive law, emanating from the state.[58] Morris R. Cohen wrote, "[t]he law of contract, then, through judges, sheriffs, or marshals puts the sovereign power of the state at the disposal of one party to be exercised over the other party."[59] Similarly, he maintained that "the law of contract may be viewed as a subsidiary branch of public law, as a body of rules according to which the sovereign power of the state will be exercised as between the parties to a more or less voluntary transaction."[60] Contract law was intended to do justice. Cohen averred: "But we also need care that the power of the state be not used for unconscionable purposes, such as helping those who exploit the dire need or weakness of their fellows."[61] He added: "We may thus view the law of contract not only as a branch of public law but also as having a function somewhat parallel to that of criminal law. Both serve to standardize conduct by penalizing departures from the legal norm."[62] In other words, contract and tort principles have merged.[63]

More recent public law approaches often consider law as a means of distributive justice. Anthony Kronmen has written,

> it has sometimes been suggested that the law of contracts should also be used as an instrument of distributive justice and that those responsible for choosing or designing rules of contract law–courts and

legislatures–should do so with an eye to their distributional effects in a self-conscious effort to achieve a fair division of wealth among the members of society.[64]

He observed, "seemingly neutral rules which purport merely to define the limits of permissible advantage-taking in the exchange process actually have a distributional effect insofar as they determine the conditions under which various valuable advantages may or may not be exploited by their possessors, . . . that these same rules ought to be evaluated by the fairness of the distributional pattern they create."[65] He argued that "instead of leaving people free to transact as they please and imposing a periodic tax on their wealth, an attempt is made to preserve the fairness of the original distribution of resources by restricting the terms on which individuals are permitted to alter their holdings through voluntary exchange–by forbidding certain transactions and, perhaps, by requiring others."[66] He gave as an example minimum wage laws, noting "such laws attempt to insure a fair distribution of wealth between workers and employers on which workers may contract to sell their labor."[67]

Courts' refusals to enforce unconscionable contracts illustrate distributive justice. In *Williams v. Walker-Thomas Furniture Co.*,[68] the court created a contract defense of unenforceability due to unconscionability. In this case, a retail furniture store leased items to customers for a monthly rental payment. Title remained in the furniture company until all payments were made, then title vested in the customer. If the customer defaulted before all payments were made, the store could repossess the item. The contract also stated that "the amount of each periodical installment payment to be made by [purchaser] to the Company under this present lease shall be inclusive of and not in addition to the amount of each installment payment to be made by [purchaser] under such prior leases, bills or accounts; *and all payments now and hereafter made by [purchaser] shall be credited pro rata on all outstanding leases, bills and accounts* due the Company by [purchaser] at the time each such payment is made."[69] Stated differently, "the effect of this rather obscure provision was to keep a balance due on every item purchased until the balance due on all items, whenever purchased, was liquidated."[70] While the trial court condemned this practice, it felt that there was no law that allowed it to void the contract.[71]

The appellate court held that under District of Columbia common law "where the element of unconscionability is present at the time a contract is made, the contract should not be enforced."[72] The court declared: "Unconscionability has generally been recognized to include an absence of meaningful choice on the part of one of the parties together with contract terms which are unreasonably favorable to the other party."[73] The Court explained:

> Ordinarily, one who signs an agreement without full knowledge of its terms might be held to assume the risk that he has entered a one-sided bargain. But when a party of little bargaining power, and hence little real choice, signs a commercially unreasonable contract with little or no knowledge of its terms, it is hardly likely that his consent, or even an objective manifestation of his consent, was ever given to all the terms. In such a case the usual rule that the terms of the agreement are not to be questioned should be abandoned and the court should consider whether the terms of the contract are so unfair that enforcement should be withheld.[74]

Professor Fried cited cases like *Williams* as examples of "redistributive zeal."[75] Regardless of whether one completely agrees with Professor Fried's criticism of these cases, they are redistributive in the sense that they restrict "the terms on which individuals are permitted to alter their holdings through voluntary exchange" based on public policy considerations. Theoretically at least, they redistribute wealth from the store owner to the poor customers.[76] Since both parties have had their rights to contract limited, one can certainly not view these cases as reflecting mutuality of agreement or even an objective approach to contracts. The state has decided on what terms parties can contract, and what the parties actually intend is irrelevant.

II. Contract Law, the Formation and Enforcement of Contracts, and Reciprocal Altruism

It is the thesis of this chapter that reciprocal altruism is the evolutionary predecessor of contract law. Contract law then "codified" reciprocal altruism, and it helped deal with the problems of reciprocal altruism, such as cheating and long-term commitments. Under the theory of behavioral biology set forth in Chapter Two, reciprocal altruism antedates formal institutions, and it appears to be hardwired into human brains.[77] In other words, there is a universal grammar of reciprocity just like there is a universal grammar of language.[78] Reciprocal altruism reduces the costs of survival and aids the continuation of the genes by allocating scarce resources and creating additional resources through cooperation. It also reduces harmful competition (serious injury and death) by creating a way of allocating resources without fighting over them.[79] Moreover, it allows for communal living because reciprocal altruism overcomes the selfish gene that tends to be altruistic only to family members. Finally, because contract law improves on reciprocal altruism by dealing with problems of cheating and long-term commitments, contract law further reduces the cost of survival and aids the continuation of the gene.

This author believes that contract rules should generally reflect their evolutionary predecessor–reciprocal altruism. It should follow the identifiable patterns that humans have traditionally used to resolve disputes over resources.[80] As mentioned in Chapter Two, this does not mean that everything that is natural is good. However, reciprocal altruism is an evolutionary trait that can "produce results of great beauty." When contract law follows reciprocal altruism, it is adopting a natural tendency that has produced good results. Because, as discussed in Chapter Two, it is easier to adopt a positive natural trait than repress it since it is part of the human behavioral system, adopting reciprocal altruism would generally produce efficient results and be easier to enforce.

This does not mean that all aspects of reciprocal altruism must be brought into contract law. Some of its characteristics might not work well in a modern world. In addition, other considerations, including other considerations from behavioral biology, may be better in determining some of the details of contract law. Nevertheless, understanding contract law's origins in reciprocal altruism can help us determine what contract rules should be.

Reciprocal altruism corresponds generally with both Solan's contract as agreement based on actual cases, Markovits's contract as collaboration, and Fried's contract as promise based on morality because all four approaches advocate the will theory of contracts. What reciprocal altruism adds to these approaches is a deeper explanation for Solan's observations, Markovits's approach, and the promise theory.

Not only is keeping promises moral because the parties willing entered into the contract and invoked the institution of contract, reciprocal altruism is part of our evolutionary past because it aided survival. Not only have the parties invoked a convention; they have invoked a convention that is part of our human behavior. The morality is not just based on convention; it is intrinsic.

Reciprocal altruism provides a significantly better explanation (or behavioral model) for contract law than the objective theories set forth in Part I, especially concerning the formation of contracts. Reciprocal altruism emphasizes individual autonomy and the need to overcome self-interest. Like Professor Solan's view of contract law, reciprocal altruism shows that contract is predicated on voluntary agreement, based on social connections created by our mirror neurons. Solan's quotation from Professor Eisenberg that "'[w]hen an offer is understood as a promise there is no need to explain why the offeror cannot walk away from the promise if his offer is accepted. He cannot walk away because by making his offer he promised to perform on stated terms if his offer was properly accepted.'"[81] fits perfectly with reciprocal altruism. Likewise, similar to Professor Markovits's view, contract under reciprocal altruism is based on cooperation. The very basis of reciprocal altruism is that parties are giving up their immediate self-interest in exchange for better rewards created by cooperation.

Broadnax v. Ledbetter[82] illustrates a situation where there was no reciprocal exchange, no subjective agreement, and thus no contract. A sheriff had publically offered a reward to anyone who returned an escaped prisoner to the Dallas county jail. The plaintiff returned the prisoner but without knowing of the reward. The sheriff refused to pay the reward because the plaintiff had not known about it when he returned the prisoner. The court held that the only way to enforce the reward was by contract and that there was no meeting of the minds since there was no acceptance.[83] The court declared: "The mere doing of the specified things without reference to the offer is not the consideration for which it calls."[84] In other words, if there has been no reciprocal altruism between the parties (no collaboration), there is no contract. You can't have reciprocal altruism when the parties are not aware of the others' acts.

Ideally, contact validity should be based solely on the subjectivity of both parties. However, contract law needs to compensate for the possibility of deception in the formation process. Therefore, a rule is needed that when the offeror makes a statement that appears to be an offer and the offeree reasonably believes it is an offer and accepts that offer, a contract is formed regardless of whether the offeror subjectively intended an offer. This does not make contract law objective; rather, it looks at the offeree's subjectivity; it protects the offeree's self-interest. In so doing, it makes agreements more secure, and it makes it more likely individuals will enter into agreements, thus creating more resources and furthering the survival of the individual and his or her genes. Accordingly, Professor Solan's suggested rule that contacts should be viewed "by a theory based on the parties' actual agreement, with a special rule carved out to bind those who give the impression that they have made a promise, if the hearer actually takes it as such" fits well with behavioral biology because it reflects reciprocal altruism and helps overcome problems of cheating.

Professor Markovits's idea of contract as collaboration generally agrees with reciprocal altruism. Reciprocal altruism is collaboration between the parties to give up their selfish interests so that both parties gain; both reciprocal altruism and contract as collaboration involve interlocking intentions. Under reciprocal altruism, the interlocking intentions are created by our mirror neurons.[85] Likewise, reciprocal altruism will not work if one party uses the other as "a means to an end" or if the parties don't cooperate as to the end. Cheating (reciprocal altruism) or lying (collaboration) destroys the bond between the contracting parties under both theories.

Reciprocal altruism is a deontological approach to contracts. It begins with pre-existing rights, and it emphasizes the parties' power to determine their destinies. Since it is based on the selfish gene and ways to produce reciprocal altruism, it works at the individual level, not the group level. In other words, contract law should be private law that is enforced by the state. Contract rules should be based on what best encourages man's positive, natural tendencies, not utilitarianism. Contract law should not be like criminal law or tort law. It is enforcing a bargain, not compensating for injuries. It should not directly punish or compensate for wrongful injuries; it should encourage and facilitate transactions that are mutually beneficial to the parties.

Unlike law and economics approaches to contracts, reciprocal altruism rejects consequentialism. It emphasizes the parties' rights, not the most efficient approach, because reciprocal altruism is concerned with individuals, not society as a whole. It is not trying to change behavior; rather, it is attempting to develop contract rules that reflect instinctive behavior.

In addition, a number of scholars have questioned whether the rational choice of law and economics reflects reality. Professor Korobkin has maintained: "Interdisciplinary behavioral science research presents substantial evidence that individuals employ decisionmaking processes that will often deviate from the predictions of narrow versions of rational choice theory."[86] Such deviations include irrationally steep discounting, mistaken probablity assessments, and endowments effects.[87] In addition, neuroscientists have shown that emotions play a role in our decisionmaking, thus further undermining the rational choice approach.[88]

Doing distributive justice through contract law is beyond reciprocal altruism. Fairness does play a significant role in reciprocal altruism, but it is a different role than in distributive justice. Contract law's purpose under behavioral biology is to facilitate reciprocal altruism, not to redistribute resources. Fairness in connection with reciprocal altruism means fairness between individuals, rather than fairness within society. In fact, redistribution is contrary to reciprocal altruism; redistribution destroys the interests of reciprocal altruism–gain through cooperation–by giving that gain back to the other party or to others. This does not mean that all the cases based on distributive justice would have different outcomes under behavioral biology, but that an alternative justification is needed for those results.

Traditional concepts of consideration (the other component for contract validity) are explainable by reciprocal altruism. Consideration comprises two factors: 1) "The consideration that in law promotes a mere promise into a contractual obligation is something, or the promise of something, given in exchange for the promise" and 2) "the law is not at all interested in the adequacy of consideration."[89] The first factor is central to the idea of bargained for exchange.[90] Under reciprocal altruism, contracts must always have some type of bargain–some type of mutuality.[91] For example, promises are given for something–cooperation in increasing both parties' resources. This need for consideration (bargained for exchange) does not mean that other types of legal relations are not enforceable, just that they are not contracts.[92] The second factor protects autonomy. An autonomous individual decides what is valuable to him or her. As Professor Markovits has asserted, "[t]he fact that one competitor is more successful in this effort than another, and that the resulting bargain might be thought substantively unfair, therefore does not undermine the bargain's collaborative character."[93]

According to traditional contract law, "[t]he principle purposes of the consideration requirement for contracts are a cautionary function of bringing home to the promisor the fact that his promise is legally enforceable and the evidentiary function of making it more likely that an enforceable promise was intended."[94] Under reciprocal altruism it is more: the consideration requirement is that there is truly a bargained for exchange because this is a part of the basic definition of reciprocal altruism.[95] This is why things like moral obligation, promises to perform past obligations, and past consideration can't be consideration;[96] there has been no exchange, no reciprocity.

Finally, courts should enforce contracts because the parties have put the enforcement of the law behind their reciprocal altruism, and they have agreed to abide by their culture's contract rules.[97] Enforcement encourages reciprocal altruism because it makes it less risky and reduces transaction costs by reducing monitoring costs.[98] This is just like the law encouraging the nuclear family through marriage. Legal enforcement of contracts is especially important in modern societies because modern societies are much larger and more impersonal than groups on the savannah, where reputation was often an effective enforcement device. In other words, law helps create trust in larger groups, impersonal exchanges, and long-term commitments.[99] Finally, human groups may have an instinct to protect an individual's things.[100] As Professor Markovits has argued, "[t]he first end of politics, including liberal politics, is therefore to sustain coordination in the face of the incentives to defect."[101] This is true under behavioral biology because cooperation helps the survival of the genes and the individual better than pure self-interest.[102]

III. Reciprocal Altruism and Contract Damages

Damages are the glue that helps contract law encourage and facilitate reciprocal altruism.[103] First, damages force cheaters to disgorge the advantages they obtained through cheating, thus influencing them to give the promised benefit. Second, they protect nonbreaching parties, thus encouraging them to enter into transactions without the concern that the other party will cheat. In sum, "[p]rofound empirical evidence shows that the possibility of sanctioning norm violators stabilizes human cooperation at a high level, whereas cooperation typically collapses in the absense of sanctioning possibilities."[104]

Unlike tort law, liability for breach of contract is strict–it does not depend on fault.[105] Under reciprocal altruism, this is because the purpose of damages is not to punish, but to cement the bargain. There are generally three types of compensatory contract damages: 1) expectation damages, which award the plaintiff the amount he or she would have been entitled to had the contract been performed; 2) reliance damages, which give the plaintiff an amount that places the plaintiff in the same position the plaintiff would have been in had the plaintiff never entered into the contract; and 3) restitution damages, which award the plaintiff an amount equal to any benefits conferred upon the defendant.[106] Expectation damages are the traditional measure of damages for breach because they give the nonbreaching party the benefit of the bargain.[107] As Professor Fried has stated, "to the extent that contract is grounded in promise, it seems natural to measure relief by the expectation, that is by the promise itself."[108] Fried based this on Kantian autonomy, rather than notions of collectivity.[109]

Expectation damages are the best measure of compensation for contract breach under reciprocal altruism. First, they give the offeror the incentive to perform the contract. If the offeror breaches the contract, he or she must give the offeree the full benefit of the agreement. Second, the offeree can feel secure in entering into the contract because the offeree will get exactly what he or she bargained for. The offeree either gets the promised for performance or the equivalent in damages. Furthermore, expectation damages allow parties to enter into long-term commitments because they help a party value a future gain as much as an immediate one. Finally, expectation damages coincide with the essence of reciprocal altruism. As Professor Markovits has pointed out, "[e]xpectation damages encompass the exact ends whose sharing enables the parties to contracts to treat each other as ends in themselves."[110]

Professors Jones and Goldsmith have developed a method for evaluating punishment based on behavioral biology that they call "The Law of Law's Leverage," which is a type of evolutionary cost-benefit analysis.[111] This law states: "The magnitude necessary to reduce or to increase the incidence of any human behavior will correlate positively or negatively, respectively, with the extent to which a predisposition contributing to that behavior was adaptive for its bearers, on average, in past environments."[112] Put differently, "behaviors that have the deepest roots in evolutionary history are most likely to be the most resistant to change."[113] Consequently, "shifting behaviors that tended to increase reproductive success in ancestral environments will generally be less costly than shifting behavior in ways that tended to decrease such success."[114] For example, "[b]ecause natural selection disfavors inbreeding among close relatives, evolutionary analysis . . . predicts that it will be far less costly to discourage incest among parents and their natural children, and between siblings reared together, than among stepparents and stepchildren."[115] One can also apply these principles to tort law since punishment affects human behavior and controlling human behavior is a part of torts.

Professors Jones and Goldsmith caution that their approach "cannot predict curves for law-relevant behaviors with precision."[116] Moreover, their theory does not create a "must." Rather, it helps evaluate the proper measure of punishment (or damages) needed to change a behavior. Other considerations may affect the choice of punishment or damages.

Expectation damages also fit with the Jones-Goldsmith cost-benefit analysis. While reciprocal altruism was adaptive, so was cheating. Consequently, significant damages are necessary to discourage cheating within reciprocal altruism. The damages must be enough so that the potential breacher will see the cost of cheating is greater than the benefit from cheating in survival terms–resources gained or lost. Expectation damages would provide this disincentive because, as stated above, it takes away all of the breachers gain from cheating.

The above does allow for efficient breaches. When the cost of the breach (expectation damages) is less then the benefit from the breach, the offeror will get the benefit of the breach, but the offeree will still be fully compensated. Actually, this is evolutionarily sound. The offeree gets the resources he or she expected, and the breaching party obtains even greater resources, thus furthering the possibility of survival. It is not unfair for the breaching party to receive the extra resources because, as noted above, contract damage are not based on fault. Thus, restitution damages should generally not be the measure of damages because, as stated earlier, the nonbreaching party is fully compensated by expectation damages and the breaching party has created greater resources for survival through his or her efforts.[117] In addition, when restitution damages are more than expectation damages they may over deter promisors, creating less reciprocal altruism.

Reliance damages, which will generally be much less than expectation damages, usually are not a proper measure of damages for contract breach. Placing a party in the same position as he or she would have been in if the contract had not been entered into is not an effective incentive to enter into a contract because it will not cause a person to trade his or her selfish interest for mutual cooperation. What the parties negotiated for was not reliance (backward looking), but the bargain–expectation (forward looking).[118] Similarly, the parties did not bargain to be compensated for injuries. In addition, a party will often pass up other opportunities when agreeing to a contract, and reliance damages will not compensate for lost opportunities. Moreover, having to pay reliance damages, rather than expectation damages, when a breaching party finds a better deal, will encourage, rather than discourage breach, because under reliance damages the breaching party will have an incentive to breach at an earlier time since the profit from breaching will occur at an earlier time.

Punitive damages are not appropriate for breach of contract under reciprocal altruism since contract damages are not based on fault.[119] Expectation damages are sufficient to perform the purpose of contract damages–to encourage the parties to enter into the contract and to discourage inefficient breach–so giving punitive damages would be overcompensation and discourage reciprocal altruism.[120] Moreover, punitive damages are not necessary because the nonbreaching party got the value that the party bargained for. In addition, as Professor Markovits has mentioned, punitive damages can "actively corrode collaboration."[121] Finally, this author believes that courts should give punitive damages only when there has been a public wrong,[122] and, as argued above, contracts are private, not public.

Courts generally give specific performance only when expectation damages would be inadequate.[123] This rule supports the autonomy behind reciprocal altruism, but still gives the nonbreaching party full compensation. Personal service contracts are generally not enforced through specific performance.[124] This is consistent with notions of autonomy. However, specific performance is usually given for the sale of real property because real property is considered unique.[125] Since property is unique, giving specific performance is the only way to give the offeree the benefit of the bargain; money cannot be a substitute.

Evolutionary biology also justifies the *Hadley v. Baxendale*[126] rule that damages should be limited to foreseeable losses. Parties enter into reciprocal altruistic relationships for their selfish interests. While each party has to give up something to get the other party to enter into the relationship, neither party intends to cover the other's unforeseeable losses. In addition, parties will be reluctant to enter into reciprocal altruistic relationships when they could be liable for significant unforeseeable damages.

Equally important, if one of the parties is acting under special circumstances, those special circumstances should be specified in the contract and the risk allocated.

Although expectation damages are usually the best measure of damages for breach under reciprocal altruism, other measures may be justified when damages are speculative, are overly burdensome, or do not fairly compensate the plaintiff. However, courts should award other measures of damages only when expectation damages are clearly improper. For example, in one case, a furnace company contracted with a shipper to deliver several packages by a date certain to a trade show in Atlantic City.[127] One of the packages did not arrive on time causing the exhibit to fail. The trial court awarded reliance damages for the cost of shipping and expenses of attending the trade show. The defendant appealed on the ground that damages were improper because the plaintiff had not put on any evidence of lost profits (the expectation). In upholding the award, the court declared: "The whole damage, therefore, was suffered in contemplation of defendant performing its contract, which it failed to do, and would not have been sustained except for reliance by plaintiff upon defendant to perform it."[128] In other words, the court had to give reliance damages, or the defendant would not have been compensated.

Finally, in *Jacobs & Young, Inc. v. Kent*,[129] Justice Cardozo refused to give specific performance or equivalent damages when a contractor used pipe that was different than specified in a building contract. The installed pipe was probably the same quality as the specified pipe, and, in any case, the difference was due to oversight, not willful conduct.[130] Cardozo wrote: "In the circumstances of this case, we think the measure of the allowance is not the cost of replacement, which would be great, but the difference in value, which would be either nominal or nothing."[131] He concluded, "the rule that gives a remedy in cases of substantial performance with compensation for defects of trivial or inappreciable importance, has been developed by the courts as an instrument of justice. The measure of the allowance must be shaped to the same end."[132] This is the correct decision under reciprocal altruism. While the non-breaching party did not get exactly what he bargained for, what he got was essentially the same. In such a circumstance, the breaching party should not be forced to pay ruinous damages.

IV. Other Contract Issues and Behavioral Biology

Reciprocal altruism and behavioral biology can also help elucidate other issues in contract law. First, the influence of "cultural differences" helps us understand the differences in gap filling between traditional contract law and the Uniform Commercial Code. Second, the personal autonomy in reciprocal altruism and the instinct for equity in reciprocal exchanges helps explain the doctrines of mutual mistake, frustration, and impossibility, as well as the requirement of good faith in performance. Finally, behavioral biology produces other explanations for unconscionability than redistributive theories.

A. Gap Filling

Gap filling is a problem for contract law because parties generally do not think of everything that might occur in connection with a contract. However, by agreeing to the contract, the parties have also agreed to allow the court to fill in the gaps.[133] In filling in gaps, courts generally try to determine the parties' intent: "In deciding how to fill gaps, they take into account what parties ordinarily intended as a surrogate for what the parties in the dispute actually intended."[134] In other words, the courts try to do the best they can to enforce the reciprocal altruism, even if they have to make reasonable guesses concerning the parties' intents.[135]

Default rules, a part of gap filling, aid reciprocal altruism. First, they make it easier to negotiate contracts because parties do not have to negotiate everything that might occur. They create a background the parties can use. More importantly, default rules provide greater security in entering into the reciprocal relationship because they make contract law more specific and certain.

However, contrasting approaches to contract fill gaps differently than others. Traditional contract law is more reluctant to fill gaps (and thus sometimes allows the contract to fail), than the Uniform Commercial Code, which is interested in upholding contracts when the parties indicate they intended to enter into the contract even if all the terms are not specified. The fact that traditional contract law fills gaps differently than the Uniform Commercial Code demonstrates that cultural differences, as discussed above in Chapter Two, can affect the details of contract law.

At the common law, a contract must be definite in its terms and conditions to be enforceable.[136] "The requirement of definiteness is designed to ensure that courts will not impose contractual obligations when the parties did not intend to conclude a binding agreement, and also to ensure that the nature of the parties' respective obligations is reasonably certain so as to enable the court to discern a breach and fashion an appropriate remedy."[137] On the other hand, under the Uniform Commercial Code, a contract for a sale does not fail for indefiniteness even though one or more terms are left open, as long as the parties have intended to make a contract and there is a reasonably certain basis for giving a remedy.[138] This applies even to important terms, such as price, time and place of delivery of goods, and time of payment.[139] Also, the UCC includes more gap filling provisions than traditional contract law.[140]

These divergences are explainable by differences between the "cultures" of traditional contract and the UCC.[141] As mentioned above, while evolution sets the outlines of reciprocal altruism, culture accounts for the details based on the culture's needs. Traditional contract emphasizes the need to protect parties from unwanted contracts and to ensure that the parties' rights and duties are clear. Traditional contract arose in a period when contracts were often between individuals and when people were less sophisticated. In contrast, the UCC is intended for commercial contracts in a modern world. It generally concerns contracts between merchants and more sophisticated individuals, who have greater access to information. In such a "culture," the emphasis is on forming contracts when the parties intended, not ensuring that all the details are specified. These details can be filled in by custom, reasonableness, default rules, etc. Thus, reciprocal altruism is the basis of both traditional contracts and UCC contracts (the ultimate causes are the same), but the details are different because of the contrasting details of their cultures (the proximate causes are different). In other words, one emphasizes the right not to contract and the other the right to contract even if all the terms aren't definite, both deriving from reciprocal altruism.

B. Mutual Mistake, Frustration, and Impossibility

Sometimes the performance of a contract will fail because of unallocated risks, such as mutual mistake, frustration, or impossibility.[142] Mutual mistake occurred in *Raffles v. Wichelhaus*,[143] where the court gave relief to a party who had refused delivery of cotton. The ship Peerless the defendant had intended the shipment to arrive in

Liverpool from India on had sailed in October, while the plaintiff's ship Peerless had left India in December. There was no contract (no subjective agreement) because the parties had intended different ships with the same name.[144] Concerning the theory behind frustration and impossibility, one commentator has written,

> the parties were said to have contemplated the continued existence of a particular state of facts. If these facts change so as to render impossible a party's performance, it is often said that the continued existence of the contemplated state of facts is a condition precedent to the promisor's duty under the contract.[145]

A classic illustration of frustration is *Krell v. Henry*,[146] where the court provided relief based on frustration of essential purpose, when a defendant had hired a room overlooking the king's coronation route at considerable cost, but the king had cancelled the procession because of an illness. Similarly, in *Taylor v. Caldwell*,[147] a court granted a musical hall owner relief for impossibility from payment to performers when the music hall burnt down before the scheduled performance.

Because of the personal autonomy involved with reciprocal altruism and the instinct for equity in reciprocal exchange, a deal should not be forced upon a party when a serious burden unforeseen by both parties falls on one of them. First, the danger of having to bear such a burden discourages individuals from entering into binding contracts.[148] Individuals will not enter into risky transactions when there is a possibility of significant loss with no return, as there was in the above examples. Parties have certain expectations in contracting, including that they will not suffer unexpected losses.[149] A chance of a heavy loss will affect the inborn cost/benefit analysis, making reciprocal altruism less frequent. Since the main reason for reciprocal altruism is mutual gain, contract law should protect both parties from harsh losses. Second, forcing a party to absorb unforeseen serious loss goes against our innate sense of fairness.[150] Bad luck should not fall on one party alone in a cooperative venture. Humans recognize the difference between bad luck and lack of effort.[151] Third, many of these cases are like the gap-filling cases above because the court is trying to determine the parties' intentions when they have not allocated the risks. Reciprocal altruism helps the court determine that neither party would have assumed significant, unforeseen losses. Finally, with some of these circumstances, especially mutual mistake of material terms, one can say that an agreement has not been entered into at all. To force an agreement in such an instance would ignore the autonomy of the parties that is the basis of reciprocal altruism.

Of course, the above does not apply to allocated risks or unilateral mistakes. When one party goes into a transaction with eyes open, that party should not be relieved from his or her contractual duty just because the party later found the duty burdensome.

C. Good Faith in Performance

Good faith in performance is central to reciprocal altruism because the parties are depending on each other to increase their resources and thus their chances for survival. The classic case on good faith is *Wood v. Lucy, Lady Duff-Gordon*.[152] In this case, the defendant was a well-known fashion designer and the plaintiff was a manufacturer and seller of clothes. The parties entered into an exclusive agreement whereby the plaintiff would have the right to use the defendant's endorsement on its clothes and the right to place her designs on sale in exchange for half the profits. The plaintiff claimed that the defendant breached this contract by placing her endorsement on other parties' clothes. The defendant defended on the ground that the agreement didn't bind the plaintiff to anything. Justice Cardozo, however, thought that there was an implied promise in the contract for the defendant to "use reasonable efforts to place the defendant's endorsements and market her designs."[153] He observed:

> Her sole compensation for the grant of an exclusive agency is to be one-
> half of all the profits resulting from the plaintiff's efforts. Unless he
> gave his efforts, she could never get anything. Without an implied
> promise, the transaction cannot have business efficacy as both parties
> must have intended that at all events it should have.[154]

In other words, Justice Cardozo found an implied promise of good faith in the contract's performance.

The defendant was correct that if the plaintiff had not acted in good faith to perform the contract she would have nothing. However, there was a background expectation that the plaintiff would perform his duties under the contract[155]–that he would act in good faith. This is a central part of reciprocal altruism because the altruism redirects self-interest since both parties gain by being altruistic. Without this background duty of good faith, reciprocal altruism would be impossible because at least one of the parties would often have no gain (no additional resources to enhance survival) and no reason to give up his or her selfish interest.[156] Similarly, a lack of duty of good faith would destroy the trust between the contracting parties that is central to Professor Markovits's approach and is also part of the incentive for reciprocal altruism.

In evaluating good faith, Professor Burton has urged courts to look at both the promisor and the promisee.[157] He has argued:

> Bad faith performance occurs precisely when discretion is used to
> recapture opportunities foregone upon contracting–when the discretion
> exercising party refuses to pay the expected cost of performance. Good
> faith performance, in turn, occurs when a party's discretion is exercised
> for purposes within the reasonable contemplation of the parties at the
> time of formation–to capture opportunities that were preserved upon
> entering the contract, interpreted objectively.[158]

Reciprocal altruism supports Burton's argument and goes further. First, Burton is correct that the duty of good faith does not extend beyond that which was within the parties' contemplation at the time of contracting. Good faith in contracting does not create a general fiduciary duty among the parties, but rather a duty of good faith concerning the performance of the contract the parties agreed to.

Second, courts should look at both parties because imposing the duty of good faith on one of them should not create unfair burdens on that party that were not allocated in the contract. Output and needs contracts are examples of such situations. In an output contract, one party agrees to sell all of their output of a certain commodity to another party. For example, a silver mine agrees to sell all of its silver to another party whose business is to make commemorative coins. The first party would have a good faith duty to mine silver under the contract at reasonable levels even if that mining became financially burdensome. However, a court would not force the mine to supply silver to the other party when the mine had exhausted its supply of silver. Under reciprocal altruism, without this limit on the good faith requirement, parties would be reluctant to enter into output contracts because such a contract could be ruinous, thus dangerously reducing their resources. This is just like the rules discussed above that relieve parties from performance when frustration of purpose or impossibility is involved.

The same applies to needs contracts. Under a needs contract, a party agrees to buy all its needs of a certain commodity from a particular supplier. There is a good faith duty under such a contract to buy a minimum quantity from the supplier. However, that good faith duty does not exist if the buyer goes out of business. Just like with output contracts, an opposite rule would dissuade parties from entering into needs contracts.

In sum, under reciprocal altruism, implying a good faith duty of performance helps give the parties what they bargained for, thus encouraging those parties and other parties to enter into future transactions. However, that duty of good faith should not go too far, which would discourage persons from entering into reciprocal exchanges.

D. Unconscionability

In Part II, this author argued that distributive justice could not be the basis of invalidating contracts for unconscionability under reciprocal altruism. However, reciprocal altruism can justify the outcome in cases like *Williams v. Walker-Thomas Furniture, Co* because reciprocal altruism is based on mutual agreement. These cases emphasize the lack of bargaining power of one of the parties–that one of the parties lacked meaningful choice.[159] As several courts have stated, "an unconscionable contract is one that no man in his senses, not under delusion, would make, on the one hand; and that no fair and honest man would accept on the other."[160] Since autonomous agreement is the basis of reciprocal altruism, one can say that when one of the parties lacked bargaining power that a contract was never created in the first place. In other words, the parties did not cooperate mutually to increase their resources, but rather that one party received a benefit without giving a benefit to the other party. There was no collaboration. Alternatively, one could say that there was a failure of consideration–that one of the parties did not receive any consideration because the terms were so harsh that that party did not receive any benefit.

Courts need to be careful with unconscionability under this theory to limit it to cases where there truly has been no agreement and one of the parties has received no benefit. That an individual has made a bad bargain is not a reason to give relief from a contract under reciprocal altruism. Thus, contracts will probably be invalidated less under reciprocal altruism than under redistributive theories.

Based on reciprocal altruism, invalidating contracts for unconscionability in proper circumstances is not redistributive zeal, as Professor Fried has labeled it in these cases.[161] This author agrees with Professor Fried that "[r]edistribution is not a burden to be borne in a random, ad hoc way by those who happen to cross paths with persons poorer than themselves."[162] However, under reciprocal altruism, the contract is void because there is no autonomous agreement, not because of policy reasons. The unfairness is private unfairness, not a desire to redistribute resources through private means. Similarly, this is not a consequentialist approach. The reason for invalidating the contract is not to change behavior but rather, as stated above, because there is no reciprocal altruism.

Some may think that the above approach to unconscionability under reciprocal altruism does not provide enough protection to consumers, especially poor ones. As stated earlier, the law does not always have to follow behavioral biology in creating legal rules; other factors may be more important in producing laws. Behavioral biology helps us understand what the law should be, but it does not create "musts." In addition, as is true in this case (see below), behavioral biology can provide alternative justifications or solutions for some problems. Unconscionability might be a place where the law wants to depart from reciprocal altruism. Just like minimum wage laws restrict employment contracts, unconscionability and similar laws protect consumers because society believes that consumers need protection in certain circumstances.

Still, strong unconscionability rules go against reciprocal altruism. Any limitation on contracting would decrease the incentive to enter into contracts. As Professor Fried has observed, such rules may limit the employment possibilities for workers or the availability of appliances for the poor.[163] However, while these considerations are important, as noted above, they create policy considerations, not musts. If lawmakers believe that such rules are necessary to protect consumers and that these considerations outweigh those of reciprocal altruism, then nothing in behavioral biology says that they cannot exist. Moreover, the enactment of such rules does not undermine reciprocal altruism as the main basis of contract; it just modifies it in limited instances.

Moreover, unconscionability and other consumer protection rules are consistent with behavioral biology in general. (In other words, behavioral biology provides an alternative justification for unconscionability.) As mentioned in Part II, cheaters are part of our evolutionary past, and mankind developed ways to deal with cheaters. Thus, unconscionability and other consumer protection rules are ways to overcome some members of society's natural inclination to cheat, which dates back to their evolutionary past.

Conclusion

Professor Markovits has argued that a theory of contract must satisfy two requirements: first, "what reasons exist for making agreements" and, second, "what reason exist for keeping such agreements as have been made?"[164] Reciprocal altruism as the basis of contract satisfies both these requirements. First, contracts are made to overcome the selfish gene and to create resources in order to reduce the costs of survival and continue the gene. Second, parties keep contracts and society enforces such agreements because it encourages further reciprocal altruism, it increases resources, it is efficient because it fosters natural tendencies, and the parties have put the force of the law behind their reciprocal altruism.

This chapter has not attempted to solve all the issues or all the details of contract law, and certainly many of the details need refinement. Nevertheless, it has shown that contract may have a basis in reciprocal altruism and behavioral biology. If legal scholars ignore this connection to man's evolutionary past, then we have an incomplete view of contract.

Notes

1. FRANS DE WAAL, THE AGE OF EMPATHY, NATURE'S LESSONS FOR A KINDER SOCIETY 45 (2009).

2. Alternatives to contract, such as promissory estoppel, are beyond the scope of this chapter. Promissory estoppel does not involve reciprocal altruism or agreement. Rather, it depends on reliance and injury. The fact that other bases exist for enforcing other obligations does not undermine this chapter's central tenet that reciprocal altruism is the main basis for contract.

3. Lawrence M. Solan, *Contract as Agreement*, 83 NOTRE DAME L. REV. 353 (2007); *see also* JOSEPH M. PERILLO, CALAMARI AND PERILLO ON CONTRACTS §2.2 at 27 (5th ed. 2003); 17 C.J.S. *Contracts* §37 (1999) ("Mental assent to the promises in a contract is not essential.").

4. GRANT GILMORE, THE DEATH OF THE CONTRACT 35 (1974) (emphasis added).

5. Solan, *supra*, at 360-61.

6. 84 S.E.2d 516 (1954).

7. *Id.* at 522.

8. *Id.* at 521.

9. *Id.* (Citations omitted).

10. *Id.* at 522.

11. *Id.*

12. Solan, *supra*, at 353.

13. *Id.* at 356. Solan has stated that "our conceptualization of contract formation changes when we look not only at the most recurrent cases, but at how we would resolve the entire matrix of possible scenarios that is generated when we take into account the few variables that seem to influence courts in the recurrent cases." *Id.* at 376.

14. *Id.* at 357.

15. *Id.*

16. *Id.* at 406.

17. *Id.* at 361.

18. *Id.* at 365 (quoting Kabil Devs. Corp. v. Mignot, 566 P.2d 505, 509 (Or. 1977)).

19. Solan, *supra*, at 362.

20. *Id.* at 363.

21. *Id.* at 384.

22. *Id.* at 363.

23. *Id.* at 363-64, 388-94.

24. *Id.* at 395.

25. *Id.* at 402.

26. *Id.*

27. Daniel Markovits, *Contract and Collaboration*, 113 YALE L.J. 1417 (2004).

28. *Id.* at 1420.

29. *Id.*

30. *Id.* at 1422.

31. *Id.* at 1424.

32. *Id.* at 1429.

33. *Id.* at 1434.

34. *Id.* at 1446.

35. *Id.* at 1447.

36. *Id.* at 1504.

37. *Id.* at 1448-49.

38. *Id.* at 1477-1514. I will discuss Markovits's ideas on consideration and expectation damages when I reach these topics below.

39. Peter A. Alces, *Law and Morality: Contract Law: The Moral Impossibility of Contract*, 48 WM. & MARY L. REV. 1647, 1656 (2007).

40. J.J.C. Smart & Bernard Williams, *An Outline of a System of Utilitarian Ethics*, *in* UTILITARIANISM: FOR AND AGAINST 1, 5 (1973).

41. JEFFERIE G. MURPHY & JULES L. COLEMAN, PHILOSOPHY OF LAW: AN INTRODUCTION TO JURISPRUDENCE 71 (2d ed. 1990).

42. LEA BRILMAYER, CONFLICT OF LAWS 225 (2d ed. 1995).

43. *Id.* at 229; *see also* Russell Korobin, *A "Traditional" and "Behavioral" Law-and-Economics Analysis of* Williams v. Walker-Thomas Furniture Co., 26 U. HAW. L. REV. 441, 446 (2004).

44. CHARLES FRIED, CONTRACT AS PROMISE: A THEORY OF CONTRACTUAL OBLIGATION (1981).

45. *Id.* at 16.

46. *Id.*

47. *Id.* at 4.

48. *Id.* at 43.

49. *Id.* at 14.

50. MURPHY & COLEMAN, *supra*, at 62.

51. FRIED, *supra*, at 2-6.

52. MURPHY & COLEMAN, *supra*, at 163.

53. FRIED, *supra*, at 4.

54. RICHARD A. POSNER, ECONOMIC ANALYSIS OF THE LAW 3 (6th ed. 2003).

55. *Id.* at 4.

56. WARNER Z. HIRSCH, LAW AND ECONOMICS: AN INTRODUCTORY ANALYSIS 6 (3d ed. 1999).

57. *Id.* at 7.

58. MORTON J. HORWITZ, THE TRANSFORMATION OF AMERICAN LAW, 1870-1960: THE CRISIS OF LEGAL ORTHODOXY (1992) ("When the state either enforced or refused to enforce agreements it was only because of considerations of public policy.").

59. Morris R. Cohen, *The Basis of Contract*, 46 HARV. L. REV. 553, 586 (1933); *see also* Arthur Linton Corbin, *Quasi-Contractual Obligations*, 21 YALE L.J. 533, 552 (1912) ("All enforceable obligations are created by the law."). Professor Horwitz has written, "Corbin's Progressive legal theory denied that even contract law embodied a pure realm of individual autonomy." HORWITZ, *supra*, at 50.

60. Cohen, *supra*, at 586.

61. *Id.* at 587.

62. *Id.* at 598.

63. HORWITZ, *supra*, at 50.

64. Anthony T. Kronman, *Contract Law and Distributive Justice*, 89 YALE L.J. 472, 472 (1980) [hereinafter Kronman, *Distributive Justice*].

65. Anthony T. Kronman, *Review: A New Champion for the Will Theory*, 91 YALE L.J. 404, 417 (1981).

66. Kronman, *Distributive Justice*, *supra*, at 499.

67. *Id.*

68. 350 F.2d 445 (D.C. Cir. 1965).

69. *Id.* at 447.

70. *Id.*

71. *Id.* at 448.

72. *Id.* at 449.

73. *Id.*

74. *Id.* at 449-50.

75. FRIED, *supra*, at 105.

76. Professor Fried has pointed out that "[s]uppose that the greater frequency of default made high prices and harsh credit terms a necessity for doing business with an often nearly destitute clientele. . ." *Id.* at 105.

77. Neel Parekh has declared: "cooperative behavior emerged as an innate tendency–an evolved algorithm naturally applied given specific environmental conditions." Neel P. Parekh, *Note: When Nice Guys Finish First: The Evolution of Cooperation, the Study of Law and the Ordering of Legal Regimes*, 37 U. MICH. J. L. REFORM 909, 920 (2004); *see also* STEVEN PINKER, THE BLANK SLATE: THE MODERN DENIAL OF HUMAN NATURE 221 (2002) (Among humans cognitive faculties is "an intuitive economics, which we use to exchange goods and favors."); John O. McGinnis, *Symposium: Originalism, Democracy, and the Constitution: The Original Constitution and Our Origins*, 19 HARV. J. L. & PUB. POL'Y 251, 260 (1996) ("Contract and commerce are not mere social artifacts, but arise from innate prepolitical aspects of human nature."). Professor Stake has made similar observations concerning fundamental principles of property. Jeffrey Evans Stake, *The Property 'Instinct,'* 359 PHIL. TRANS. ROYAL SOC'Y LONDON 1763 (2004); *see also* E. O. Wilson, *Foreword from the Scientific Side, in* THE LITERARY ANIMAL: EVOLUTION AND THE NATURE OF NARRATIVE 87 (Jonathan Gottschall & David Sloan Wilson eds., 2005). Stake has added: "An ability to recognize and, in appropriate contexts, adhere to specific conventions may be part of our behavioral repertoire." Stake, *supra*, at 1764. For example, he believes humans may have an innate sense of alienability. *Id.*; *see also* Thomas A. Smith, *Equality, Evolution and Partnership Law*, 3 J. BIOECONOMICS 99 (2001) (Human nature includes a complex predisposition toward egalitarianism in certain situations, such as partnerships.).

78. PINKER, *supra*, at 438; *see also* Stake, *supra*, at 1764 ("These rules reflect what we could call a 'deep property structure' akin to the deep language structure.").

79. Professor Stake holds a similar view of property rules. Stake, *supra*, at 1763.

80. Professor Stake believes similarly concerning property. *Id.* ("Embedded in the idea of property is the presumption that there are identifiable patterns in the resolution of disputes over resources.").

81. Solan, *supra*, at 391 (quoting Melvin A. Eisenberg, *The Revocation of Offers*, 2004 WISC. L. REV. 271, 275).

82. 99 S.W. 1111 (Tex. 1907).

83. *Id.* at 1111-12.

84. *Id.* at 1112.

85. MARCO IACOBONI, MIRRORING PEOPLE: THE NEW SCIENCE OF HOW WE CONNECT WITH OTHERS 76, 267 (2008) ("[N]eurons code the intentions." *Id.* at 267).

86. Russell Korobkin, *Bounded Rationality, Standard Form Contracts, and Unconscionability*, 70 U. CHI. L. REV. 1203, 1290 (2003); *see also* Parekh, *supra*, at 929 ("But behavioral economics and evolutionary studies of the brain as a cognitive processor demonstrate that man is far from rational.").

87. Owen D. Jones & Sarah F. Brosnan, *Law, Biology, and Property: A New Theory of the Endowment Effect*, 49 WM. & MARY L. REV. 1935, 1939 (2008).

88. Alan G. Sanfey et. al., *The Neural Basis of Economic Decision-Making in the Ultimatum Game*, 300 SCIENCE 1755, 1755 (2003).

89. FRIED, *supra*, at 29.

90. Solan, *supra*, at 395 ("Contract law rests on obligation imposed by bargain.") (quoting *Rich Prods. Corp. v. Kemutec Inc.*, 241 F.3d 915, 918 (7th Cir. 2001)).

91. Professor Markovits views consideration similarly under his collaboration theory of contract: "The bargain form is intimately connected to the conception of collaboration that lies at the root of the morality of contract–indeed, that the bargain form is characteristic of collaborative relations–and that contract law therefore is right to enforce this form." Markovits, *supra*, at 1482.

92. Professor Markovits has written similarly in connection with his theory of contract as collaboration: "The consideration doctrine's emphasis on bargains also serves to exclude certain noncollaborative classes of voluntary obligations from the realm of contract." *Id.* at 1484.

93. *Id.* at 1483. He added, "[t]he bargain form is sufficient for collaboration, and the consideration doctrine, attending to the intrinsic value of this form, properly places bargains at the core of contract." *Id.*

94. 17 C.J.S. *Contracts* §84 (1999).

95. Professor Solan has noted "the inconsistency between an objective approach to contract formation on the one hand, and the consideration requirement on the other." Solan, *supra*, at 395.

96. PERILLO, *supra*, at §§4.3, 4.9, 5.2 at 177-78, 188-89, 229; 17 C.J.S. *Contracts* §§102, 120, 125.

97. Professor Randy E. Barnett has written, "by manifesting their consent to be legally bound, parties necessarily–that is, as a conceptual matter, consent to the jurisdiction of some adjudicative and enforcement mechanism." Randy E. Barnett, *The Sound of Silence: Default Rules and Contractual Consent*, 78 VA. L. REV. 821, 861 (1992).

98. *See* Terrence R. Chorvat & Kevin McCabe, *The Brain and the Law*, 359 PHIL. TRANS. R. SOC. LOND. B. 1727, 1730, 1733 (2004) ("Legal regimes that allow one to seek restitution even from parties one does not know personally increases willingness to deal with those whom one has not yet had repeated dealings." *Id.* at 1733.).

99. *Id.* at 1733.

100. Stake, *supra*, at 1767.

101. Markovits, *supra*, at 1515.

102. Professor Markowitz has averred: "Too frequent defections undermine coordination entirely, render public order and social stability unsustainable, and introduce a state of affairs that is worse, for every person, than the coordinated state that it replaces." *Id.*

103. As Professors Jones and Goldsmith have stated: "Contract law ensures that people who behave in a certain way in the past (creating obligation) will behave in a particular way in the future (performing or

paying compensation)–all so that still other people will have requisite confidence to engage in future transactional behavior with yet other people." Owen D. Jones & Timothy H. Goldsmith, *Law and Behavioral Biology*, 105 COLUM. L. REV. 405, 413 (2005). Contract damages under any theory can never be perfect because of competing interests and uncertainty in evidence. Reciprocal altruism and other aspects of behavioral biology can help illuminate what will affect behavior, but the exact measure of damages must be determined by weighing all considerations.

104. Özgür Güreck et. al., *The Competitive Advantage of Sanctioning Institutions*, 312 SCIENCE 108, 108 (2006).

105. HENRY MATHER, CONTRACT LAW AND MORALITY 111 (1999); E. Allan Farnsworth, *Legal Remedies for Breach of Contract*, 70 COLUM. L. REV. 1145, 1146-47 (1970).

106. A. MITCHELL POLINSKY, AN INTRODUCTION TO LAW AND ECONOMICS 28 (2d ed. 1989); FRIED, *supra*, at 17-18; Farnsworth, *supra*, at 1148.

107. MATHER, *supra*, at 111; FRIED, *supra*, at 17.

108. FRIED, *supra*, at 18.

109. *Id.* at 19.

110. Markovits, *supra*, at 1505.

111. Jones & Goldsmith, *supra*, at 459-65.

112. *Id.* at 461.

113. *Id.* at 463.

114. *Id.*

115. *Id.* at 464.

116. Jones & Goldsmith, *supra*, at 465.

117. As Professor Markovits has noted, the parties can allocate this benefit through the contract. Markovits, *supra*, at 1497-1500.

118. As Professor Markovits has observed, "[h]arm-based views fit uncomfortably with the experience that promissory obligation extends to encompass promisees' forward-looking expectations in the promised performance and not just their backward-looking reliance." *Id.* at 1443.

119. Punitive damages might be appropriate in cases where there has been intentional tortuous conduct, such as fraud in the inducement or duress. These are more like torts than contract characteristics because they go against the very basis of reciprocal altruism. Instead of one party cooperating with another party, the first party is taking advantage of the second party in the bargaining process.

120. Professor Markovits has written that punitive damages "do not serve to secure or complete the collaboration or to protect the promisee's interest or expectation in the collaborative venture, but instead look to burden the breaching promisor with a punishment or reprimand. The collaborative ideal rejects punitive damages for breach of contract because it rejects the suggestion that a promisor who breaches a contract–but does nothing more–acts wrongfully in any sense that might justify punishing her." Markovits, *supra*, at 1508-09. However, courts might consider awarding attorney's fees to fully compensate the plaintiff.

121. *Id.* at 1509.

122. *See* Chapter Six.

123. MATHER, *supra*, at 115-16; Farnsworth, *supra*, at 1153-54.

124. Farnsworth, *supra*, at 1153.

125. *Id.* at 1154-55.

126. 156 ENG. REP. 154 (1854).

127. Security Stove & Mfg. Co. v. American R.E. Co., 51 S.W.2d 572 (1932).

128. *Id.* at 577.

129. 129 N.E. 889 (1921).

130. *Id.* at 890.

131. *Id.* at 891.

132. *Id.* at 892.

133. *See* Barnett, *supra*, at 862 ("[W]hen courts enforce these background rules [default rules], they do so with actual, not merely hypothetical, consensual authorization.").

134. Solan, *supra*, at 385.

135. As Professor Solan has stated, "[w]e privilege the ordinary meaning because, by doing so, we are more likely to enforce the ex ante intent of the contracting parties." *Id.* at 401.

136. PERILLO, *supra*, at §2.9 at 414; 17 C.J.S. *Contracts* §42.

137. 17 C.J.S. *Contracts* §42 (1999).

138. UCC §2-204(3).

139. UCC §§ 2-305, 2-308, 2-309, 2-310; *see also* 77A C.J.S. *Sales* §74 (1994).

140. 77A C.J.S. *Sales* §84a (1994).

141. Cosmides and Tooby have pointed out that "our social exchange psychology should be highly context-dependant." Leda Cosmides & John Tooby, *Cognitive Adaptions for Social Exchange*, in THE ADAPTED MIND: EVOLUTIONARY PSYCHOLOGY AND THE GENERATION OF CULTURE 211 (Jerome H. Barkow, Leda Cosmides, & John Tooby eds., 1992).

142. "'Impossibility' is the rubric used when the carrying out of a promise is no longer 'physically possible,' and 'frustration of purpose' is when performance of the promise is physically possible but the underlying purpose of the bargain is no longer attainable." Richard A. Posner & Andrew M. Rosenfield, *Impossibility and Related Doctrines in Contract Law: An Economic Analysis*, 6 J. LEG. STUD. 83, 85 (1977).

143. 2 HURL. & C. 906 (Exch. 1864).

144. *Id.*

145. PERILLO, *supra*, at §13.1 at 513.

146. 2 K.B. 740 (C.A. 1903).

147. 3 Best and S. 826 (Q.B. 1863).

148. Professor Solan has stated concerning these types of cases "[t]o rule otherwise would result in an unduly harsh (and inefficient) outcome since the contractor would forfeit a great deal more than the owner would realize." Solan, *supra*, at 401.

149. *See* FRIED, *supra*, at 88, 91. Professor Kar has proposed that there are standard excuses that are part of the deep structure of law and morality. Robin Bradley Kar, *The Deep Structure of Law and Morality*, 84 TEX. L. REV. 877, 924 (2006).

Law & Human Behavior

150. According to Professors Jones & Goldsmith, "[r]esearch suggests that there are biological underpinnings of a sense of fairness." Jones & Goldsmith, *supra*, at 441.

151. Leda Cosmides & John Tooby, *Evolutionary Psychology, Moral Heuristics, and the Law, in* HEURISTICS AND THE LAW 191 (Gerd Gigerenzer & Christoph Enge eds., 2006).

152. 118 N.E. 214 (1917).

153. *Id.*

154. *Id.* at 214-15.

155. As Professor Fried has stated, "[p]romises, like every human expression, are made against an unexpressed background of shared purposes, experiences, and even a shared theory of the world." FRIED, *supra*, at 88.

156. Professor Burton has pointed out that "[c]ontract parties rely on the good faith of their exchange parties partners because detailed planning may be ineffectual or inadvisable." Steven J. Burton, *Breach of Contract and the Common Duty to Perform in Good Faith*, 94 HARV. L. REV. 369, 371 (1980).

157. *Id.* at 369.

158. *Id.* at 373.

159. *E.g., Williams*, 350 F.2d at 449. As one commentator has stated, "[a] lack of genuine assent makes these transactions more akin to robbery than contract." Richard L. Barnes, *Rediscovering Subjectivity in Contracts: Adhesion and Unconscionability*, 66 LA. L. REV. 123, 125 (2005).

160. Rodman Elfin, *The Future Use of Unconscionability and Impracticality as Contract Doctrines*," 40 MERCER L. REV. 937, 938-39 (1989).

161. FRIED, *supra*, at 105.

162. *Id.* at 106. Professor Fried believes that redistribution should be done by taxation. *Id.*

163. *Id.* at 105-06 ("Presumably we want the poor to be able to buy refrigerators on credit; we want unskilled workers to have a chance to work.").

164. Daniel Markovits, *Symposium: Political Theory and Private Law: Making and Keeping Contracts*, 92 VA. L. REV. 1325, 1325 (2006).

Chapter Five

A Biological Basis of Rights

I wish my life and my decisions to depend on myself, not on external
forces of whatever kind. I wish to be the instrument of my own,
not of other men's acts of will. I wish to be a subject, not an object.

Isaiah Berlin[1]

Rights are an essential part of a modern legal system.[2] Yet, scholars have had great
difficulty developing a convincing source for rights. Traditionally, scholars have based
rights on natural rights–rights that come from God or nature. However, God is based on
faith, and no scholar has been able to demonstrate conclusively that rights exist externally
in nature. Modern moral rights theories, in contrast, are generally deontological, rejecting
metaphysical or theological foundations.[3] In other words, they retain classical natural
law's relationship between law and morality, but they reject a connection with the natural
order.

Ronald Dworkin is probably the most important twentieth-century legal
philosopher to have developed a deontological, moral-based conception of rights, which
rejects their source in nature.[4] Dworkin has argued that

> [i]ndividual rights are political trumps held by individuals. Individuals
> have rights when, for some reason, a collective goal is not a sufficient
> justification for denying them what they wish, as individuals, to have or
> to do, or not a sufficient justification for imposing some loss or injury

upon them.[5]

He has stated: "Political rights are creatures of both history and morality; what an individual is entitled to have, in a civil society, depends on both the practice and the justice of its political institutions."[6]

Dworkin's theories appear in his approach to constitutional adjudication:

> Our constitutional system rests on a particular moral theory, namely, that men have moral rights against the state. The difficult clauses of the Bill of Rights, like the due process and equal protection clauses, must be understood as appealing to moral concepts rather than laying down particular conceptions: therefore a court that undertakes the burden of applying these clauses fully as law must be an activist court, in the sense that it must be prepared to frame and answer questions of political morality.[7]

More recently, Alan Dershowitz has developed a system of rights based on experience with wrongs, which he calls "nurtural" rights.[8] He asserts that "rights are those fundamental preferences that experiences and history–especially of great injustices–have taught are so essential that the citizenry should be persuaded to entrench them and not make them subject to easy change by shifting majorities."[9] He views the essential problem of a system of rights as the source of those rights; otherwise, they could not trump majoritarian (democratic) preferences.[10] He rejects both God and nature as the source of rights.[11] He also refuses to use the ideal as a basis of rights, declaring "[i]t is more realistic to try to build a theory of rights on agreed-upon wrongs of the past that we want to avoid repeating, than try to build a theory of rights on idealized conceptions of the perfect society about which we will never agree."[12] Instead, he "identifies the most grievous wrongs whose recurrence we seek to prevent, and then asks whether the absence of certain rights contributed to those wrongs."[13] Dershowitz acknowledges that, because his system has no external source, he can only advocate his theory.[14] However, he declares, "[i]f there can be agreement that certain rights are essential to reduce injustice, such agreement constitutes a solid theory of rights."[15]

Neither Dworkin's nor Dershowitz's approach is convincing because both approaches lack a source for their rights.[16] One cannot accept rights based on faith; faith often becomes ideology. Rights should be unchangeable (or at least not easily changed), and rights cannot be unchangeable without a source. Dworkin is not clear concerning his source of rights, and, as noted above, Dershowitz admits that his theory has no external source, and his optimism concerning obtaining a consensus on rights is questionable.

This chapter advocates rights based on a different kind of "natural law," rights which come not from God or externally from nature, but from human behavior–how our minds evolved.[17] Under this approach, there are two kinds of truth: anthropocentric truth and non-anthropocentric truth.[18] Non-anthropocentric truths are the laws of physical nature and mathematics; they are unassailable truths that "are true regardless of what we happen to think about them."[19] Anthropocentric truths are "truths that are true only because of the kinds of minds that we happen to have and the cultural worlds in which our minds developed."[20] In other words, anthropocentric truths are not unassailable in the universe, but they are truths shared by all mankind.

This chapter proposes that rights can be based on anthropocentric truths–that rights arose from human nature. In particular, anthropocentric rights developed to deal with specific adaptive problems in the Environment of Evolutionary Adaptedness ("EEA"). The fundamentals of rights derived from how our brains evolved with the details of rights arising from how a particular culture reacted to how differing geography, ecology, and social conditions affected survival.

Part I of this chapter will present a biological basis for rights. It will first demonstrate the need for rights based on biological factors and introduce the sources of rights in human nature. Next, it will discuss the biological basis of four kinds of rights–property rights, rights to fairness, liberty rights, and rights to equal treatment. Finally, it will examine some implications of a biological basis of rights.

Part II will illustrate how biological rights exist in different cultures. It will first examine how rights based on human behavior developed in the American constitutional system, then it will compare the concept of liberty in American and German law.

I. A Biological Basis of Rights

A. Introduction

It is the thesis of this chapter that a universal system of basic rights is hardwired into our brains (a universal grammar of rights), just like morality is hardwired into our brains. In fact, rights relate to our innate ability to tell right from wrong. Like morality,[21] our hardwired rights are general principles with the details of these rights being specified by particular cultures. In other words, we have an innate toolkit for building a system of rights.[22] Among these rights are 1) property rights, 2) a right to basic fairness, 3) liberty rights, and 4) a right to be treated equally.[23] These innate rights are not a minimum, but rather a foundation.

Behavioral biology demonstrates the need for rights. First, behavioral biologists have established that humans are sentient, autonomous beings who have a moral sense.[24] As Professor Haidt has declared, "Thomas Jefferson's declaration that certain truths are 'self-evident' is an example of ethical intuitionism."[25] As discussed in Chapter Three, despite the traditional (and now totally discredited) social science theory of man as culturally constructed, the human mind is not a blank slate that allows for easy social engineering–human nature can not be rewritten. Rather, all humans are defined by the inner workings of their minds, and they share a similar genetic makeup. In addition, as Kant believed, human beings are morally special because they have the capacity for rational choice and the freedom of rational beings should be respected.[26] For example, psychology experiments, such as the trolley and footbridge problems discussed in Chapter Two have shown that "it is permissible to cause harm as a by-product of achieving a greater good, but it is impermissible to use harm as a means to a greater good."[27] Finally, autonomy helps the individual survive.[28]

Second, rights help hold the social contract together. Social contracts involve "commitment" problems, which are "any dynamic, strategic problem in which an individual can obtain more desirable or self-interested results by giving up certain options or by guaranteeing others–in short, by making commitments."[29] A person will not voluntarily give up her selfish interest (commit or remain committed) when that person is subject to the tyranny of a majority of which that person is not a part. Similarly, part of our evolved nature is the freedom to leave our group and join another one to avoid coercion by dominants.[30] In other words, "[e]xit freedom had the effect of imposing constraints on dominant individuals in the group; if a few powerful individuals got too powerful, they risked loss of members, and thus some of the net advantage of living in groups. Likewise, even the majority in any group had to keep a keen eye on majoritarian excess."[31]

Rights help solve the commitment and exit problems by protecting individuals from the tyranny of a majority and creating trust in large groups.[32] While an individual will not always win what he or she wants in the political process, rights will protect that individual from overreaching by the majority. In other words, rights grant a minimum for each person under the social contract, which encourages that person to give up his or her selfish interest, to remain a member of that community, and to further both the individual's and community's ability to survive. As Judge Hoffman has declared:

> [t]he deepest social connections that bind us bind us only because, in the end, we are free to disregard them. They have become powerful precisely because they must have had enough long-term utility to overcome their short-term costs, and to keep us from exercising our freedom to exit the group.[33]

Of course, in order for rights to help hold the social contract together, society must punish those who violate others' rights.

A third reason for the existence of rights is to prevent violence and increase the chances for survival. Professor Barash has declared: "What isn't arbitrary is the underlying idea: the success of strategies that settles conflicts with a minimum of violence."[34] In other words, when rules settle disputes, no one is harmed and genes are passed on.

Another justification for rights is to compensate for flaws in human nature.[35] As Professor Pinker has written, "[i]n the Tragic Vision, humans are inherently limited in knowledge, wisdom, and virtue, and all social arrangements must acknowledge those limits."[36] Society must protect individuals from nepotism, selfishness, competition for social status, and power seeking. Hierarchy is part of human nature, and while it is necessary for a functioning society, rights must be protected within the hierarchy.[37] Individuals must be safeguarded from those who govern; otherwise, the social contract will break down. Similarly, humans need to be protected from group coercion. Finally, societies with a system of rights work better and further the survival changes of its inhabitants. For example, "no functioning democracy with political rights has ever suffered a famine."[38]

While the above demonstrates justifications for rights, the question remains what is their source within human biology. As will be show in detail below, rights come from the following sources: 1) the autonomy of human beings (liberty rights; a right to equal treatment), 2) reciprocal altruism, which is part of the social contract (rights are what an individual gets from entering into the social contract–property rights, fairness, etc.), 3) rights that arose as a solution to an evolutionary problem (certain property rights arose as a method to avoid harm and violence), and 4) our innate morality (most rights). Some rights have a combination of sources as their basis. In addition, our inner sense of morality helps define these rights, and these rights aided survival.

B. Property Rights

Several scholars believe that property rights are hardwired into human brains–that there are "identifiable patterns in the resolutions of disputes over resources."[39] Professor Stake thinks that property rights evolved to avoid harm to individuals: "Rivals can reduce the costs of competition by adopting strategies for determining the outcome of fights without physical damage."[40] "Thus, a body is more likely to survive if the brain is equipped with rules of property incorporating ESSs [evolutionary stable strategies] for reducing the costs of allocating resources among competitors."[41] Other scholars give additional reasons for the development of property rights including that they involved territorial possession,[42] they developed as a method to control cheating,[43] they evolved as an incentive to get people to work,[44] and survival is based on the use of things.[45] This author believes that the last two reasons are particularly important; an individual should generally be able to keep the fruits of his labor because they are necessary for his survival. Finally, all these reasons contribute to the cohesiveness of the social contract by motivating cooperation and cutting down on freeriders.

Professor Stake proposes that "humans might be programmed with three rules for initially allocating rights to a thing: to the first person to touch the thing, or to the older contestant, or to the dominant member of the group. . ."[46] Particular cultures would then determine the details of these rules.[47] For example, a "first-in-time convention" (possession) might have developed because humans fight harder for something they already possess, which means that deferring to the person who was first in time can avoid harmful violence for both parties.[48] Part of this convention would be rules for determining who is first in time, such as a person who first had actual control of a wild animal had title in it.[49] Thus, "[t]he result is that most of us descended from beings who could correctly determine who was first in time according to the convention."[50]

Our mirror neurons and the related ability to form triadic mental representations of mental states were involved in the development of property rules. Professor Stake has written,

> [W]e may be programmed to recognize when we have a certain proximate relationship to a physical object and, by mirroring, to recognize when others have a similar relationship to an object. Our brains may then determine 'ownership' by combining the relational data with information about previous relationships, such as information about who was first in time and what voluntary transfers have occurred.[51]

For example, actual grasping may cause an individual to recognize that the grasper has possession of the grasped object through the above process.[52]

If property rules exist to help hold the social contract together, then society must protect individuals' property. Animal studies have suggested that group protection of individual property may have ancient roots.[53] Professors Merrill and Smith have noted that property rights work because a significant majority of people recognize property as moral rights.[54] These authors think that law, without morality, cannot create a system of property rights and that, if property rights are based on morality, they can be secure with minimal legal enforcement.[55] This accords with the present author's theory that much of our modern law is based on practices that developed on the savannah as survival advantages and that modern law helps reinforce these evolutionary behaviors and makes them work in large groups.[56]

In addition, property rights are not based on a utilitarian, cost-benefit analysis.[57] For example, the property right to prevent trespass to land is absolute; it does not depend on a cost-benefit analysis that the trespass would or would not be beneficial to society.[58]

Accordingly, economic development takings where the government takes property from an innocent party and awards it to another party who can make better use of it are not justified.   While the new use might create a bigger pie and produce favorable externalities, such as better business in the neighborhood, such takings go against our basic instincts concerning the sanctity of property.   Eminent domain under such circumstances constitutes immoral coercion of innocent parties.[59]   While the Supreme Court disagreed in *Kelo*,[60] the strong criticism of this case[61] supports the proposition that property is an instinctive, moral right.   As Professors Merrill and Smith have declared: "Coercing innocent persons to give up their homes and farms in order to bestow favors on the select few, however, crosses the line of what most persons are prepared to countenance, consistent with popular perceptions of morality."[62]

Behavioral biology also supports intestate succession (and similar inheritance by will).   Intestate succession is a way of transferring property (resources for survival) to those who share a person's genes, thus furthering the survival of the individual's genes.[63] Since closer relatives, such as children and parents, share more of the donor's genes, intestate succession laws favor closer relatives rather than distant ones.[64] These laws also favor spouses, who are unrelated genetically to the donor, because favoring spouses increases the spouse's investment in their children.[65]   Furthermore, "[e]volutionary pressure could have shaped brains to send property where it will be more efficiently deployed"–where it has a greater change of furthering the donor's genes.[66] For example, primogeniture may have arisen because "[u]nder primogeniture, a decedent's land passed to a single son, thereby maximizing that son's chances of becoming an alpha male and, hence, his reproductive opportunities."[67]   Of course, under different cultural conditions, different rules will develop.

Society often limits a person's ability to leave property to one's relatives through inheritance taxes.   Such taxes are often necessary for the good of the society–to support public projects.   However, when a society takes too much of a person's property upon death, it negates human nature.   Part of the incentive to work is to leave property to those who share one's genes.   Studies have shown that the elderly do not consume all of their resources so that they can transfer those resources to their kin.[68]   Taking too much of a person's property upon death destroys the incentive to work and save.

In sum, because property rights are a basic part of human evolution and morality, they have greater importance than many modern courts and writers have given them.   Not only are they hardwired into our brains, they are also tied into our personhood and autonomy.[69] Accordingly, they are equal to other basic rights, such as the right of liberty or the right of equal treatment. As Professor McGinnis has asserted: "If property is natural to man, a government that ignores the interests of mankind in property and exchange does so at its own peril."[70]

C. A Right to Fairness

Fairness is universal, and mankind's sense of fairness is based on the "Golden Rule" ("Do unto others as they would do unto you" and "Don't do unto others as you would not have them do to you").[71] Our sense of fairness derives from our theory of mind working through our mirror neurons that allows us to identify with others.[72] As mentioned in Chapter Two, the parts of the mind that we use in doing an action are often the same parts that perceive that action when it involves others. Professors Chorvat and McCabe have written that "[a] relatively simple version of a TOM would be to assume that the other person will do what we would do in the same situation."[73] Similarly, Professor Pinker has asserted: "No creature equipped with circuitry to understand that it is immoral for you to hurt me could discover anything but that it is immoral for me to hurt you."[74] Like the other rights mentioned in this chapter, our sense of fair play helped individuals and groups survive because it produced evolutionary advantages over those individuals and groups that lacked a sense of fairness.[75]

Humans innately sense when they are being treated fairly or unfairly by others.[76] People judge fairness "both on the distribution of gains and on the possible alternatives to a given outcome;"[77] "reciprocal exchanges must be relatively equal."[78] In other words, one derives the fairness of an outcome (e.g., property, money, goods) from a comparison of one's outcome/input ratio to the outcome/input ratio of another.[79] Individuals have positive emotions when they are treated fairly and strong negative emotions when they believe that they have been treated unfairly.[80] The most common reactions to unfairness are anger, protest, spite, and outrage.[81] Similarly, "when a worker perceives that another with similar inputs receives greater rewards, that worker will reduce effort."[82] People are also sympathetic to those who have treated them fairly.[83]

In addition, reciprocal altruism is a part of our sense of fairness: "whenever people treat each other in a fair, sympathetic manner, they are exhibiting an essential understanding of the importance of reciprocity."[84] Cooperation is connected with reward-related neural activity,[85] and it also depends on the other person's reputation.[86] Our sense of fair play probably first developed in sexual love and parental love and then spread to others in society.[87] In addition, our sense of fear, anxiety, and danger generally keeps us from harming others.[88] Similarly, "[p]eople define their norms of fairness through social processes; groups of people create norms and work to enforce them."[89]

Evolutionary psychologists have used the "ultimatum game" to study fairness in humans.[90] The ultimatum game is a two player game in which A is given money to be divided between A and B in any portion A wants. If B accepts the offer, the players split the money, but if B rejects the offer, the players get nothing. One might expect that A would keep a very large portion (say 90%) for selfish reasons and B would accept a small portion (say 10%) because at least he would get something. However, A generally offers an average of 40%, and B usually rejects offers below 30%. This shows that "[h]umans have built-in regulators, evolved over aeons of intense social interaction, that tells us not to be unfair to each other, lest today's player A will become tomorrow's player B."[91] In addition those who receive unfair offers (those in the position of B) will often reject those offers even if he loses something, too, due to B's sense of fairness and the desire to punish those who are unfair.[92]

Our sense of fair play appears in brain activity that neuroscientists have detected and tracked.[93] For example, neuroscientists have observed that unfair offers active areas of the brain connected with both cognition and emotions.[94] In addition, some neuroscientists believe that there is a Golden rule hormone–oxytocin, which is produced in the hypothalamus and which may have evolved in connection with motherly love.[95] As mentioned in Chapter Two, oxytocin increases feelings of trust, both in being willing to trust and creating trust in others.[96]

Finally, studies have shown that when humans have strong moral convictions concerning a matter, they are more interested in substantive fairness than procedural fairness.[97] This occurs because "people's affective reactions [especially outrage] to outcomes color their judgment of fairness."[98] Accordingly, "[p]rocedural information may do little to offset the feelings of incensed outrage in reaction to an outcome that threatens a moral mandate: instead, anger and outrage may lead people to paint the entire situation as unfair."[99]

D. Liberty Rights

Liberty rights derive from the autonomy of human beings. Man has a natural desire for liberty because it helps the autonomous individual survive by allowing choice.[100] "Evolutionary theorists realize that there is more than one possible goal or end to human life and that end which is chosen may depend in large part on the circumstances in which an individual finds himself."[101] In other words, "[w]e need liberty in order to make up for our lack of knowledge of diverse human ends, and the diverse understanding of human ends leads to a justice in which each man lives according to his own conscience, as opposed to that of another."[102] Furthermore, "[a] just society recognizes when it has squelched the individual, deleting the political conception of the self."[103] Finally, liberty is necessary for diversity in society; a group needs individuals who can perform specialized functions. In sum, liberty facilitates the natural genetic and experience variations among human beings.

Mirror neurons facilitated the development of liberty rights. Through our theory of mind along with our emotions of empathy, sympathy, and responsibility, an individual can see that others should be treated in the same way that the individual is (given the same liberty).

On the savannah, man was completely free (liberty is prior to the state), but, by entering into a social contract (which increases an individual's ability to survive), man must give up some liberty, but only that liberty that is necessary for society's protection.[104] Liberty is what man gets from the social contract in exchange for what he gives society; liberty is part of reciprocal altruism on the societal level. In addition, the more liberty a society allows its inhabitants, the more likely those inhabitants are to remain part of that society. Liberty also breeds personal responsibility: "By taking away freedom we essentially deny that the individual has any responsibility for himself, negating the moral worth, and further negating the possibility for political friendship between citizens."[105] As Professor Hall has noted: "As autonomous individuals, selected by natural selection, we alone hold the responsibility for our own survival and that of our children."[106] Moreover, since liberty is part of human nature, groups that grant more liberty will generally work more efficiently and require less coercion.[107] Finally, when people have liberty rights, they do not have to fight for liberty, thus increasing their survival chances.

That liberty is a central part of human nature does not mean that individuals should be allowed to do whatever they please.[108] As Professor Rawls recognized, "arguments for restricting liberty proceed from the principle of liberty itself."[109] By entering into society, individuals must obey the group's rules, or the group will collapse. While this may restrict the individual somewhat, it increases the survival chances for all.

Society can also limit liberty when that liberty interferes with someone else's liberty.[110] As discussed in detail in the next section, individuals are equal under the social contract, which increases their chances of survival. For example, criminal laws interfere with liberty, but such laws are necessary to protect other individuals. Similarly, government can step in when someone is overreaching in the marketplace.

Society, however, should only restrict liberty when it is necessary for the good of society. This means that there should be few restrictions on "morality." For example, since homosexuality does no real harm to society, it should be permitted. On the other hand, society can restrict sexual activity when there is the danger of harm, such as protecting children by banning sex between adults and children.

Slavery is the opposite of liberty because it takes away all liberty rights. It also treats an individual as a means to an end. As Professor Arnhart has noted, humans are not naturally adapted for slavery.[111] A slave has no autonomy and no dignity, which are central to man's nature. Slavery also goes against mankind's natural moral sense, which was shaped by natural selection.[112] In particular, slavery contradicts man's moral sense not to be exploited.[113] In addition, a master/slave relation lacks the reciprocity that is central to society based on human nature. Slavery also interferes with liberty because it interferes with the subcategories of liberty discussed below, such as the right of association, the right to choose one's mate, and the right of parents to raise their children as they please.

Liberty rights are the basis of many of our more detailed rights like the right to privacy or the right to free speech. "What makes liberty different from other human goods is that it embraces more political goods than any other good can, and it leaves man to choose the goods which fit his particular circumstances and attributes."[114] Fundamental to liberty is the right of privacy–the right to be left alone. In *Lawrence v. Texas*, the Supreme Court formulated a broad concept of the right of privacy:

Liberty protects the person from unwarranted government intrusions into a dwelling or other private places. In our tradition the State is not omnipresent in the home. And there are other spheres of our lives and existence, outside the home, where the State should not be a dominant presence. Freedom extends beyond spatial bounds. Liberty presumes an autonomy of self that includes freedom of thought, belief, expression, and certain intimate conduct.[115]

This broad concept of privacy is consistent with the right to liberty that is intrinsic to human behavior and the social contract. The state should not be a dominant presence in areas where it has no interest; man did not give up all his natural freedom when he entered into society. The state should not interfere with a person's home, unless there is a significant reason to do so, such as protection of a child or a spouse. Because intimacy between human beings is an essential part of human nature, intimacy should be especially protected from state interference. Also, outside the home we should be able to do as we please, as long as it does not interfere with a significant state interest or another person's liberty. As *Lawrence* noted, freedom of thought, belief, and expression are essential to autonomous human beings. Man was free before the social contract to think, believe, and express himself as he pleased, and society does not have a reason to interfere with those natural freedoms except in extreme circumstances.

Another part of liberty is the right of free association. Free association furthers productivity and thus survival because it allows individuals to work with whomever they please. It allows an individual to develop his life plan with the help of others. It also helps hold society together because a lack of free association could cause individuals to exit that society.

Another part of liberty is the freedom to choose one's spouse. As noted above, mate selection is a central part of evolution because it affects reproductive success.[116] A related liberty is the liberty for parents to raise their children as they please, unless the children are in danger from the parents. Experiments in kibbutzim where children were raised communally were failures because of human nature–mothers did not want to give up their children.[117] In addition, children are better off with their parents because parents give more attention to their children because they carry their genes.

E. Right to Equal Treatment

There is no equality in the natural world. The powerful rule, and the weak are eaten. This is, of course, part of evolution.

Equal treatment came into the biological picture when man created the social contract. As stated earlier, when mankind developed societies, individuals gave up some of their liberty in exchange for the survival benefits of living in a society. Although individuals gave up some liberty, equal treatment from the government was part of the bargain because no one would enter into a society to be treated as an inferior, especially if this would decrease survival chances. Professor Nagel has summarized this basis of equality best:

> The pure ideal of political legitimacy is that the use of state power
> should be capable of being *authorized* by each citizen–not in direct detail
> but through acceptance of the principles, institutions, and procedures
> which determine how the power will be used. This requires the
> possibility of unanimous agreement at some significantly high level for
> if there are citizens who can legitimately object to the way state power
> is used against them or in their name, the state is not legitimate.[118]

Similarly, the sense of fairness discussed above requires that leaders treat their subjects equally. Individuals demand equal treatment from their sovereigns, and our emotions are brought into play when we see that others are not treated equally. Finally, equal treatment is required as part of the respect that autonomous human beings deserve–all persons are moral equals.[119] Professor Dworkin has written, "majoritarianism does not guarantee self-government unless all members of the community in question are moral members. . ."[120] Further, as Professor Weinreb has asserted: "Each person should be able to develop and grow as a person; he should have a sense of his own capacity as an actor in the world, who makes things happen according to his own plan."[121] This is Thomas Jefferson's "pursuit of happiness."

Equality under behavioral biology means equality of opportunity, not equality of outcome. Equality of outcome is contrary to the evolutionary process.[122] If everyone were made equal, the survival chances of all would diminish. Incentives to help society would disappear because individuals who worked hard would not reap the benefits of their work. Moreover, if individuals did not receive a significant portion of their labors, they would leave the society, and the social contract would fall apart. As Professor Hall has argued: "While there are certainly evils in inequality, the coercion necessary to create absolute equality (if even possible) would be worse for human psychology and the overall quality of human life than the inequality which presently exists."[123]

Similarly, equality of outputs ignores individual autonomy, which is basic to humans and necessary for survival. As Professor Weinreb has asserted: "Unlike equality of opportunity, which recognizes persons as distinct actors who exercise individual capacities, the central significance of equality of result is that it denies the relevance of individuality in some respect. Where equality of result applies, persons are not actors who determine for themselves; they are recipients (or donors) who, whatever their individual characteristics, receive (or donate) according to a general rule that they are individually unable to vary."[124] He has added that "[o]ur common humanity does not consist of or depend on particular characteristics that all have alike. On the contrary, its essence is our common capacity for individual self-determination as a unique person."[125] Finally, differences in outputs is not unfair. As Professor Hayek has noted, "[a] bare fact, or state of affairs, which no one can change, may be good or bad, but not just or unjust."[126] More specifically, Professor Rubin has asserted that inequality exists generally because "some individuals are vastly more productive than others. . ." and that productivity is good for society as a whole.[127]

While a few scholar have noted that some hunter-gatherer societies were egalitarian, this is a different type of egalitarianism than is sometimes advocated for today.[128] This egalitarianism was not a concern for others, but rather a desire not to be dominated by dominants.[129] Thus, individuals banded together to avoid creation of a dominant hierarchy.[130] Accordingly, this type of egalitarianism, which was dominance avoiding, supports the argument that human behavior resists attempts to impose artificial equality by dominance, as was argued in the previous paragraph.

Mankind does have a sense of minimal distributional fairness,[131] which is probably the result of our theory of mind. Studies have suggested that mankind has adopted the "principle that maximized the overall resources of the group while preventing the worst off from dropping below some preestablished level of income."[132] This allows "for extra benefits to flow toward those who contribute more to society," while providing "a safety net for those who are disadvantaged. . ."[133] Also, primitive humans recognized the difference between lack of effort and bad luck.[134] In sum, while equality in human nature is equality of inputs, not outputs, there may be a right to minimum subsistence.

Having equality of opportunity as the basis of equal treatment does not mean the adoption of "Social Darwinism." Social Darwinism, which is generally associated with Herbert Spencer, is not consistent with behavioral biology or for that matter with Darwin himself. Darwin's theory was not a theory about progress and his evolution was not to a positive end.[135] More importantly, Social Darwinism is contrary to the biological basis of rights set forth in this chapter. A concept of human nature that views certain individuals as superior interferes with natural property rights, fairness rights, liberty rights, and equal treatment rights.

Equality means that society cannot discriminate based on superficial differences such as race. As noted in Chapter Two, behavioral biology demonstrates that one should be judged by individual characteristics, not as members of an artificial group to which one belongs. "One of the downsides to essentialist thinking and certain aspects of categorization more generally is that we readily develop stereotypes and prejudices."[136] Because there are an astronomical number of possible genetic combinations, each human is genetically unique. On the other hand, as noted in Chapter Three, behavioral biology also demonstrates that there is little difference between the races;[137] there hasn't been enough time in the human evolutionary process for significant differences to occur among localized populations.[138]

In addition, equal treatment under behavioral biology should not be limited to a traitist approach, but should protect all individuals from differing treatment by the government. For example, the Jeffersonians stood for "equal rights for all, special privileges for none."[139] In other words, the minority should be protected from the majority, regardless of the characteristics of the minority and majority. As the court declared in *State v. Goodwill*,

> the rights of every individual must stand or fall by the same rule of law
> that governs every other member of the body politic under similar
> circumstances; and every partial or private law which directly proposes
> to destroy or affect individual rights, or does the same thing by
> restricting the privileges of certain classes of citizens and not others,

when there is no public necessity for such discrimination, is unconstitutional or void. Were it otherwise, odious individuals or corporate bodies would be governed by one law, and the mass of the community, and those who make the law by another one.[140]

The court, of course, is stating a version of the rule of law.

F. Some Implications

From the above, it should be clear that there is sometimes not just one right answer to rights questions. Different-right creating behaviors (from different modules in the brain) can conflict. In addition, different cultures realize fundamental rights in different ways.

For instance, behavioral biology sometimes does not supply an answer when equality rights and liberty rights clash. Both are vital for human survival and holding together the social contract. As Professor Weinreb has remarked, "[i]n a just social order we believe, liberty and equality are consistent, because the law establishes what we call equality of opportunity: not equality as such but the proper bounds of liberty, within which all persons alike are allowed to exercise their individual capacities."[141] However, he also admitted that in any society there will inevitably be clashes between liberty and equality.[142] While liberty rights are probably much older than equality rights since liberty rights probably existed before the social contract, equality rights are also important because, as stated above, they help hold the social contract together and they relate to mankind's sense of fairness. In addition, the answer to the question of how liberty relates to equality varies by culture, with the emphasis on liberty or equality probably being determined by that culture's combination of the Haidt-Joseph five moral modules.

Another implication from the above is that anthropocentric rights should generally prevail over utilitarianism (cost-benefit analysis).[143] Darwinists are individual oriented.[144] Under Darwinism, society grows out of the individual, not the other way around. While the social contract is important, under behavioral biology, individuals are more important because they are autonomous beings and they had total liberty before the social contract. Individuals are the basic unit of the social contract. In addition, utilitarianism can interfere with property rights, liberty rights, fairness rights, and the right to equal treatment. For example, while it may be better for society for the government to turn over someone's house to a developer who will build a mall that will bring economic improvement to the neighborhood, this violates an individual's property rights as discussed above. As Professor Rawls had declared: "Each person possesses an inviolability founded on justice that even the welfare of society as a whole cannot override."[145] In other words, "utilitarianism does not take seriously the distinction between persons."[146] In addition, a neuroscientific study of patients with damage to the ventrodemial prefronal cortex, a part of the brain involved with social emotions, supports that humans value the individual over the utilitarian answer.[147] These brain-damaged patients acted in a much more utilitarian manner than normal individuals when faced with a high-conflict personal dilemma, such as the footbridge problem, than did a control group.[148]

A striking example of when rights should overcome collectivism concerns female genital mutilation. Jomo Kenyatta, the founding father of Kenya, once wrote that the abolition of female genital circumcision would "destroy the tribal symbol which identifies the age-groups, and prevent the Gikuyu from perpetuating that spirit of collectivism and national solidarity which they have been able to maintain from time immemorial."[149] To justify female genital mutilation upon countless young woman based on collectivism and nationalism is abhorrent to this author. Human nature protects the individual, not the collective.

Thus, a system of rights based on human behavior will adopt the Kantian notion of not using an individual as a mean to an end.[150] On the other hand, when basic behavioral rights are not involved, it is perfectly legitimate to adopt a cost-benefit utilitarian approach to law making.[151]

II. Biological Rights in Particular Cultures

A. Biological Rights and the American Constitution

Professor Hoffman believes that there is an evolutionary link between justice and democracy:

The ability of any justice system to accommodate the biological tension between individual freedom and social norms depends to a great extent on its own ability to develop those norms as a free expression of social consensus. The best laws work because they efficiently confer, and express, enough long-term benefits on enough individuals that those individuals are willing to remain in the group and pay the short-term price of compliance. The genius of democracy is that it provides a continuous feedback mechanism on those social norms, constantly recalibrating them to current individual preferences.[152]

Thus, "democracy creates a market for the governed, in which conflicting preferences for individual freedom and social restraint compete freely to obtain optimal results."[153] This connection between justice and democracy is not an artificial social construct, but rather how mankind evolved with our conflicting notions of individual freedom and social constraints.[154] In addition, a free market economy furthers this connection because it allows for reciprocal exchanges, which, as noted above, are essential to human nature.[155]

More specifically, Professor McGinnis believes that "biology–the interaction of genetically shaped behavior with particular environments–better explains the structure of the [United States] Constitution than other theories. . ."[156] He continues: "The vocabulary with which the Framers discussed human nature is in fact close to that now used to describe the elements of human nature from an evolutionary point of view."[157] Similarly, "Jefferson argued that American colonists 'felt their rights before they had thought through their explanation.'"[158]

We actually have two constitutions: 1) the original Constitution, which mainly dealt with the imperfections of human nature though a division of sovereignty, and 2) the Bill of Rights and other amendments, which granted specific rights. In the original Constitution, the Framers were trying to deal with four human factors (all of which have been discussed above): 1) that self-interest created limitations on altruistic behavior among unrelated individuals, 2) that self-interest could be consistent with "gains from trade through cooperation because man has a natural sense of exchange and property," 3) that "individuals have substantial differences in their natural endowments, creating peculiar risks of expropriation through politics," and 4) that "the natural desire to increase status may, in some circumstances, be less beneficial to society as a whole than wealth production."[159] Stated differently, "[t]he Framer's whole new science of politics was premised on this view of human psychology: government could not depend on man's benevolence or virtue."[160] In particular, "[w]hat was unique about James Madison and the Founding Fathers, however, was not just that they based government on the consent of the people, but that they based government on individuals and a people that they understood to be not always virtuous."[161]

On one hand, the framers believed that man's self-interest worked well in the private sphere because it created gains in commerce, so they protected the private sphere by giving Congress the authority to regulate trade through the Commerce Clause, rather than allowing states to do this separately, and by protecting property and trade through the Contracts Clause and the Takings Clause [part of the Bill of Rights].[162] On the other hand, the Framers feared factions and abuses of power in the public sphere.[163] The Framers were particularly concerned about the protection of property.[164] As Professor McGinnis has written, "[u]nder the Framer' system, national democracy was primarily an attempt to preserve wealth from public expropriation that could result from coalition building."[165] In other words, "[n]atural inequality exacerbates the danger of factions because it creates a reserve of individuals readily persuaded to expropriate the property of the more talented."[166] The Framers dealt with this problem through separation of power between the federal and state governments (federalism), bicameralism, and separation of power between the federal government's three branches.

While the original Constitution mainly protected against human nature by division of authority, the Bill of Rights directly created rights, some of which are very specific while others are abstract. As this part will show, these rights are details of the rights discussed in Part I based on the cultural of late eighteenth-century America.

Our freedom of speech right in the First Amendment flowed from the natural right to liberty. As noted in Part I, freedom of thought and expression are part of man in the EEA, and man did not give up this liberty when he entered into the social contract, although it can be limited when harm to others is involved, such as defamation or falsely shouting fire in a crowded theater. Freedom of speech also arises from individual autonomy and dignity. "We retain our dignity as individuals, only by insisting that no one–no official and no majority–has the right to withhold an opinion from us on the ground that we are not fit to hear and consider it."[167] Likewise, government interferes with our autonomy and dignity when it prevents us from expressing our opinions to others. Finally, free speech promotes reciprocity and cooperation.[168]

The details of freedom of speech differ among cultures. For example, the United States generally limits speech less than European nations. "[T]he U.S. First Amendment is far more protective than other countries' laws of hate speech, libel, commercial speech, and publication of national security information," and this greater protection grew out of America's "peculiar social, political, and economic history."[169]

Other constitutional rights are less obviously grounded in biology, but most of the Bill of Rights relates to human behavior. The Third Amendment states, "No soldier shall, in time of peace, be quartered in any house, without the consent of the owner, nor in time of war, but in a manner to be prescribed by law."[170] Obviously, there was no specific right against quartering soldiers in a home on the savannah.[171] However, this right is a specification of the right to liberty and privacy. The British quartering soldiers in colonists' homes was a specific problem to the Founders regarding liberty so they wrote protection against it into the Constitution. Notice that this right is less in war time when greater incursions on liberty might be justified for survival.

Similarly, our Second Amendment right to bear arms[172] was not a part of mankind's early rights. Nevertheless, it relates to an individual's interest in personal autonomy and liberty. Under these concepts, an individual has the right to protect herself.[173] As Professor Hauser has stated, "[o]ur moral faculty judges" that "self defense . . . is justifiable" because "[t]he agent's intention . . . is not to kill the thief but to defend himself from being killed."[174] Thus, the Second Amendment right to bear arms is a late eighteenth-century manifestation of the right to protect oneself. Likewise, the criminal procedure rights in the Fourth, Fifth, and Sixth Amendments and the Seventh Amendment right to a trial by jury are manifestations of the rights to fairness and liberty discussed above. For example, while the right to a jury trial is not universal,[175] it is one of America's methods of insuring the biological right to fairness.

Finally, the Ninth Amendment supports that, for the Founders, rights are in the people (individuals), and individuals did not give up their basic rights when they entered society. The Ninth Amendment states: "The enumeration in the Constitution of certain rights shall not be construed to deny or disparage others retained by the People."[176] Thus, the people created the government and gave it its authority. The government did not grant rights to individuals; they already had these rights. As Professor Barnett has written, the Founders' view was "first came rights, then comes the Constitution."[177] Professor Barnett thought that those rights were liberty rights, and he has proposed a

"Presumption of Liberty" when interpreting the Constitution.[178] This corresponds with the arguments above that one gives up only a necessary portion of liberty when entering into the social contract.

B. Liberty in American and German Law

One can see how different cultures created different kinds of liberty by comparing our Constitution's idea of liberty with that of the German Constitution. Our constitutional liberty is a negative liberty (a freedom from government)–"the freedom to pursue one's own vision in life as one chooses."[179] American liberty is value-neutral and is based on individuality and personal choice.[180]

In contrast, German freedom is based on the Kantian notion of human dignity–"that each person is valuable per se as an end in himself, which government and fellow citizens must give due respect."[181] German rights center on the free development of personality and thus on a person's integrity and security.[182] For example in one case, the German Constitutional Court "invalidated a court-ordered sampling of a defendant's spinal column to test his involvement in a crime on the ground it violated his physical integrity."[183] Similarly, confidentiality and inquiry into certain personal matters are carefully protected under the German system.[184] This idea of dignity affects both public and private law.[185] For instance the German Constitutional Court recast "the private law interests of reputation and privacy into the capacious language of human dignity and personality, thereby constitutionalizing the doctrine."[186] In addition, German freedom rejects the American notion of the atomistic individual, and instead it views individuals as being connected.[187] In other words, "[i]ndividual choice is bounded by community, civility norms and a sense of the responsibility."[188]

Consequently, unlike American liberty, German freedom creates both rights against the state and duties for citizens.[189] Under the German conception of freedom: "people are spiritual-moral beings who act freely, but their actions are bound by a sense of moral duty. Actions are to be guided by a sense of social solidarity, human and social need, and personal responsibility."[190] This coupling of rights and duties developed from Kant's notion of universal law that applies to all.[191] Examples include a parent's rights and duties in raising children and the German notion of academic freedom that doesn't release anyone from his allegiance to the constitution.[192]

The German version of the rule of law (Rechtsstaat) applies to both law and justice, and justice can include natural or moral law.[193] Another important idea under German freedom is the "Social State (Sozialstatt), which obligates the state to provide for the security of its citizens, including a minimal level of existence."[194]

In sum, in Germany, "[t]he state became the focus for the fount of freedom, in comparison to the American idea that the state is the object against which freedom is directed: limiting state power to empower individual liberty."[195] This is because under the American system, "man comes from the state of nature and then forms a social contract," while, the German system "does not exclusively rely upon a social foundation for a view of man as the founding element of society. . . ."; [r]ather, man is conceived as a social animal who is part of a community."[196]

Neither the American concept of liberty based on freedom from government nor the German concept of freedom based on dignity is superior. Rather, each developed from human behavior based on the needs of the particular society. Americans were rebelling from an English king and parliament, which limited their freedom. They also feared factions within their own country. Consequently, they were most interested in protection from government. Based on the existence of slavery, the eighteen-century status of women, and differences between landowners and nonlandowners and other class differences, the idea of universal human dignity was not central to the Founders.[197] Similarly, because individuals had abundant access to land they could farm and other natural resources, providing for each member of society was a foreign concept.

The German idea of dignity is based both on the German reaction to the atrocities of Naziism and Germany's intellectual history.[198] After World War II, Germany had to face the horrors of Naziism, and its reaction was to emphasize the dignity and autonomy of human beings. Freedom from government was not enough to protect society; rather, freedom needs positive action from the government and duties by citizens. Also, part of the intrusion of the Nazis was into the sphere of privacy, which helped them identify Jews and other "undesirables." Likewise, in an industrialized society with a dense population, equality is a more serious problem and not all people have access to basic resources.

Conclusion

Rabbi Joseph Telushkin has declared: "To this day there is ultimately no philosophically compelling answer to the question 'Why was Hitler wrong?' Aside from 'Because God said so.'[199] This chapter has tried to counter this argument by showing that there a universal, innate set of rights that evolved to help mankind survive. While the details of rights differ by culture, the fundamental rights that exist in all societies, especially the autonomy of all humans, demonstrates that Hitler was wrong.

Similarly, Professor Dershowitz has argued against natural law: "But we must remind ourselves that natural law has also been invoked in support of slavery, racism, sexism, homophobia, terrorism, the blocking of abortion clinics, and the refusal to pay taxes."[200] First, almost all philosophies have been used to justify evil. If a philosophy is misused, it doesn't make that philosophy bad. More importantly, earlier versions of natural law were mainly based on opinion, not science. For example, homosexuality is not against scientifically-supported natural law or natural morality. On the other hand, the anthropocentric version of rights employed in this chapter is based on extensive scientific studies.

Notes

1. *Quoted in* MATT RIDLEY, THE AGILE GENE: HOW NATURE TURNS ON NURTURE, 270-71 (2003).

2. As Max Weber noted, pluralistic societies must generally be based on legal authority in contrast to homogenous societies, which are usually predicated on kinship descent or charismatic social organization. MAX WEBER, THE THEORY OF SOCIAL AND ECONOMIC ORGANIZATION 328 (1921).

3. JEFFRIE G. MURPHY & JULES L. COLEMAN, PHILOSOPHY OF LAW: AN INTRODUCTION TO JURISPRUDENCE 37 (rev. ed 1990); LLOYD L. WEINREB, NATURAL LAW AND JUSTICE 3 (1987).

4. RONALD DWORKIN, LAW'S EMPIRE (1986); RONALD DWORKIN, TAKING RIGHTS SERIOUSLY (1977, 1978) [hereinafter DWORKIN, RIGHTS].

5. DWORKIN, RIGHTS, *supra*, at xi.

6. *Id.* at 87.

7. *Id.* at 147.

8. *See generally* ALAN DERSHOWITZ, RIGHTS FROM WRONGS: A SECULAR THEORY OF THE ORIGIN OF RIGHTS (2004).

9. *Id.* at 81.

10. *Id.* at 5. *See also id.* at 15-91.

11. *Id.* at 8.

12. *Id.* at 7.

13. *Id.* at 82.

14. *Id.* at 9.

15. *Id.* at 82. He also states, "the reality is that rights are legal constructs devised by the minds of human beings, based on human experience, and they must be constantly defended in the court of public opinion." *Id.* at 8.

16. Professor Dershowitz has written concerning Dworkin's approach: "Accepting his source of rights requires one to accept the brilliance of his logic (or some hidden metaphysical truth) rather than being persuaded that experience demonstrates the utility (broadly defined of rights)." *Id.* at 117. He has also argued, "[u]nless there is a compelling source of rights that trumps majoritarian preferences, the default position in a democracy should be a vote of the majority." *Id.* at 5.

17. Professor Keane has also advocated rights based on human nature, partially using this author's theories. David Keane, Survival of the Fairest? Evolution and the Geneticization of Rights, 30 Oxford J. Legal Stud. 467 (2010).

18. *See* Jonathan Haidt, *Invisible Fences of the Moral Domain*, 28 BEHAV. & BRAIN SCI. 552, 552 (2005) [hereinafter Haidt, *Invisible Fences*]; *see also* Jonathan Haidt & Fredrik Bjorklund, *Social Intuitionists Answer Six Questions About Moral Psychology*, in 2 MORAL PSYCHOLOGY 181, 213-14 (W. Sinnott-Armstrong ed., 2006). *See also* Chapter Three.

19. Haidt, *Invisible Fences*, *supra*, at 552.

20. *Id.* at 552-53; *see also* Haidt & Bjorklund, *supra*, at 214 ("We would expect intelligent creatures from another planet to show little agreement with us on questions of humor, beauty, good writing, or morality."). These authors note that the only other ultrasocial mammals are naked mole rats, but their ultrasociality, like that of bees and ants, is based on kin altruism since all are siblings. Haidt & Bjorklund, *supra*, at 192. Consequently, their social system is radically different from that of humans.

21. MARC D. HAUSER, MORAL MINDS: HOW NATURE DESIGNED OUR UNIVERSAL SENSE OF RIGHT AND WRONG 47 (2006). *See* Chapter Two of this study.

22. Professor Hauser makes a similar comment concerning morality. *Id.* at xvii.

23. I am not claiming that this is a definitive list of basic rights. However, our current state of knowledge concerning behavioral biology suggests that these are the most important rights.

24. STEVEN PINKER, THE BLANK SLATE 425 (2002).

25. Jonathan Haidt, *The Emotional Dog and Its Rational Tail: A Social Intuitionist Approach to Moral Justice*, 108 PSYCHOL. REV. 814 , 814 (2001) [hereinafter Haidt, *Emotional Dog*].

26. MURPHY & COLEMAN, *supra*, at 77-79.

27. HAUSER, *supra*, at 33, 120.

28. Lauren K. Hall, *The Liberated Beast: An Evolutionary Justification for Political Liberty*, http://www.allacademic.com//meta/p_mla_apa_research_citation/1/3/8/9/0/pages138908/p138908-1.php at *13 (2006).

29. Robin Bradley Kar, *The Deep Structure of Law and Morality*, 84 TEX. L. REV. 877, 898 (2006). Judge Hoffman has noted that "living in groups requires rather sophisticated mechanisms to regulate relationships between members." Morris B. Hoffman, *The Neuroeconomic Path of the Law*, 359 PHIL. TRANS. R. SOC. LOND. B. 1667, 1670 (2004).

30. PAUL RUBIN, DARWINIAN POLITICS: THE EVOLUTIONARY ORIGIN OF FREEDOM 97-98 (2002); *see also* Hoffman, *supra*, at 1673 ("[T]he small groups in which we evolved contained an important element of

freedom–the freedom to enter into mutually beneficial social institutions, the freedom to decline to do so, and, as Rubin points out, the freedom to leave the group and to join another."); THOMAS NAGEL, EQUALITY AND PARTIALITY 24 (1991). One might ask why more civilized societies have not had a strong system of rights. The answer is that a dictator can often limit exit freedom, Hoffman, *supra*, at 1673, and that to exit, there must be somewhere to go.

31. Hoffman, *supra*, at 1673.

32. Professor Stake has noted that "no strategy will be [evolutionarily stable] in situations where it would make permanent reproductive losers of one group." Jeffrey Evans Stake, *The Property "Instinct,"* 59 PHIL. TRANSACTIONS ROYAL SOC'Y LONDON 1763, 1766 (2004).

33. Hoffman, *supra*, at 1673.

34. DAVID P. BARASH, THE SURVIVAL GAME: HOW GAME THEORY EXPLAINS THE BIOLOGY OF COOPERATION AND COMPETITION 232 (2003).

35. As Professor Pinker has noted, "[t]he checks and balances of democratic institutions were explicitly designed to stalemate the often dangerous ambitions of imperfect humans." PINKER, *supra*, at 128.

36. *Id.* at 287; *see also* RUBIN, *supra*, at 113 ("[I]ndividuals prefer to be dominants and reduce the freedom of others.").

37. Professors Grady and McGuire argue that constitutions arise from subordinates' agreements with each other to prevent excessive appropriations by dominants. Mark F. Grady & Michael T. McGuire, *The Nature of Constitutions*, 1 J. BIOMETRICS 227 (1999).

38. DERSHOWITZ, *supra*, at 163.

39. Stake, *supra*, at 1763; *see also* Thomas W. Merrill & Harry E. Smith, *Law and Morality: Property Law: The Morality of Property*, 48 WM. & MARY L. REV. 1849, 1894 (2007) ("The points establish, we believe, that property rights must be moral rights if they exist at all, and that the moral right to property is not qualitatively different from those moral rights we describe as human or civil rights."); Herbert Gintis, *The Evolution of Private Property*, 64 J. ECON. BEHAV. & ORG. 1, 15 (2007); John O. McGinnis, *The Human Constitution and Constitutive Law: A Prolegomenon*, 8 J. CONTEMP. LEGAL ISSUES 211, 222 (1997) ("[P]roperty is a phenomenon that exists apart from any organized government."); Ori Friedman & Karen Neary, *First Possession Beyond the Law: Adults' and Young Children's Intuitions About Ownership*, 83 TUL L. REV. 679 (2009). Professor Pipes has noted that there has never been a society so primitive as to not have some form of ownership. RICHARD PIPES, PROPERTY & FREEDOM 76 (1999). He has added that the idealized notion of primitive communism has no basis in fact. *Id.* at 117.

40. Stake, *supra*, at 1763; *see also* Gintis, *supra*, at 3; Peter DeScioli & Bart J. Wilson, Mine and Thine: The Territorial Foundations of Human Property, http://www1.chapman.edu/~bjwilson/papers/FoundationsProperty%203%2029%2010.pdf (2010).

41. Stake, *supra*, at 1763; *see also* Merrill & Smith, *supra*, at 1858 ("This 'possession' or 'bourgeois' convention is an evolutionary stable strategy.").

42. Gintis, *supra*, at 2 ("[P]reinstitutional 'natural' private property has been observed in many species, in the form of the recognition of territorial possession.").

43. HAUSER, *supra*, at 80.

44. PINKER, *supra*, at 290.

45. Hoffman, *supra*, at 1675, n.3. Philosopher Ayn Rand wrote, "Without property rights no rights are possible. Since man has to sustain his own life by his own effort, the man who has no right to the product of his effort has no means to sustain his life." AYN RAND, THE VIRTUE OF SELFISHNESS 110 (1964).

46. Stake, *supra*, at 1764.

47. *Id.*

48. *Id.* For a scientific study of first possession, see Friedman & Neary, *supra*.

49. Stake, *supra*, at 1765.

50. *Id.*

51. *Id.*; *see also* Merrill & Smith, *supra*, at 1858-60 ("Rules making nearness and physical control the criteria for possession have a psychological basis, and the convention of respecting possession stems from people's mutual expectations that they will respect the right to control these things." *Id.* at 1858.).

52. Stake, *supra*, at 1765.

53. *Id.* at 1767.

54. Merrill & Smith, *supra*, at 1850.

55. *Id.*; *see also* Gintis, *supra*, at 2.

56. For example, as noted in Chapter Four, this author believes modern contract law derived from reciprocal altruism ("tit for tat"), which developed during the EEA. A person would give up his selfish aims in order to cooperate with another person so that both parties would benefit, thus increasing both their chances for survival.

57. Merrill & Smith, *supra*, at 1851. They add that "we will argue that the forms of utilitarianism that undergird modern law and economics which assume a degree of plasticity of property and have underplayed the information and coordination problems present in core property situations are inconsistent with the nature of the rights in question." *Id.* at 1856-57.

58. *Id.* at 1871-74.

59. Merrill & Smith, *supra*, at 1882-84.

60. Kelo v. City of New London, 545 U.S. 469 (2005).

61. *See generally* Janice Nadler & Shari Seidman Diamond, *Eminent Domain and the Psychology of Property Rights: Use, Subjective Attachment, and Taken Identity*, 5 J. Empirical Legal Stud. 713 (2008). These authors have noted that the disapproval rating for *Kelo* was around 80-90%. *Id.* at 720. They added: "Our experiments suggest that subjective attachment to property looms far larger [than public purpose] in determining the perceived justice of a taking." *Id.* at 713.

62. Merrill & Smith, *supra*, at 1884. Professors Haidt and Bjorklund have argued: "Traditional utilitarianism, for example, does an admirable job of maximizing moral goods derived from the harm/care foundation. However, it often runs afoul of moral goods derived from the fairness/reciprocity foundation (e.g., rights), to say nothing of its violations of the ingroup/loyalty foundation (why treat outsiders equal to insiders?), the authority/respect foundation (it respects no tradition or authority that demands anti-utilitarian practices), and the purity sanctity foundation (spiritual pollution is discounted as superstition)." Haidt & Bjorklund, *supra*, at 215.

63. Stake, *supra*, at 1768.

64. *Id.*

65. *Id.* at 1772.

66. *Id.* at 1770.

67. *Id.*

68. McGinnis, *supra*, at 215. Alan Wolfe has noted that Americans disfavor inheritance taxes because leaving property to one's spouse and children is a type of family-related altruism that people understand. Alan Wolfe, *The Moral Sense in Estate Tax Repeal*, NY Times A19 (July 24, 2000).

69. Merrill & Smith, *supra*, at 1859.

70. McGinnis, *supra*, at 222.

71. DONALD PFAFF, THE NEUROSCIENCE OF FAIR PLAY: WHY WE (USUALLY) FOLLOW THE GOLDEN RULE 4, 10-12 (2007); HAUSER, *supra*, at 410. For this paper, fairness is "the equitable distribution of goods or outcomes." Golnaz Tabibnia & Matthew D. Lieberman, *Fairness and Cooperation are Rewarding: Evidence from Social Cognitive Neuroscience*, 1118 ANN. N.Y. ACAD. SCI. 90, 91 (2007).

72. As Professor Iacoboni has written, mirror neurons "show that we are not alone, but are biologically wired and evolutionarily designed to be deeply interconnected with one another." MARCO IACOBONI, MIRRORING PEOPLE: THE NEW SCIENCE OF HOW WE CONNECT WITH OTHERS 267 (2008). Philosopher Thomas Nagel recognized that "[a]ny social arrangement governing the relations among individuals, or between the individual and the collective, depends on a corresponding balance of forces within the self–its image in microcosm." NAGEL, *supra*, at 4.

73. Chorvat & Kevin McCabe, *The Brain and the Law*, 359 PHIL. TRANS. R. SOC. LOND. B 1727, 1729 (2004).

74. PINKER, *supra*, at 193.

75. PFAFF, *supra*, at 7; Timothy Ketel & Bryan Koenig, *Justice, Fairness, and Strategic Emotional Commitment, in* ADVANCES IN THE PSYCHOLOGY OF JUSTICE AND AFFECT 133, 133 (David De Cremer ed., 2007).

76. *See generally* Tabibnia & Lieberman, *supra*, at 94 ("Numerous behavioral and self-report studies using the ultimatum game have established that people dislike unfair treatment."). *See also* John Richardson, *How Negotiators Choose Standards of Fairness: A Look at Empirical Evidence and Some Steps Toward a Process Model*, 12 HARV. NEGOT. L. REV. 415, 417, 421 (2007); Sarah F. Brosnan & Frans B. M. De Waal, *Monkeys Reject Unequal Pay*, 425 NATURE 297, 297 (2003) ("During the evolution of cooperation it may have become critical for individuals to compare their own efforts and pay-offs with those of others.").

77. Brosnan & de Waal, *supra*, at 299.

78. Hoffman, *supra*, at 1671.

79. David De Cremer, *Justice and Affect: When Two Friends Meet, in* ADVANCES IN THE PSYCHOLOGY OF JUSTICE AND AFFECT 1, 3-4 (David De Cremer, ed. 2007); *see also* Tabibnia & Lieberman, *supra*, at 90; JAMES Q. WILSON, THE MORAL SENSE 70 (1993) ("Equity: People who are equal with respect to contributing should be equal with respect to outcomes.").

80. Tabibnia & Lieberman, *supra*, at 91. In addition to human studies, Professors Brosnan & de Waal have demonstrated that monkeys have a sense of fairness. Brosnan & de Waal, *supra*, at 297 ("Here, we demonstrate that a nonhuman primate, the brown capuchin monkey . . ., responds negatively to unequal

reward distribution in exchanges with a human experimenter. Monkeys refused to participate if they witnessed a cospecific obtain a more attractive reward for equal effort, an effect amplified if the partner received such a reward without any effort at all.").

81. Richardson, *supra*, at 418-422.

82. *Id.* at 418.

83. Tabibnia & Lieberman, *supra*, at 95 ("When viewing fair partners who appeared to be in pain, men and women both exhibited increased activity in insular and anterior cingulate regions, suggesting an empathetic response to pain."); Richardson, *supra*, at 416.

84. PFAFF, *supra*, at 118.

85. Tabibnia & Lieberman, *supra*, at 95.

86. *Id.* at 95-97 ("Faces of cooperators, regardless of intention, were rated as more likable than neutral faces; and faces of defectors, particularly intentional defectors, were rated as less likeable than neutral faces." *Id.* at 97.).

87. PFAFF, *supra*, at 5, 81.

88. *Id.* at 22 ("Fear can spur the Golden Rule circuitry into action, causing people to opt for ethical choices in a variety of situations." *Id.* at 23.).

89. Richardson, *supra*, at 421.

90. *E.g.*, Hoffman, *supra*, at 1671.

91. *Id.*

92. *Id.*

93. RIZZOLATTI & CORRADO SINIGAGLIA, MIRRORS IN THE BRAIN–HOW OUR MINDS SHARE ACTIONS AND EMOTIONS 173-93 (2008); PFAFF, *supra*, at 7.

94. Chorvat & McCabe, *supra*, at 1731.

95. PFAFF, *supra*, at 100-01. Vasopressin may also be involved with the Golden Rule, especially in males. *Id.* at 104.

96. *Id.* at 104-05.

97. Elizabeth Mullen and Linda J. Skitka, *Exploring the Psychological Underpinnings of the Moral Mandate Effect: Motivated Reasoning, Group Differentiation, or Anger?*, 90 J. PERSONALITY AND SOC. PSYCH. 629, 629 (2006).

98. *Id.* at 631.

99. *Id.*

100. Hall, *supra*, at *11, *13, *16 ("Hunter-gatherer societies, with relatively egalitarian social structures, would have allowed little direct physical coercion since few would have the requisite power necessary to exert such control." *Id.* at *10). Throughout history, humans have taken great risks to protect their freedoms. RUBIN, *supra*, at 113.

101. Hall, *supra*, at *10. Professor Arnhart has written that "[t]he human good is variable insofar as what is desirable for human beings varies according to individual temperament, individual history, social custom, and particular circumstances." LARRY ARNHART, DARWINIAN NATURAL RIGHT: THE BIOLOGICAL ETHICS OF HUMAN NATURE 17 (1998). He has identified twenty natural desires that are rooted in human nature and

which vary in the individual and a particular society based on the above factors: "a complete life, parental care, sexual identity, sexual mating, familial bonding, friendship, social ranking, justice as reciprocity, political rule, war, health, beauty, wealth, speech, practical habituation, practical reasoning, practical arts, aesthetic pleasure, religious understanding, and intellectual understanding." *Id.* at 29); *see also* RUBIN, *supra*, at 14 ("[H]umans are highly individualistic.").

102. Hall, *supra*, at *10.

103. HAUSER, *supra*, at 187.

104. According to John Locke, "[a]nything that is not transferred remains beyond the government's authority, still as a matter not of power but of right." WEINREB, *supra*, at 132. This is based on "the assumption that the individual is fully formed prior to any action of the state." *Id.* at 133.

105. Hall, *supra*, at *17, *25.

106. *Id.* at *25.

107. *Id.* at *2.

108. Professor Hall has asserted that "[j]ust as in the classical liberal tradition, evolutionary liberty is not simply license, doing whatever one wants to win the evolutionary race." *Id.* at *3. She had added: "Evolutionary liberty . . . is liberty within the constraints of other aspects of human nature. . . . To protect social relationships, natural selection has instilled in us a moral sense which prevents (most of the time) our desire for liberty becoming a desire for license." *Id.* at *22.

109. John RAWLS, A THEORY OF JUSTICE 213 (2d ed. 1999).

110. Herbert Spencer "took it for granted that restraints to prevent a person from 'directly or indirectly aggressing on his fellows' were not only consistent with liberty but essential to it." WEINREB, *supra*, at 232. Similarly, J. S. Mill wrote, "the only purpose for which power can be rightfully exercised over any member of a civilized community, against his will, is to prevent harm to others." JOHN STUART MILL, ON LIBERTY 96 (1951). Although this author agrees with Mill on this point, Mill's statement is based on a utilitarian view of law, while this author's view derives from biology.

111. ARNHART, *supra*, at 161.

112. *Id.*

113. *Id.* at 163, 169.

114. Hall, *supra*, at *10.

115. Lawrence v. Texas, 539 U.S. 558, 562 (2003).

116. ARNHART, *supra*, at 132-33.

117. Hall, *supra*, at *7; ARNHART, *supra*, at 95-101 ("Mammalian young need social interaction with a primary caretaker for their physical and emotional health, and most Mammalian mothers desire to provide such care." *Id.* at 100.); Haidt & Bjorklund, *supra*, at 201 ("The resistence of children to arbitrary or unusual socialization has been the downfall of many utopian efforts.").

118. NAGEL, *supra*, at 8.

119. Writers have generally based equality on an individual's humanity. WEINREB, *supra*, at 167; RAWLS, *supra*, at 442 ("The capacity for moral personality.").

120. RONALD DWORKIN, FREEDOM'S LAW: THE MORAL READING OF THE AMERICAN CONSTITUTION 23 (1996) [hereinafter DWORKIN, FREEDOM'S LAW]. Professor Dworkin has added that "[m]oral membership involved reciprocity: a person is not a member unless he is treated as a member by others, which means that they treat the consequences of any collective decision for life as equally significant a reason for or against that decision as comparable consequences for the life of anyone else." *Id.* at 25.

121. WEINREB, *supra*, at 175.

122. In addition, Professor Weinreb believes that equality of result "is not a comprehensible human goal." *Id.* at 161. He continues: "Since measures to eliminate various kinds of designated group inferiority, such as racial and sexual discrimination are strongly supported on moral grounds, the principle of equality itself acquires moral credentials. Nevertheless, the achievement of equality between one human being and another or among human beings generally, for its own sake, is not a possible moral objective." *Id.* at 179. Similarly, Professor Pinker has written, "[p]olicies that insist that people be identical in their outcomes must impose costs on humans who, like all living things, vary in their biological endowment." PINKER, *supra*, at 425.

123. Hall, *supra*, at *19; *see also* McGinnis, *supra*, at 222 ("[R]edistributive efforts decrease the incentives to engage in productive activity because some of the property created will be taken by others.").

124. WEINREB, *supra*, at 177. Professor Pinker has gone further: "Many atrocities of the twentieth century were committed in the name of egalitarianism, targeting people whose success was taken as evidence of their criminality." PINKER, *supra*, at 152; *see also* RUBIN, *supra*, at 87.

125. WEINREB, *supra*, at 180; *see also* PINKER, *supra*, at 425. ("The ideal of political equality is not a guarantee that people are innately indistinguishable.").

126. 2 F. A. HAYEK, LAW, LEGISLATION, AND LIBERTY: THE MIRAGE OF SOCIAL JUSTICE 31 (1974).

127. RUBIN, *supra*, at 93-94. Professor De Waal has added: "When citizens are pampered by the state, they lose interest in economic advancement. They become passive players more interested in taking than in giving." FRANS DE WAAL, THE AGE OF EMPATHY: NATURE'S LESSONS FOR A KINDER SOCIETY 37 (2009).

128. *Id.* at 70.

129. *Id.*

130. *Id.*

131. HAUSER, *supra*, at 83.

132. *Id.* at 88.

133. *Id.*

134. Leda Cosmides & John Tooby, *Evolutionary Psychology, Moral Heuristics, and the Law*, in HEURISTICS AND THE LAW 191 (Gerd Gigerenzer & Christoph Enge eds., 2006).

135. Bernd Graefrath, *Darwinism: Neither Biologistic nor Metaphysical*, in DARWINISM & PHILOSOPHY 364, 363, 373 (Vittorio Hösle & Christian Illies eds., 2005).

136. HAUSER, *supra*, at 212; Owen D. Jones & Timothy H. Goldsmith, *Law and Behavioral Biology*, 105 COLUM. L. REV. 405, 496 (2005) ("Yet biology offers no support for the existence of discrete genetically distinct populations of humans different from each other in important ways.").

137. PINKER, *supra*, at 143.

138. Jones & Goldsmith, *supra*, at 477.

139. V. F. Nourse & Sarah A. Maguire, *The Lost History of Governance and Equal Protection*, 58 DUKE L.J. 955, 963-64 (2009).

140. 10 S.E. 285, 286 (1889).

141. WEINREB, *supra*, at 10.

142. *Id.*

143. Professor Greene has shown that emotions cause us to value our nonutilitarian intuitions over a cost benefit analysis. Joshua Greene, *Cognitive Neuroscience and the Structure of the Moral Mind*, *in* THE INNATE MIND: STRUCTURE AND CONTENTS 338, 344-50 (Peter Carruthers et. al. eds., 2005). In addition, utilitarian rights do not protect minorities, while rights based on human behavior are for all individuals. Thus, rights based on human behavior are better at protecting against racism, sexism, etc., than other bases of rights, especially those rights that are considered social constructs. *See* Chapter Three of this study.

144. Bailey Kuklin, *Evolution, Politics and Law*, 38 VAL. U.L. REV. 1129, 1216 (2004); *see also* McGinnis, *supra*, at 225.

145. RAWLS, *supra*, at 3; *see also* DERSHOWITZ, *supra*, at 156 ("The greatest crises for a constitutional democracy occur when the majority demands that minority rights be abridged in the name of strongly held preferences or claims of necessity.").

146. NAGEL, *supra*, at 66-67.

147. Michael Koenigs et. al., *Damage to the Prefrontal Cortex Increases Utilitarian Moral Judgements*, 446 NATURE 908 (2007).

148. *Id.*

149. JOMO KENYATTA, FACING MOUNT KENYA: THE TRIBAL LIFE OF THE GIKUYU 130 (1965).

150. MURPHY & COLEMAN, *supra*, at 79.

151. For example, a city may have several acres of vacant land that it wants to put to a productive use. Some citizens want to employ the land for a basketball stadium so that the city can attract an NBA team. Others may think that the best use for the land would be as an industrial park to improve the city's economy. Still others may want it to be a public park for recreation. None of these reasons involve basic human rights. Therefore, the city can make its decision based on democratic and/or cost/benefit grounds.

152. Hoffman, *supra*, at 1674.

153. *Id.*

154. *Id.*

155. *Id.*

156. McGinnis, *supra*, at 212.

157. *Id.* at 212-13.

158. Deshowitz, *supra*, at 42. Professor Strahlendorf has elaborated: "Natural-law philosophers have stated that there are a set of basic human values that are 'self-evident.' This means that humans sense that these values are good. . . . The point here . . . is . . . to suggest that there must be sets of biological mechanisms (epigenetic rules and Darwinian algorithms) that make things 'self-evidently' good." Peter Strahlendorf, *Legal Concepts from an Evolutionary Perspective*, *in* THE SENSE OF JUSTICE: BIOLOGICAL FOUNDATIONS OF LAW 154 (Roger D. Masters & Margaret Gruter eds., 1991).

159. McGinnis, *supra*, at 231.

160. *Id.* at 232.

161. JAMES H. RUTHERFORD, *The Moral Foundations of United States Constitutional Democracy, in* MORAL AND POLITICAL PHILOSOPHY 76 (2004).

162. McGinnis, *supra*, at 232.

163. *Id.* at 232-235; *see also* G. Edward White, *Revisiting the Ideas of the Founding*, 77 U. CIN. L. REV. 969, 979 (2009) ("It was only when Americans began to reflect upon factionalism in state legislatures, and to consider how to avoid the evils of that phenomenon, in a revised federal government, that more robust concentrations of separate branches and powers in a single government began to be emphasized."). As James Madison wrote,

> [i]n the compound republic of America, the power surrendered by the people is first divided between two distinct governments, and then the portion is allotted to each subdivided among distinct and separate departments. Hence a double security arises to the rights of the people. The different governments will control each other, at the same time that each will be controlled by itself. THE FEDERALIST PAPERS No. 51, at 357 (James Madison) (Benjamin Fletcher Wright ed., 1961).

164. White, *supra*, at 981-84. Professor White has continued: "the idea of protection for the property rights of individuals can be said to have been implicitly understood by Americans as part of their heritage as British subjects. . . . As resistance to British policy toward the colonies widened in the 1770s, Americans began to assert that because they were not represented in Parliament that body had no authority over them at all. In the evolution of this argument, protection of property rights of individuals became a way of concretizing the theory that government existed to secure the 'natural' rights of citizens, and when it transgressed on those rights it lost its legitimacy." *Id.* at 981-82.

165. McGinnis, *supra*, at 235.

166. *Id.* at 234.

167. DWORKIN, FREEDOM'S LAW, *supra*, at 200.

168. Jason Mazzone, *Speech and Reciprocity: A Theory of the First Amendment*, 34 CONN. L. REV. 405, 406 (2002).

169. Harold Hongju Koh, *On American Exceptionalism*, 55 STAN. L. REV. 1479, 1482 (2003); *see also* DWORKIN, FREEDOM'S LAW, *supra*, at 195.

170. U.S. CONST. amend. III.

171. As Professor Dershowitz has noted, "[t]here can be no rational claim to a natural right not to have troops quartered in one's home except during wartime." Dershowitz, *supra*, at 50.

172. "A well regulated militia, being necessary to the security of a free state, the right of the people to keep and bear arms, shall not be infringed." U.S. CONST. amend. II.

173. Professor Dershowitz has declared that "[i]f the right to bear arms is narrowed to include only the right to defend oneself and one's family–thus excluding the right to revolt, hunt, collect guns, and possess them for other reasons–a stronger case can be made for its near-universality. . ." Dershowitz, *supra*, at 55.

174. HAUSER, *supra*, at 149.

175. Dershowitz, *supra*, at 52.

176. U.S. CONST. amend. IX.

177. RANDY E. BARNETT, RESTORING THE LOST CONSTITUTION: THE PRESUMPTION OF LIBERTY 4 (2004). The main argument against including a bill of rights in the original Constitution was that it was unnecessary because rights were in the people. For example, Alexander Hamilton argued that bills of right "have no application to constitutions professedly founded upon the power of the people, and executed by their immediate representatives and servants. Here, in strictness, the people surrender nothing, and as they retain everything, they have no need of particular reservations." THE FEDERALIST PAPERS No. 84, at 578 (Alexander Hamilton) (Benjamin Fletcher Wright ed., 1961).

178. BARNETT, *supra*, at 253-69.

179. Edward J. Eberle, *The German Idea of Freedom*, 10 OR. REV. INT'L L. 1, 2-3 (2008).

180. *Id.* at 3.

181. *Id.* at 3-4

182. *Id.* at 4.

183. *Id.* at 17.

184. *Id.* at 25.

185. *Id.* at 5.

186. *Id.* at 31.

187. *Id.* at 14.

188. *Id.*

189. *Id.* at 4-5.

190. *Id.* at 13.

191. *Id.* at 36.

192. *Id.* at 38.

193. *Id.* at 46.

194. *Id.* at 5-6, 52. Of course, American law deals with welfare through legislation. *Id.* at 52.

195. *Id.* at 59.

196. *Id.* at 66.

197. Professor White has noted that modern civil liberties were not a concern of the drafters and that the idea of equality was muted in the founding era. White, *supra*.

198. *Id.* at 18.

199. JOSEPH TELUSHKIN, JEWISH WISDOM 43 (1994).

200. Dershowitz, *supra*, at 66-67.

Chapter Six

Analysis of Constitutional Cases

How comes it that human beings, whose contacts with the world are brief and personal and limited, are nevertheless able to know as much as they know?

Bertrand Russell[1]

This chapter will use behavioral biology to analyze constitutional cases in the areas of takings/property, parental rights, and punitive damages.

I. Property, Reciprocal Altruism, and Kelo v. City of New London

Behavioral biology, particularly its analysis of reciprocal altruism and its emphasis on property ownership as a basic human instinct, can help us understand *Kelo v. City of New London*,[2] which concerned the application of the Takings Clause of the Fifth Amendment of the United States Constitution. The issue in *Kelo* was whether a taking for economic development was a "public use" under the Takings Clause.[3] The Takings Clause states: "[N]or shall private property be taken for public use, without just compensation."[4]

New London, Connecticut approved an economic development plan that was "projected to create an excess of 1,000 jobs, to increase tax and other revenues, and to revitalize an economically distressed city, including its downtown and waterfront areas."[5] New London had seen decades of economic decline including high unemployment, and, in 1996, the federal government had closed the Naval Undersea Warfare Center in Fort Trumbull, which had employed over 1,500 people.[6] In 1998, Pfizer, a major pharmaceutical company, decided to construct a $300 million dollar facility adjacent to Fort Trumbull.[7] In May 1998, New London created a plan to develop 90 acres of the Fort Trumbull area for commercial, recreational, and residential use.[8] The area included 115 privately-owned properties, as well as 32 acres from the former naval facility.[9] New London approved the plan in January 2000, and it authorized the use of eminent domain to acquire property for the project.[10]

The City commenced condemnation proceedings against nine owners who owned 15 properties in the area, including the house of a person who had lived there since 1918.[11] There was no allegation that the properties were blighted or in poor condition.[12] The owners brought suit in superior court, and the court ruled in favor of the owners for part of the property (park or marina support), but not another part of the property (office space).[13] The Connecticut Supreme Court held that all the takings were valid, and the United States Supreme Court affirmed this ruling.[14]

Justice Stevens began his opinion by stating the extremes of the Takings Clause:

> it has long been accepted that the sovereign may not take the property of *A* for the sole purpose of transferring it to another private party *B*, even though *A* is paid just compensation. On the other hand, it is equally clear that a State may transfer property from one private party to another if future "use by the public" is the purpose of the taking; the condemnation of land for a railroad with common-carrier duties is a familiar example.[15]

Neither extreme was involved in this case.[16] In this case, the taking would be executed pursuant to a carefully considered development plan, but not all the land was to be used by the general public, nor was the land to be used by a common carrier, whose services would be open to all comers.[17]

Rather than requiring that condemned property be put to use for the general public, which the Court had considered impractical, at the end of the nineteenth century, the Court "embraced the broader and more natural interpretation of public use as 'public purpose.'"[18] For example, in *Berman v. Parker*,[19] the Court had upheld a redevelopment plan that had targeted a blighted area of Washington, even though the particular condemned department store was not blighted itself. The Court deferred to a legislative and agency determination that the area must be planned as a whole.[20] Similarly, the Court had upheld a Hawaii statute under which "fee title was taken from lessors and transferred to lessees (for just compensation) in order to reduce the concentration of land ownership."[21] Concerning this case, *Kelo* declared: "reaffirming *Berman's* deferential approach to legislative judgments in this field, we concluded that the State's purpose of eliminating the 'social and economic evils of a land oligopoly' qualified as a valid public use."[22] Likewise, in *Ruckelshaus v. Monsanto Co.*,[23] the Court upheld the Federal Insecticide, Fungicide, and Rodenticide Act that allowed the Environmental Protection Agency to consider data, including trade secrets, "submitted by a prior pesticide applicant in evaluating a subsequent application, so long as the second applicant paid just compensation for the data."[24] Although the main beneficiaries of the Act were subsequent applicants, the Court found "Congress' belief that sparing applicants the cost of time-consuming research eliminated a significant barrier to entry in the pesticide market and thereby enhanced competition."[25]

The Court concluded:

> Viewed as a whole, our jurisprudence has recognized that the needs of society have varied between different parts of the Nation, just as they have evolved over time in response to changed circumstances. Our earliest cases in particular embodied a strong theme of Federalism, emphasizing the "great respect" that we owe to the state legislatures and state courts in discerning local public needs . . . For more than a century, our public use jurisprudence has wisely eschewed rigid formulas and intrusive scrutiny in favor of affording legislatures broad latitude in determining what public needs justify the use of the takings power.[26]

Concerning the present facts, the Court concluded that the City's "determination that the area was sufficiently distressed to justify a program of economic rejuvenation is entitled to our deference."[27] The Court continued: "Given the comprehensive character of the plan, the thorough deliberation that preceded its adoption, and the limited scope of our review, it is appropriate for us, as it was in *Berman*, to resolve the challenges of the individual owners, not on a piecemeal basis, but rather in the light of the entire plan.

Because that plan unquestionably serves a public purpose, the takings challenged here satisfy the public use requirements of the *Fifth Amendment*."[28]

The Court rejected the owners' argument that it should create a bright-line rule that economic development is not a public use.[29] The Court noted that promoting economic development is a traditional governmental function and that the Court had upheld similar takings in agriculture and mining that had been important to the states' welfare.[30] The Court also rejected the owners' argument that employing eminent domain for economic development impermissibly blurred the boundary between public and private takings on the ground that a government's pursuit of a public purpose will often benefit private parties.[31] Finally, the Court rejected the owner's contention that the Court "should require a 'reasonable certainty' that the expected public benefits will actually accrue."[32] The Court declared: "When the legislature's purpose is legitimate and its means are not irrational, our cases make clear that empirical debates over the wisdom of other kinds of socioeconomic legislation—are not to be carried out in the federal courts."[33] The Court added: "A constitutional rule that required postponement of the judicial approval of every condemnation until the likelihood of success of the plan had been assured would unquestionably impose a significant impediment to the successful consummation of many such plans."[34]

Justice Steven's opinion in *Kelo* contravenes basic principles of human behavior—principles which, as mentioned in Chapter Five, this author thinks the Framers used to draft the Constitution. First, the Supreme Court should not defer to the legislature when fundamental principles are involved. This author believes that behavioral biology supports a Kantian notion of rights—"the view that the rational choice in ethics is always the choice that respects the rights of autonomous persons freely to determine their own destinies, even if this respect is bought at the cost of loss of happiness or well-being."[35] Human beings are autonomous because they have the capacity for rational choice.[36] That an individual is mainly determined by the inner workings of his or her mind backs up Kant's notion that humans should be respected because they can make rational choices. Thus, in matters of basic principle, the Court should not defer to policy decisions of the other branches.[37]

More fundamentally, New London's taking of private property interferes with the basis of human nature. As mentioned in Chapter Five, property developed as part of humans' social relations behavioral system,[38] and it is hard-wired into our brains.[39] Thus, "contrary to legal realists, property is a phenomenon that exists apart from any organized government."[40] Behavioral biology scholars, including the present author, believe that property evolved to avoid harm to individuals,[41] that it developed as a method to control cheating,[42] that it involved territorial possession,[43] that it evolved as an incentive to get people to work,[44] and that survival is based on the use of things.[45] Finally, when people have an interest in property, they protect that property and put the property to beneficial use, thus creating more resources and benefitting the community.[46]   Our Constitution protects property because it is a social contract that is rooted in reciprocal altruism. A social contract is "an arrangement negotiated by rational, self-interested individuals," which evolved for the protection of individuals.[47] Professor Pinker has written that "[r]eciprocal altruism, in particular, is just the traditional concept of the social contract restated in biological terms."[48] Other biologists have theorized that our legal institutions developed "to compensate for the fact we are not programmed by biological evolution to behave cooperatively in large groups of non-kin."[49]

Part of the social contract that is our Constitution is the protection of property. Similarly, as mentioned earlier, protection of property is essential to reciprocal altruism and human nature. One of the Constitution's goals was to protect private property from those who would use governmental mechanisms to appropriate what is not theirs. As Professor McGinnis has observed: "Thus under the Framers' system, providing public power to a continental people paradoxically was an attempt to protect wealth created by private enterprise from public expropriation."[50] He has added: "If property is natural to man, a government that ignores the interests of mankind in property and exchange does so at its own peril."[51]

In ruling that a taking for economic development did not violate the Takings Clause, Justice Stevens violated these basic principles of human nature, as well as the Framers' carefully-balanced social contract. The government has taken property from one individual and given it to another. Instead of the government protecting private property, the government is being used to appropriate private property. Government is breaking the social contract and encouraging cheating. *All* private property is now subject to condemnation after *Kelo*, a result that is not consistent with human nature because it interferes with security in property.

As mentioned in Chapter Five, property rights are not based on a utilitarian, cost-benefit analysis. For example, the property right to prevent trespass to land is absolute;

it does not depend on a cost-benefit analysis that the trespass would or would not be beneficial to society. As one scholar has noted, "when the government has broad eminent domain powers that can be 'lent' to commercial actors, property is no longer protected by a 'property rule' requiring voluntary transactions, but instead by a 'liability rule' that permits nonconsensual transfer at judicially determined prices."[52] Accordingly, economic development takings, where the government takes property from an innocent party and awards it to another party who can make better use of it, are not justified. While the new use might create a bigger pie and produce favorable externalities, such as better business in the neighborhood, such takings go against our basic instincts concerning the sanctity of property.[53] Eminent domain under such circumstances constitutes immoral coercion of innocent parties.[54] Utilitarian considerations should not trump basic individual rights.

The Framers knew what they were doing when they put "public use" instead of "public purpose" into the Takings Clause. This allowed the government to take property (for just compensation) when the government needed it, but it prevented the government from overreaching by taking property when it was for the benefit of private individuals. This was part of the Framers' protection against factions–factions using the government for their individual gain.[55] Notably, under the economic development theory, private property is being redistributed to persons with influence in the political process, such as large corporations.[56]

In addition, this violation of the social contract can affect the individual initiative that the Framers wanted to protect and that is part of human nature. As Professor McGinnis has noted: "Such redistributive efforts decrease the incentives to engage in productive activity because some of the property created will be taken by others."[57] In addition, as Donald Elliot has stated, "What a person is willing to do or how much of a particular activity a person will engage in is often dependent on his or her perception about what others in the community are doing."[58] Moreover, "relative control over resources is important to [human's] reproductive success."[59] Finally, there is biological basis to fairness.[60] Professor Stake has written, "the property instinct connects with an instinct for equity in reciprocal exchanges and thus can be seen as one part of a sense of fairness or justice."[61] In sum, by reading "public purpose" for "public use" and deferring to legislative wisdom, the Court has read the Takings Clause out of the Constitution, and it has used a notion of human nature that is contrary to science and the Framers' intent.

Behavioral biology does not always provide one right answer, and, in this case, behavioral biology provides an alternative argument that supports Justice Stevens's opinion. Human beings do not always act rationally.[62] "[B]ehavior is substantively rational when it is appropriate for achieving particular goals, given conditions and constraints, regardless of how the behavior was actually chosen."[63] Substantive irrationality occurs because the brain is partially designed for the environment of an earlier time.[64] Professors Jones and Goldsmith have pointed out that "[b]ecause long lives, reliable futures, and reliable rights to future payoffs were not part of the environment in which the modern brain was slowly built, it is not particularly surprising that the modern brain tends to steeply discount the value of a future benefit compared to an immediate one and is not particularly well equipped to reach the outcome currently deemed most rational."[65] More importantly for this issue, for reasons unrelated to sentimental attachment, "people tend to value an object more highly, often twice as highly, as soon as they possess it compared to how they value the same object if they had to purchase it."[66] Similarly, humans are concerned more with losses than gains.[67]

Based on the above, one could argue that when the government allows takings for economic development, it is compensating for substantive irrationality that is built into the human mind. It is forcing a rational exchange that would occur were it not for the fact that the owner values his or her property more than its actual value because humans value what they have more than what they could obtain.

Of the two arguments set forth above, I believe the one that would prevent the taking is the better one. Although an owner may be overvaluing his or her property, as was stated above, the protection of property is basic to human nature, reciprocal altruism, and our social contract. Equally important, this outcome favors the Framers' intent to prevent individuals from exploiting others by using governmental mechanisms. Nevertheless, the fact that behavioral biology can be used to support arguments on both sides of the takings issue demonstrates that the best use of behavioral biology is often to better understand a problem rather than come to one right answer.

II. Behavioral Biology and Michael H. v. Gerald D.

Behavioral biology is helpful in understanding what is important about the family. In *Michael H. v. Gerald D*,[68] the main issue was whether application of a California statute (Cal. Evid. Code Ann. §621) that presumes a child born to a married woman living with her husband is a child of that marriage violated the due process rights of a man who was almost certainly the child's natural father.[69] Carole D. and Gerald D. were married in 1976.[70] Carole had an affair with Michael H. beginning in 1978.[71] In 1981, she conceived a child, Victoria, and the birth certificate listed her husband Gerald as the father, and he always acted like Victoria's father.[72] Over the next few years, Carole and Victoria lived at different times with Gerald, Michael, and another man.[73] In 1983, Michael filed a filiation action in California, and Carole withdrew a motion for summary judgment that she had filed in that action when she again became involved with Michael.[74] In April 1984, Carole and Michael signed a stipulation that Michael was Victoria's father.[75] However, two months later, Carole reconciled with Gerald.[76]

Michael and Victoria, through a *guardian ad litem*, sought visitation rights for Michael with his daughter, which the court granted.[77] Gerald then intervened and moved for summary judgment, claiming that under Cal. Evid. Code Ann § 621 there was no triable issue concerning Victoria's paternity.[78] Under the statute, "[t]he presumption [of paternity] may be rebutted by blood tests, but only if a motion for such tests is made, within two years of the child's birth, either by the husband or, if the natural father has filed an affidavit acknowledging paternity, by the wife."[79] The court granted Gerald's motion for summary judgement, and it also denied Michael visitation rights during the pendency of the appeal.[80]

Michael's appeal asserted that the court's application of § 621 violated his procedural and substantive due process rights, and Victoria raised due process and equal protection claims.[81] The Court of Appeals rejected Michael's and Victoria's arguments, and the California Supreme Court denied their petition for discretionary review.[82] They then appealed to the United States Supreme Court, which granted certiorari.[83]

Justice Scalia began the main part of the plurality opinion with an observation based on nature: "California law, like nature itself, makes no provision for dual fatherhood."[84] He noted that, although Michael was initially seeking only visitation, under California law, if he were successful in establishing paternity, he could sue for custody.[85] Scalia rejected Michael's procedural due process claim on the ground that § 621 was actually the implementation of substantive law.[86]

Scalia began the substantive due process part of his opinion with the observation that "[i]t is an established part of our constitutional jurisprudence that the term 'liberty' in the Due Process Clause extends beyond freedom from physical restraint."[87] Scalia found some need for constraint because of the possibility of an expansive reading of the clause under this interpretation.[88] He found that constraint in tradition: "[T]he Due Process Clause affords only those protections 'so rooted in the roots and conscience of our people as to be ranked as fundamental.'"[89] He then stated, "the legal issue in the present case reduces to whether the relationship between persons in the situation of Michael and Victoria has been treated as a protected family unit under the historic practices of our society, or whether on any other basis it has been accorded special protection."[90] After examining common law authorities dating back to the eighteenth century, like Blackstone's *Commentaries*, he concluded that there was no such tradition.[91] He declared: "The primary policy rationale underlying the common law's severe restrictions on rebuttal of the presumption appears to have been an aversion to declaring children illegitimate . . . thereby depriving them of their inheritance and succession, . . . and likely making them wards of the state. A secondary policy concern was the interest in promoting the 'peace and tranquility' of States and families, . . . a goal that obviously is impaired by facilitating suits against husband and wife asserting that their children are illegitimate."[92] He continued, "even in modern times–when, as we noted, the rigid protection of the marital family has in other respects been relaxed–the ability of a person in Michael's position to claim paternity has not been generally acknowledged."[93] In addition, what Michael is trying to assert in this case is the right to obtain parental prerogatives, and "[w]hat he must establish, therefore, is not that society has traditionally allowed a natural father in his circumstances to establish paternity, but that it has traditionally accorded such a father parental rights, or at least not traditionally denied them."[94] He concluded: "This is not the stuff of which fundamental rights qualifying as liberty interests are made of."[95]

He responded to Justice Brennan's criticism in the dissent that the plurality opinion "'squashes' the liberty that consists of 'the freedom not to conform'" by stating "to *provide* protection to an adulterous natural father is to *deny* protection to a marital father, and vice versa."[96] In other words, the expansion of one liberty interest contracts another.[97] He concluded: "Our disposition does not choose between those two 'freedoms,' but leaves that to the people of California."[98]

Scalia also rejected Victoria's due process claim, asserting that her claim was even weaker than her father's.[99] Despite any psychological benefits to Victoria, Scalia thought that "the claim that a state must recognize multiple fatherhood has no support in the history or traditions of this country."[100] Scalia also denied Victoria's equal protection claim, rejecting her argument for strict scrutiny analysis on the ground that the state was discriminating against her because she was illegitimate, because she was not illegitimate under California law. He noted that "[i]llegitimacy is a legal construct, not a natural trait."[101]

Behavioral biology shows the problem with Scalia's evaluation of liberty through the lens of tradition. Tradition concerns a continuation of the past for the past's sake. It is anti-change. However, mankind's nature can change as the environment changes, which includes technological change. The rule that one could not generally attack the paternity of a child of a marriage may have been a good rule for Blackstone's time because at that time there were no blood tests that could determine paternity. Today, the environment has "changed"; we have such tests. Consequently, the traditional rule should be altered. In addition, even in Blackstone's time, there were exceptions to the rule; the presumption could be rebutted if the husband was sterile or had no access to the wife at the relevant time.[102] This means that, if it were impossible for the husband to be the father, paternity could be attacked. Thus, the rule isn't different today; rather, the methods of establishing paternity have expanded.

In addition, tradition is not the best choice as a basis for liberty; something is not fundamental solely because it has been done a long time. There are traditions that go against human nature or that encourage behavior that are remnants of a different environment. Slavery was a tradition, but our leaders in the nineteenth-century eliminated it because it was repugnant to human nature.

Justice Scalia argued that the peace and tranquility of the family was another reason for the rule.[103] Of course, the peace and tranquility of the family is also different today from what it was in Blackstone's time. There is a much greater incidence of divorce, and living arrangements exist that Blackstone would not recognize. In *Michael H.*, the mother separated from her husband several times, and she lived with at least two other men.[104] There was little peace and tranquility to interfere with in that marriage. More importantly, it is not the adjudication of paternity that interferes with the peace and tranquility of the family, but the accusation or knowledge of the paternity.

Nor does the stigma of illegitimacy continue as a basis for the traditional rule. It is true that in Blackstone's time illegitimacy was a real stigma, and it caused numerous other problems, such as loss of inheritance or the danger that the child would become a ward of the state.[105] Today, however, that stigma does not exist, and the law has changed to treat illegitimate children in the same manner as children born of a marriage.[106]

The real problem here is that Scalia holds too narrow a concept of liberty that ignores human nature. This author believes that, because individuals are autonomous, human nature supports that the government should not interfere with a person's liberty unless there is harm to another. Moreover, the right of a father to have a relationship with his natural child is a liberty that the government should not generally interfere with.[107] As Professor McGinnis has remarked, "family affections are not mere social constructs but are deeply rooted in our behavior and psyche."[108] In fact, unlike most other mammals, human fathers have strong parental bonds with their children.[109] It is the natural relationship between father and child that is fundamental, not the legal one, which is contrary to nature in this instance.

However, as Scalia pointed out, the husband had a liberty, too.[110] Nevertheless, the answer is not to let the state decide, as Scalia suggested. Rather, this is a constitutional question that the Supreme Court must decide. In other words, basic liberty is a question of principle, not policy.

Clashes of liberty occur all the time. Which is a more important liberty, a person's right to not associate with a race of people he dislikes or the right of a person of that race to have a fair opportunity for a job? Such questions can be answered with the help of behavioral biology. In the case of the above discrimination hypothetical, a person's right to equal opportunity in the job market to feed himself and his family should trump a person's liberty of nonassociation in the public sphere, especially when it is based on a taboo mentality.[111] In private life, a person might have the liberty to not associate with whomever he likes for whatever reason, but this liberty is restricted in public life when it harms others.

In *Michael H.*, Michael had an interest in a paternal relationship with his daughter because he was Victoria's natural father–she shared his genes–and because of the paternal bond that is essential to human nature.[112] As mentioned above, human fathers have strong parental bonds with their children. Victoria also had a liberty interest in a relationship with her father because she shared his genes; it will usually be in the best interest of the child to have a relationship with her father, absent an abusive relationship.[113] Gerald did have the liberty of association with anyone he pleased, and it is certainly reasonable that he would want a relationship with his wife's daughter.

However, since paternity and the paternal bond are central to human nature, Michael's and Victoria's liberty trumps Gerald's. Carole also had a liberty in protecting her daughter, but there was no harm here because it had never been alleged that Michael was a threat to Victoria in any way.[114]

Scalia also had it backwards in favoring the sanctity of the marriage over Michael's paternal interest. Marriage is a way that society protects paternity and the paternal bond that are essential to human nature.[115] Accordingly, paternity and the paternal bond are more important than marriage.[116] The pair-bond between Gerald and Carole are also essential to human nature, but it is not an adjudication of paternity that threatened that pair-bond, but Victoria's unfaithfulness to her husband. Scalia also ignored Victoria's interest.[117] It was not the psychological benefit from having two fathers that was important, it was the fact that Michael shared her genes, which is the most essential connection in human nature.

In sum, Justice Scalia came to the wrong outcome in *Michael H.* because he favored tradition over evolution, a choice that ignored human nature. He should have seen that technology had eliminated the foundation for the rule that the paternity of a child born in a marriage should be challenged only in limited circumstances. Moreover, he wrongly favored marriage over protecting paternity and the paternal bond because paternity and the paternal bond are essential to human nature, while marriage is only a way to protect those attributes. Scalia had it right that there is no dual fatherhood in nature. However, in nature Michael was Victoria's father.[118] If California law interferes with Michael's relationship with his natural daughter, it has violated his due process rights under the Fourteenth Amendment.

III. Behavioral Biology and Due Process Limits on State Punitive Damages

In recent years, the Supreme Court has placed strict due process limits on the ability of states to award punitive damages.[119] In addition, as Professor Anthony J. Sebok has declared, "American tort law . . . is in a major reexamination of punitive damages–the final chapter of which has not been written."[120] This section will analyze these cases from the viewpoint of behavioral biology.

These cases start from the principle that: "[t]he Due Process Clause of the Fourteenth Amendment prohibits a state from imposing a 'grossly excessive' punishment on a tortfessor."[121] According to the Supreme Court, the purpose of punitive damages is deterrence and retribution: they "may properly be imposed to further a State's legitimate interest in punishing unlawful conduct and deterring its repetition."[122] Most states that authorize exemplary damages afford the jury similar latitude, requiring only that the damages awarded "be reasonably necessary to vindicate the State's legitimate interests in punishment and deterrence."[123] As Justice Stevens has observed: "Whereas compensatory damages are measured by the harm the defendant has caused the plaintiff, punitive damages are a sanction for the public harm the defendant's conduct has caused or threatened. There is little difference between a justification for a criminal sanction, such as a fine or term of imprisonment, and an award of punitive damages."[124]

   BMW held that a state could not base punitive damages on conduct that was legal in other states, and it created a three-part test to determine whether punitive damages were excessive.[125] This case involved a policy by BMW not to advise its customers of predelivery damages to automobiles when the repair cost comprised less than 3% of the automobile's suggested retail price.[126] The plaintiff had purchased a BMW that had been repainted prior to delivery at a cost of approximately 1.5% of the car's suggested retail price.[127] After hearing that the value of the car after being repainted was approximately 10% less ($4,000) than if it had not been repaired, the jury returned a verdict of $4,000 in compensatory damages and $4 million in punitive damages.[128] The trial judge rejected BMW's post-trial motion to set aside the punitive damages award, and the Alabama Supreme Court held that the award did not exceed a constitutionally permissible amount.[129] The Alabama Supreme Court, however, reduced the punitive damages to two million dollars on the ground that they were incorrectly computed.[130]

   The Supreme Court stated,"[p]unitive damages may properly be imposed to further a State's legitimate interests in punishing unlawful conduct and deterring its repetition," and "[o]nly when an award can fairly be categorized as 'grossly excessive' in relation to these interests does it enter the zone of arbitrariness that violates the Due Process Clause of the Fourteenth Amendment."[131] In awarding punitive damages, a state cannot impose its policy choice on other states.[132] The Court declared, "one State's power to impose burdens on the interstate market for automobiles is not only subordinate to the federal power over interstate commerce, but is also constrained by the need to respect the interests of other States."[133] Thus, Alabama could not use BMW's similar conduct in other states when computing punitive damages.[134]

The Court then stated: "elementary notions of fairness enshrined in our constitutional jurisprudence dictate that a person receive fair notice not only of the conduct that will subject him to punishment, but also the severity of the penalty a State may impose."[135] The Court developed a three-part test to analyze fair notice in punitive damages cases: "(1) the degree of reprehensibility, (2) the disparity between the harm or potential harm suffered by the plaintiff and the punitive damages, and (3) the differences between the award and civil penalties authorized or imposed in comparable cases."[136]

Concerning reprehensibility, the Court noted that some wrongs are more blameworthy than others; for example, nonviolent crimes are less serious than violent crimes and fraud is more reprehensible than negligence.[137] The Court felt that BMW's conduct was not particularly reprehensible because the harm was purely economic.[138] The Court concluded: "That conduct is sufficiently reprehensible to give rise to tort liability, and even a modest award of exemplary damages does not establish the high degree of culpability that warrants a substantial punitive damages award."[139]

Concerning the second requirement that the punitive damages must bear a reasonable relationship to the compensatory damages, the Court observed that the $2,000,000 award was 500 times the compensatory damages, and there was no suggestion that the plaintiff or any other purchaser was faced with any other potential harm from the nondisclosure policy.[140] The Court added, however, a higher ratio between punitive damages and compensatory damages might be justified when an egregious act has produced a small amount of damages or where the injury is hard to detect.[141] Concerning the third requirement, a comparison between the punitive damages award and the civil or criminal penalties that could be imposed for comparable misconduct, the Court believed the award was substantially greater than statutory fines available in Alabama and elsewhere for similar conduct.[142]

In *Campbell*, the Court applied the three-part test to an award of punitive damages in a case involving claims of bad faith, fraud, and intentional infliction of emotional distress.[143] Campbell had been involved in a wrongful death and tort action involving an automobile accident.[144] Although Campbell insisted he was not at fault, the investigators came to a consensus that he had caused the crash.[145] His insurance company refused settlement offers for the policy limit ($50,000), and they litigated the action. The insurance company assured the Campbells "their assets were safe, that they had no liability for the accident, that [State Farm] would represent their interests, and that they did not need to procure separate counsel."[146] The jury returned a verdict against Campbell for $185,849, and State Farm refused to cover the excess liability.[147] State Farm told the Campbells: "You may want to put for sale signs on your property to get things moving," and they refused to post a supersedeas bond.[148] Eighteen months later, after the Utah Supreme Court denied Campbell's appeal, the insurer paid the entire judgement.[149]

Campbell filed suit against his insurer for bad faith, fraud, and intentional infliction of emotional distress, and he won a verdict of $2.6 million in compensatory damages and $145 million in punitive damages, which the court reduced to $1 million and $25 million, respectively.[150] Using the three-part test from *Gore*, the Utah Supreme Court reinstated the $145 million in punitive damages, noting that because of the insurer's clandestine actions, its conduct would be punished at most in one out of 50,000 cases.[151]

Applying the three-part test, the Court reversed.[152] Although the Court thought that "State Farm's handling of the claims against the Campbell merits no praise," it held that the size of the award was excessive because the insurer was being punished for its nationwide conduct, much of which was lawful where it occurred.[153] The Court argued that "[a] defendant should be punished for the conduct that harmed the plaintiff, not for being an unsavory business or individual."[154] The Court also remarked the ratio between punitive and compensatory damages should usually be in the single digits.[155] The Court also pointed out that the emotional distress was covered in the compensatory damages and should not be duplicated in the punitive damages.[156] The Court concluded: "Here the argument that State Farm will be punished in only the rare case, coupled with reference to its assets . . . had little to do with the harm sustained by the Campbells."[157]

Philip Morris, the most recent case, radically altered a state's ability to impose punitive damages when it ruled that such an award could not be based on a desire to punish the defendant for harming persons who were not before the court.[158] This case concerned a wrongful death from smoking, with compensatory damages of $821,000 and punitive damages of $79.5 million.[159] The jury had found "that Williams smoked in significant part because he thought it was safe to do so and that Philip Morris knowingly and falsely led him to believe that this was so."[160]

The Court held that "the Constitution's Due Process Clause forbids a State to use a punitive damages award to punish a defendant for injury that it inflicts upon nonpareils or those whom they directly represent, *i.e.*, injury that it inflicts upon those who are, essentially, strangers to the litigation."[161] The Court noted, "the Due Process Clause prohibits a State from punishing an individual without first providing that individual with an opportunity to present every available defense. Yet a defendant threatened with punishment for injuring a nonparty has no opportunity to defend against the charge, by showing, for example in a case such as this, that the other victim was not entitled to damages because he or she knew that smoking was dangerous or did not rely upon the defendant's statements to the contrary."[162] Such a rule would be standardless and speculative.[163] Moreover, there is no authority to support punitive damages for the purpose of punishing a defendant for harm to others.[164] Finally, a state court cannot permit procedures that would allow an unreasonable risk of confusion concerning whether the jury has punished the defendant for causing harm to others.[165]

As noted in earlier chapters, punishment is the glue that holds together reciprocal altruism and the social contract. Punishment exists in all legal systems.[166] In a system based on reciprocal altruism, self-interest encourages cheating, so there is a need to punish cheaters (or free riders).[167] As noted in earlier chapters, humans can detect cheating,[168] and there is a fundamental urge in humans to punish cheaters based on an innate sense of fairness.[169] There is a need to punish cheaters, even at a cost to the punisher, to benefit the group and consequently individual members.[170] As Professors Hoffman & Goldsmith have observed, "[a]s our cognitive abilities evolved in tandem with the emergence of culture, our urge to punish individuals who break the social contract appeared as an important stabilizing feature."[171] Thus, punishing cheaters was an evolutionary advantage because it helped hold the group together.[172]

One can evaluate punishment by a cost-benefit analysis: "one can consider legal sanctions as prices imposed on behaviors that will tend to decrease the incidence of those behaviors."[173] As stated in Chapter Four, Professors Jones and Goldsmith have developed a cost-benefit rule based on behavioral biology for determining the proper level of punishment, which they call "The Law of Law's Leverage": "The magnitude of legal intervention necessary to reduce or to increase the incidence of any human behavior will correlate positively or negatively, respectively, with the extent to which predisposition contributing to that behavior was adaptive for its bearers, on average, in past environments."[174] In other words, "behaviors that have the deepest roots in evolutionary history are likely to be the most resistant to change. . . . [S]hifting behavior in ways that tended to increase reproductive success in ancestral environments will generally be less costly than shifting behavior in ways that tended to decrease such success."[175] For example, "[b]ecause natural selection favors predispositions to direct parental resources principally toward offspring and other close relatives, we can explain and anticipate that the cost of reducing child abuse will be greater, per capita, for stepparent households than for nonstepparent households."[176]

As noted throughout this study, there is a biological basis to our sense of fairness.[177] Our innate sense of fairness limits punishment when the costs exceeds the benefits; no one should be punished more than they deserve.[178] Humans also consider certain actions to be more and less blameworthy.[179] For example, societies distinguish between a violent act that is premeditated and one that is not.[180] Similarly, self-defense is justifiable,[181] actions are worse than omissions,[182] and intentional conduct is worse than accidental acts.[183]

Behavioral biology supports the notion that punitive damages reinforce a state's legitimate interest in deterrence and retribution. Concerning retribution, Professors Hoffman and Goldsmith have written: Punishment "is the crux of social living. The very instincts that make us human–to survive and excel as individuals but in a social context that often requires us to empathize and care for others–obligate us to punish those whose selfishness is unacceptably antisocial."[184] Elsewhere they have stated, "we have deep urges to punish free riders, quite apart from whether punishment accomplishes any utilitarians goals, and in fact those urges are bound up with our nature as social creatures." [185] In addition, punitive damages "may reflect the 'sense of the community' about the egregious character of defendants' actions."[186]

Behavioral biology also supports the deterrence basis of punitive damages. Deterrence counteracts man's selfish nature; it protects the motivations for reciprocal altruism.[187] It forces "defendants to internalize the full expected cost of its conduct to others."[188] Through punishment "the law gives us selfish reasons to act unselfishly."[189] This may be especially true for large corporations–a modern day faction. For example Professors Rustad and Koenig have argued that punitive damages are necessary to control abuses of power by the economic elite.[190]

Behavioral biology also supports limits on punitive damages (what is "grossly excessive punishment"), although not necessarily the limits set forth by the Supreme Court. Behavioral biology corroborates the Supreme Court's notion that punitive damages should not be awarded for conduct that is legal in other jurisdictions and that punitive damages should not be granted for conduct in other jurisdictions. Retribution punishes for damages to the community; out-of-state conduct that has no effect in the community has no free rider problem. Thus, courts should not grant punitive damages for conduct outside a community. The same is true for a deterrence-basis of punishment; punitive damages for out-of-jurisdiction conduct would provide too much deterrence. Accordingly, punitive damages can be awarded for nationwide conduct under federal statutes, but they should be limited to a state's jurisdiction for state statutes.

On the other hand, the Supreme Court went too far when it held that punitive damages could not be based on a desire to punish the defendant for harming persons who are not before the court. Punitive damages under a retribution theory are for harm to the community. To ignore that harm contravenes the very nature of human beings and fails to punish free riders. Similarly, it is unlikely that awarding punitive damages only for harm to the plaintiff before the court will have the necessary deterrence effect. There will be too many cases where the harm goes undetected.

Under behavioral biology, the maximum punitive damages should normally be the amount necessary to deter the negative conduct–the amount needed to overcome individual selfishness. Under traditional law and economic theory, "the formula to establish optimal deterrence is the amount of loss multiplied by the inverse of the possibility that the injurer will be found liable."[191] On the other hand, as noted above, the maximum amount under behavioral biology might vary considerably depending on whether the negative behavior had a "predisposition contributing to that behavior was adaptive for its bearers, on average, in past environments."[192] Thus, the punishment needed for rape, which at one time had an evolutionary advantage for males because they could produce more offspring, will need much more deterrence than incest between brothers and sisters who grew up with each other because natural selection disfavors inbreeding between relatives.[193] In addition, to satisfy the Due Process Clause, the punishment must be reasonably effective, and behavioral biology can help with this determination. As Professor Jones has written, "if chemical castration is an aspect of state punishment, it can run afoul of the constitution if it is either unnecessary or applied arbitrarily. Again, whether chemical castration is sufficiently necessary and nonarbitrary depends, in part, on the extent to which rape is typically influenced by sexual desire."[194]

Under the above standard, the *Gore* three-part test–(1) the degree of reprehensibility, (2) the disparity between the harm or potential harm suffered by the plaintiff and the punitive damages, and (3) the differences between the award and civil penalties authorized or imposed in comparable cases"[195]–is a poor measure of punitive damages, especially the second and third elements. Reprehensibility of the defendant's conduct is obviously important in determining punitive damages; reprehensibility is important for both retribution and deterrence. However, "the disparity between the harm or potential harm suffered by the defendant and the punitive damages" is irrelevant because, as noted above, punitive damages are for harm to the community. The defendant may have suffered a small harm, but the community may have suffered a significant harm. In addition, the danger of instances where the defendant's conduct may go undetected often justifies a larger ratio between compensatory and punitive damages. Finally, "the differences between the award and civil penalties authorized or imposed in comparable cases" is also irrelevant. A state can choose how it punishes offenders, and it may choose to do so by punitive damages, rather than civil penalties or criminal sanctions. Legislatures have the authority to limit punitive damages, and in those states that they have not done so, one can assume that they approve of their state's punitive damages system.

The Supreme Court's emphasis on notice is also unfounded. If a state often gives punitive damages in cases of intentional or similar conduct that is notice that if one commits fraud or other intentional harm in that state that punitive damages might be awarded. The size of punitive damages in a particular state is a matter of public record.

The defendant, of course, must be protected from multiple punitive damages awards from multiple litigations. If the maximum amount to deter is awarded in one law suit in a jurisdiction, then fairness dictates that it cannot be awarded again. This is partially prevented by the rule from Gore and State Farm that a jurisdiction cannot base punitive damages on conduct outside the state that does not cause harm in the state. However, a state must do something to prevent multiple awards for conduct or harm in that state.[196]

Similarly, a defendant needs to be protected from arbitrary punitive damages awards–similarly-situated persons should receive or give similar damages. Professors Sunstein, Kahneman, and Schkade have suggested that the problem with arbitrary punitive damages may be with a jury's ability to map their outrage onto a dollar scale.[197] On the other hand, they have found that juries "have a remarkably high degree of moral consensus on the degrees of outrage and punishment that are appropriate for punitive damages cases," which cuts across class, race, gender, etc.[198] Consequently, they suggest that juries map their response in terms other than dollars, and let the judge set the exact dollar award.[199]

One criticism of punitive damages is that they provide a windfall for the plaintiff.[200] Viewing punitive damages as compensation for injury to the public, as behavioral biology supports, backs up this criticism. A possible solution would be to have punitive damages awards go to the state treasury, except for a small amount for the plaintiff for uncompensated expenses, such as attorney's fees.[201]

More innovatively, Professor Sharkey has proposed "a new category of damages: compensatory societal damages assessed to redress widespread harms caused by the defendant, harms that reach far beyond the individual plaintiff before the court."[202] She has added: "the concept of societal damages expands the boundaries of a single lawsuit's ability to achieve the tort systems varied goals by allowing a jury to access damages against a defendant whose conduct has had harmful effects radiating far beyond the particular plaintiff who has initiated the suit."[203] Such damages force wrongdoers to internalize costs.[204] Depending on the circumstances, the damages could be distributed to parties who were harmed but are not yet before the court, they could be a kind of tax for the general welfare, such as for CAT scans for smokers to detect cancer, or there could be an ex post class action.[205] Regardless of the exact solution to the windfall problem, this author believes that most of the punitive damages should go to either other persons who were harmed by the defendants' conduct or the public treasury.

Although behavioral biology is useful in determining the maximum amount of punitive damages–the Due Process limitations, it does not dictate the exact amount of punitive damages. The exact amount of punitive damages (or even whether punitive damages is the most effective deterrent) is a policy decision that is left up to the state; it is not a constitutional issue. States may not want to go to the full limits of deterrence, and they may consider other factors, such as other types of punishment or administrative costs. Behavioral biology, however, can help illuminate that process; it can aid in the cost-benefit analysis.[206] It can show what is behind human behavior, what humans consider fair, and what might be an effective deterrent. For example, it can show that selfishness is an evolutionary trait that can be deterred, that humans consider intentional harm more blameworthy than negligent harm, and that punitive damages might be an effective deterrent for fraud because punitive damages forces a wrongdoer to internalize costs.

In sum, behavioral biology supports a statement in punitive damages cases that is often written, but also often ignored–"that the damages awarded be reasonably necessary to vindicate the State's legitimate interests in punishment and deterrence."[207] In other words, the constitutional limit on punitive damages should be the amount of damages necessary to deter the defendant's conduct. Thus, the Supreme Court was correct in *Gore* and *State Farm* when it held a state should be able to impose punitive damages only for conduct that occurred in that state or that caused harm in that state. However, it went too far in Philip Morris when it said a state could not impose punitive damages based on a desire to punish the defendant for harming persons who are not before the court.

Notes

1. BERTRAND RUSSELL, HUMAN KNOWLEDGE: ITS SCOPE AND LIMITS v (1948).

2. 545 U.S. 469 (2005).

3. *Id.*

4. U.S. Const. amend. 5.

5. *Kelo*, 545 U.S. at 472.

6. *Id.* at 473.

7. *Id.*

8. *Id.* at 473-74.

9. *Id.* at 474.

10. *Id.* at 475.

11. *Id.*

12. *Id.*

13. *Id.* at 475-76.

14. *Id.* at 476.

15. *Id.* at 477.

16. *Id.*

17. *Id.* at 478.

18. *Id.* at 479-80.

19. 348 U.S. 26 (1954).

20. *Id.* at 34.

21. Hawaii Housing Auth. v. Midkiff, 467 U.S. 229 (1984).

22. *Kelo*, 545 U.S. at 482.

23. 467 U.S. 986 (1984).

24. *Id.* at 1014.

25. *Kelo*, 545 U.S. at 482.

26. *Id.* at 483.

27. *Id.*

28. *Id.* at 484.

29. *Id.*

30. *Id.*

31. *Id.* at 485.

32. *Id.* at 478-88.

33. *Id.* at 488.

34. *Id.*

35. JEFFRIE G. MURPHY & JULES L. COLEMAN, PHILOSOPHY OF LAW: AN INTRODUCTION TO JURISPRUDENCE 71 (rev. ed 1990); *see also* STEVEN PINKER, THE BLANK SLATE: THE MODERN DENIAL OF HUMAN NATURE 425 (2002).

36. MURPHY & COLEMAN, *supra*, at 77-79; *see also* Chapter Five.

37. In her *Kelo* dissent, Justice O'Connor declared: "But were the political branches the sole arbiters of the public-private distinction, the Public Use Clause would amount to little more than hortatory fluff." *Kelo*, 545 U.S. at 497 (O'Connor, J., dissenting); *see also Kelo*, 545 U.S. at 518 (Thomas, J., dissenting) ("Still worse, it is backwards to adopt a searching standard of constitutional review for nontraditional property interests, such as welfare benefits, while deferring to the legislature's determination as to what constitutes a public use when it exercises the power of eminent domain, and thereby invades individuals' traditional property interests in real property."); Timothy Sandefur, *Mine and Thine Distinct: What* Kelo *Says About Our Path*, 10 CHAP. L. REV. 1, 47 (2006) ("It is most implausible that the Framers intended to defer to legislatures to what satisfies the Public Use Clause, uniquely among all the express provisions of the Bill of Rights.").

38. "The term behavior system refers to functionally and causally related behavior patterns and the systems responsible for them." MICHAEL MCGUIRE AND ALFONSO TROISI, DARWINIAN PSYCHIATRY 60 (1998).

39. Jeffrey Evans Stake, *The Property 'Instinct,'* 359 PHIL. TRANSACTIONS ROYAL SOC'Y LONDON 1763, 1763 (2004); *see also* Thomas W. Merrill & Harry E. Smith, *Law and Morality: Property Law: The Morality of Property*, 48 WM. & MARY L. REV. 1849, 1894 (2007); Herbert Gintis, *The Evolution of Private Property*, 64 J. ECON. BEHAV. & ORG. 1, 15 (2007).

40. John O. McGinnis, *The Human Constitution and Constitutive Law: A Prolegomenon*, 8 J. CONTEMP. LEGAL ISSUES 211, 222 (1997).

41. Stake, *supra*, at 1763 ("Rivals can reduce the costs of competition by adopting strategies for determining the outcome of fights without physical damage."); *see also* Gintis, *supra*, at 3.

42. MARC D. HAUSER, MORAL MINDS: HOW NATURE DESIGNED OUR UNIVERSAL SENSE OF RIGHT AND WRONG 24 (2006).

43. Gintis, *supra*, at 2.

44. PINKER, *supra*, at 290.

45. Morris B. Hoffman, *The Neuroeconomic Path of the Law*, 359 PHIL. TRANS. R. SOC. LOND. B. 1667, 1675 n.3 (2004).

46. *See* MICHAEL S. GAZZANIGA, HUMAN: THE SCIENCE BEHIND WHAT MAKES US UNIQUE 154-55 (2008).

47. PINKER, *supra*, at 285; *see also* HAUSER, *supra*, at 411; *see also* Chapter Two.

48. PINKER, *supra*, at 285; *see also* HAUSER, *supra*, at 274.

49. E. Donald Elliot, *Law and Biology: The New Synthesis*, 41 ST. LOUIS L.J. 595, 609 (1997); *see also* McGinnis, *The Human Constitution*, *supra*, at 218 ("[T]he innate tendency to be reciprocally altruistic provides a strong foundation on which to erect institutions to enforce obligations that serve mutual self-interest.).

50. McGinnis, *The Human Constitution*, *supra*, at 222.

51. *Id.*; *see also* Raymond R. Coletta, *The Measuring Stick of Regulatory Takings: A Biological and Cultural Analysis*, 1 U. PA. J. CONST. L. 20, 24 (1998) ("Strong feelings surround the sense of ownership and any attack on its inviolability generates visceral reactions at the expense of rational, unbiased inquiry."). As noted in Chapter Five, *Kelo* produced a great deal of outrage. *E.g.*, Julia D. Mahoney, Kelo's *Legacy: Eminent Domain and the Future of Property Rights*, 2005 SUP. CT. REV. 103, 104 (2005) ("This anger may be especially acute in settings where the acquired property is to be transferred to developers or other commercial interests, thereby creating an opportunity for profit-seeking firms to acquire property for less than they would have to pay in a negotiated purchase.").

52. Mahoney, *supra*, at 106.

53. And, a stretched reading of the Constitution. The Takings Clause says public <u>use</u>, not public purpose. U.S. CONST. amend. V.

54. Merrill & Smith, *supra*, at 1882-84.

55. As Professor Goldsmith has noted: "Human history is largely the record of struggles for control of resources by one group at the expense of others." TIMOTHY H. GOLDSMITH, THE BIOLOGICAL BASIS OF HUMAN NATURE: FORGING LINKS BETWEEN EVOLUTION AND BEHAVIOR 120 (1991). Similarly, Professor Sandefur has declared: "Whenever government has power to redistribute benefits and burdens between constituents, interest groups will compete for control of that power in order to secure benefits for themselves or to impose burdens on their competitors." Sandefur, *supra*, at 34.

56. Justice Thomas has pointed out that economic development eminent domain disproportionately affects poor and minority communities. *Kelo*, 545 U.S. at 521 (Thomas, J., dissenting). For examples of eminent domain abuse, see Sandefur, *supra*, at 35.

57. McGinnis, *supra*, at 222. Notably, the redistribution with economic development eminent domain is usually from those with less resources to those with more resources. As Justice O'Connor noted in her dissent to *Kelo*, "the founders could not have intended this perverse result." *Kelo*, 545 U.S. at 505.

58. Elliot, *The New Synthesis*, *supra*, at 611.

59. McGinnis, *supra*, at 223; *see also* Coletta, *supra*, at 69 ("Economic stability similarly reinforces a sense of personal stability as well as a feeling of well-being and security.").

60. Owen D. Jones & Timothy H. Goldsmith, *Law and Behavioral Biology*, 105 COLUM. L. REV. 441 (2005); *see also* HAUSER, *supra*, at 84; Douglas A. Terry, *Don't Forget About Reciprocal Altruism: Critical Review of the Evolutionary Jurisprudence Movement*, 34 CONN. L. REV. 477, 507 (2002) ("In a situation in

which an individual suspects that the distribution is not in accord with a particular distributive rule, he may experience a feeling of moral outrage (that's not fair). This quick and simple Darwinian algorithm, and its accompanying strong emotional response, is adaptive because [a] hunter gatherer who is not quick to complain about the distribution of meat will find his or her objections addressed to a pile of gnawed bones.").

61. Stake, *supra*, at 1164.

62. Jones & Goldsmith, *supra*, at 443-455.

63. *Id.* at 443.

64. *Id.* at 448.

65. *Id.* at 450.

66. *Id.* at 452; *see also* Stake, *supra*, at 1167.

67. Jones & Goldsmith, *supra*, at 444, 453.

68. 491 U.S. 110 (1988).

69. *Id.* at 113.

70. *Id.*

71. *Id.*

72. *Id.*

73. *Id.* at 114.

74. *Id.*

75. *Id.* at 114-15.

76. *Id.* at 115.

77. *Id.*

78. *Id.*

79. *Id.*

80. *Id.* at 115-16.

81. *Id.* at 116.

82. *Id.*

83. *Id.*

84. *Id.* at 118. Notably, Justice Scalia provided no citation for his observation about nature.

85. *Id.*

86. *Id.* at 119.

87. *Id.* at 121.

88. *Id.* at 121-22.

89. *Id.* at 122 (citing Snyder v. Massachusetts, 291 U.S. 97, 105 (1934).

90. *Michael H.*, 491 U.S. at 124.

91. *Id.* at 124-27.

92. *Id.* at 125.

93. *Id.*

94. *Id.* at 126.

95. *Id.* at 127.

96. *Id.* at 130.

97. *Id.*

98. *Id.*

99. *Id.*

100. *Id.* at 130-31.

101. *Id.* at 131.

102. *Id.* at 124.

103. *Id.* at 125.

104. *Id.* at 115.

105. AM.JUR.2D *Illegitimate Children* § 7 (1995).

106. *Id.*; C.J.S. *Child Born Out of Wedlock* §§5, 63 (1991).

107. Of course, the government should be able to interfere with this liberty if the father were abusing the child, but there was no such allegation here.

108. McGinnis, *supra*, at 215.

109. ANTHONY WALSH, BIOSOCIOLOGY: AN EMERGING PARADIGM 209 (1995). ("Most primate fathers are unable to identify their offspring, let alone form a bonded relationship with them." *Id.* at 211.); *see also* PINKER, *supra*, at 252.

110. *Michael H.*, 491 U.S. at 130.

111. Taboo mentality refers to irrational prejudices. Professor Pinker has written that "the design of the moral sense leaves people in all cultures vulnerable to confusing defensible moral judgements with irrelevant passions and prejudices." PINKER, *supra*, at 272.

112. Justice Brennan's dissent noted that Michael H. had lived with his daughter, supported her, and maintained a relationship with her. *Michael H.*, 491 U.S. at 143 (Brennan, J., dissenting).

113. Professor Mary Kay Kisthardt has observed that, despite the fact that Victoria was the focus of the case, it became a battle over the rights of the parents, with "the plurality simply defin[ing] her individual existence out of existence." Mary Kay Kisthardt, *Of Fatherhood, Families and Fantasy: The Legacy of* Michael H. v. Gerald D., 65 TULANE L. REV. 585, 628 (1991); *see also* Lawrence C. Nolan, *"Unwed Children" and their Parents before the United States Supreme Court from* Levy *to* Michael H: *Unlikely Participants in Constitutional Jurisprudence*, 28 CAPITAL U. L. REV. 1, 67 (1999) ("Often, in cases dealing with parental rights, the child is subjected to the adult's claim, or it is ignored."). Professor Kisthardt has also noted that "the continuity of relations [which had been established in this case] is extremely significant for healthy psychological development of children." Kisthardt, *supra*, at 630.

114. In addition, Professor Kisthardt has pointed out that Carole had at one point encouraged the contact between Victoria and Michael. Kisthardt, *supra*, at 626. She has stated: "The reader is left with the sad feeling that the mother is the only person whose rights were truly vindicated in this case and that she is, in all likelihood, the least deserving of vindication." *Id.* at 627.

115. WALSH, *supra*, at 212-13.

116. Justice Brennan's dissent also criticized the plurality's emphasis on the "unitary family," noting that the only difference between the relationship among Michael, Victoria, and Carole and that of Gerald, Victoria, and Carole was the fact of marriage. *Michael H.*, 491 U.S. at 143-44 (Brennan, J., dissenting). He added: "It is a bad day for due process when the State's interest in terminating a parent-child relationship is reason to conclude that that relationship is not part of the 'liberty' protected by the Fourteenth Amendment." *Id.* at 146-147.

117.   Professor Janet Dolgin has pointed out that "[i]n order to preserve traditional families, in general, or one family, courts have been willing to manipulate, even to dismiss, the biological facts." Janet L. Dolgin, *Just a Gene: Judicial Assumptions About Parenthood*, 40 U.C.L.A. L. REV. 637, 644 (1993). She has noted that a natural father's paternity is often ignored because the law defines fathers, in contrast to mothers, through their cultural selves, rather than through their biological selves. *Id.* at 669.

118. As Professor Dolgin has remarked: "Thus, in effect, Justice Scalia argued that a child's stepfather is a more 'natural' father than the child's genitor." *Id.*

119.   *Philip Morris v. Williams*, 549 U.S. 346 (2007); *State Farm Mut. Auto Ins. Co. v. Campbell*, 538 U.S. 408 (2003); *BMW of N. Am., Inc. v. Gore.*, 517 U.S. 559 (1996).

120.   Anthony J. Sebok, *Punitive Damages: From Myth to Theory*, 92 IOWA L. REV. 957, 959 (2007); *see also generally* Victor E. Schwartz, Mark A. Behrens, & Cary Silverman, *I'll Take That: Legal and Public Policy Problems Raised by Statutes that Require Punitive Damages*, 68 MO. L. REV. 525 (2003); Michael Rustad & Thomas Koenig, *The Historical Continuity of Punitive Damages Awards: Reforming the Tort Reformers*, 42 AM. U.L. REV. 1269 (1993); Dan Quayle, *Civil Justice Reform*, 41 AM. U.L. REV. 559 (1992); Cass R. Sunstein, Daniel Kahneman, & David Schkade, *Assessing Punitive Damages (with Notes on Cognition and Valuation in Law)*, 107 YALE L. REV. 2071 (1998); John Calvin Jefferies, Jr., *Commentary: A Comment on the Constitutionality of Punitive Damages*, 72 VA. L. REV. 139 (1986).

121.   *BMW*, 517 U.S. at 562.

122.   *Philip Morris*, 549 U.S. at 352; *BMW*, 517 U.S. at 568; *see also State Farm*, 538 U.S. at 416.

123.   *BMW*, 517 U.S. at 568.

124.   *Philip Morris*, 549 U.S. at 358-59 (Stevens, J., dissenting); *see also State Farm*, 538 U.S. at 416.

125.   *BMW*, 517 U.S. at 559.

126.   *Id.* at 562.

127.   *Id.* at 563-64.

128.   *Id.* at 565.

129.   *Id.* at 566.

130.   *Id.* at 567.

131.   *Id.* at 568.

132.   *Id.* at 571.

133.   *Id.*

134.   *Id.* at 572-74.

135.   *Id.* at 574.

136.   *Id.* at 574-75.

137. *Id.* at 575-76.

138. *Id.* at 576.

139. *Id.* at 580.

140. *Id.* at 582.

141. *Id.*

142. *Id.* at 583-84.

143. *Campbell*, 538 U.S. at 408.

144. *Id.* at 412.

145. *Id.* at 413.

146. *Id.*

147. *Id.*

148. *Id.*

149. *Id.* at 414.

150. *Id.* at 415.

151. *Id.*

152. *Id.* at 419-26.

153. *Id.* at 419-20.

154. *Id.* at 423.

155. *Id.* at 425.

156. *Id.* at 426.

157. *Id.* at 427.

158. *Philip Morris*, 349 U.S. at 346.

159. *Id.* at 350.

160. *Id.*

161. *Id.* at 353.

162. *Id.* at 353-54.

163. *Id.* at 354.

164. *Id.*

165. *Id.* at 355.

166. Morris B. Hoffman & Timothy H. Goldsmith, *The Biological Roots of Punishment*, 1 OHIO ST. J. CRIM. L. 627, 627 (2004).

167. *Id.* at 630; *see also* PINKER, *supra*, at 261 ("In the real world, people differ genetically in their selfish tendencies.").

168. HAUSER, *supra*, at 243, 254, 272, 319 ("It could be that our ability to detect cheaters is part of a more general ability to figure out when someone or something has violated a rule." *Id.* at 272.); Owen D. Jones, *Time-Shifted Rationality and the Law of Law's Leverage: Behavioral Economics Meets Law and Biology*, 95 N.W. U.L. REV. 1180 (2001); GOLDSMITH, *supra*, at 231 ("Your interests are also well served if you are skillful in detecting when others are deceiving you.").

169. Hoffman & Goldsmith, *supra*, at 630-31.

170. *Id.* at 631; *see also* HAUSER, *supra*, at 81 ("[T]he only way to guarantee stable, cooperative societies is by ensuring open inspection of reputation and providing opportunities for punishing cheaters."); Jones & Goldsmith, *supra*, at 441.

171. Hoffman & Goldsmith, *supra*, at 633; *see also* HAUSER, *supra*, at 99 (Behavioral biology "highlight[s] the importance of punishment in the evolution of cooperation, and, in particular, in the unique forms of human civilization that have emerged and persisted over thousands of years in the face of temptations to break them apart.").

172. Hoffman & Goldsmith, *supra*, at 634; *see also* HAUSER, *supra*, at 285, 398 ("Members of this self-interested societies adhere to commitments and other social norms because of the ever-pending threat of punishment." *Id.* at 285. "In the absence of such punishment, cooperation deteriorates as individuals defects." *Id.* at 398); Erin O'Hara and Douglas Yarn, *On Apology and Consilence*, 77 WASH. L. REV. 1121, 1153 (2002) ("The emotional urge to retaliate sometimes called a retributive instinct, can therefore be adaptive.").

173. Jones & Goldsmith, *supra*, at 459-60. Elsewhere they stated, "law is a lever for moving behavior that has a model of human behavior as its fulcrum." *Id.* at 415.

174. *Id.* at 462.

175. *Id.* at 463.

176. *Id.*

177. *Id.* at 441; HAUSER, *supra*, at 79.

178. Hoffman & Goldsmith, *supra*, at 637, 639.

179. HAUSER, *supra*, at 124, 125, 143, 149, 207.

180. *Id.* at 143.

181. *Id.* at 149.

182. *Id.* at 207.

183. *Id.* at 398, 404.

184. Hoffman & Goldsmith, *supra*, at 640.

185. *Id.* at 639-40.

186. Sunstein et. al., *supra*, at 2075.

187. Professor McGinnis has written, "we can expect many individuals to behave in some circumstances as if they will reciprocate when, instead, they intend to defect." McGinnis, *The Human Constitution, supra*, at 218.

188. Catherine M. Sharkey, *Punitive Damages as Social Damages*, 113 YALE L.J. 347, 359 (2003); *see also* Sunstein et. al., *supra*, at 2075 ("Punitive damages can, in theory, take account of the infrequency of private suits by penalizing defendants enough ex post that they will undertake optimal precautions ex ante."); *see also* HAUSER, *supra*, at 109 ("To ignore the potential deterrence function of punishment, in any form, is to ignore one of its most significant educational functions.").

189. Elliot, *supra*, at 610 ; *see also* O'Hara & Yarn, *supra*, at 1156 ("retaliation can make non-cooperation too costly. . .").

190. Rustad & Koenig, *supra*, at 1277 ("The doctrine of punitive damages is one of the few remedies that can constrain a giant corporation that is willing and able to take advantage of its less powerful 'adversaries.'").

191. A. Mitchell Polinsky & Steven Shavell, *Punitive Damages: An Economic Analysis*, 111 HARV. L. REV. (1998); *see also* Sharkey, *supra*, at 367.

192. Jones & Goldsmith, *supra*, at 462.

193. Jones & Goldsmith, *supra*, at 459, 464.

194. Owen D. Jones, *Book Review: Realities of Rape: Of Science and Politics, Causes and Meanings: A Natural History of Rape: Biological Bases of Sexual Coercion. By Randy Thornhill & Craig T. Palmer*, 86 CORNELL L. REV. 1386, 1418 (2001).

195. *BMW*, 517 U.S. at 574-75.

196. For example, Alabama law in reviewing punitive damages awards considers whether "there have been other civil actions against the same defendant, based on the same conduct." *Gore*, 517 U.S. at 612 n.4 (Ginsburg, J., dissenting). Alternatively, Professor Sharkey has suggested that instead of going to a single plaintiff that punitive damages be kept to compensate for harm to others. Sharkey, *supra*, at 433.

197. Sunstein et. al., *supra*, at 2078, 2100.

198. *Id.* at 2077-78.

199. *Id.* at 2078, 2142.

200. Sharkey, *supra*, at 370-73,.

201. Some states already do something similar to this. *See Gore*, 517 U.S. at 616-18 (appendix to opinion of Ginsburg, J. dissenting).

202. Sharkey, *supra*, at 389.

203. *Id.* at 391.

204. *Id.* at 354.

205. *Id.* at 391-414.

206. PINKER, *supra*, at ix ("I believe that controversies about policy almost always involve tradeoffs between competing values, and that science is equipped to identify the tradeoffs but not to resolve them. Many of these tradeoffs, I will show, arise from features of human nature, and by clarifying them I hope to make our collective choices, whatever they are, better informed.").

207. *BMW*, 517 U.S. at 568.

Chapter Seven

Conclusion: The Threat

In the distant future I see open fields for far more important researches.
Psychology will be based on a new foundation that of the necessary
acquirement of each mental power and capacity by graduation.

Charles Darwin[1]

Using the wrong model of human behavior for law and society can have enormous destructive consequences. The history of the twentieth century has often been the history of wrong human behavioral choices. Totalitarian societies, like Soviet Russia, Communist China, and Nazi Germany, have killed millions and caused millions more terrible suffering. Similarly, other collectivist and utopian experiments have failed miserably. Finally, having even the details of human behavior wrong can cause unnecessary suffering.

To begin with, a totalitarian government goes against human nature. Totalitarianism is defined as "of or relating to a political regime based on subordination of the individual to the state and strict control of all aspects of the life and productive capacity of the nation especially by coercive measures (such as censorship and terrorism)."[2] First, as mentioned throughout this study, humans formed societies and governments for human protection. The role of government was to enforce the social contract, not impose social engineering on individuals. Second, subordinating individuals to the collective is opposite of human nature. In nature, it is the individual that matters, not the collective. Third, having strict control of the life and productive capacity of the

185

nation is counterproductive. Mankind got where it is through reciprocal altruism, not coercion. Finally, control by a few goes against man's natural rights of liberty, fairness, and equality.

Marxism also goes against human behavior. Marx wanted to reshape humanity.[3] He adopted a type of materialism–which meant "the denial that there is any Mind or Idea which is prior to Nature and expresses itself in nature."[4] He rejected fixed categories, eternal truths, and natural laws, as elements of bourgeois economics.[5] At one point he stated, "it is not the consciousness of human beings which determines their being, but it is, on the contrary, their social being which determines their consciousness."[6] He also rejected Capitalism, which he viewed as exploitation of workers.[7] Central to Marxism was the rejection of private property.[8] His credo was: "from each according to his ability, to each according to his need."[9]

Marx viewed the history of man as the history of class struggle.[10] In analyzing history, Marx used a version of the Hegalian dialectic, which was negation and its negation into a higher stage.[11] He saw at the beginning of history a state of primitive communism in which land was held in common and there were no classes.[12] However, the introduction of private property created economic classes, and the State became the instrument of the dominant class, which tries to impose its moral conceptions on the lower classes.[13] When the forces of production, especially property, have become "a drag and a fetter," the rising class will overthrow the dominant class.[14] At this point, primitive sharing will reemerge because human minds reflect the material conditions of existence.[15] The new dominant class will eliminate private property and thus class distinctions.[16] A temporary dictatorship of the proletariat will be necessary until the classless society is created.[17]

Marxism founders on the illusion that man can be culturally engineered.[18] As has been shown throughout this book, the mind is not a blank slate that can be molded. Rather, human nature is largely inherited, and it is difficult to change inherited human nature. Behaviorist conditioning cannot change man's basic nature. Two and two does not equal five.

Marx's notion that an individual should work for the collective good goes against principles of human behavior, especially the idea of the selfish gene and reciprocal altruism, as illustrated throughout this study.[19] In addition, studies have shown that free riders and lack of punishment of free riders causes less production of resources and even breaks down a society.[20]   Obviously, participation in such a society is not evolutionarily sound.

Moreover, scientists have proven Marx's view on primitive man wrong. While the hunting of large animals was a collective action, most labor and sharing was done on the individual and family level.[21]   Sharing outside the family was generally based on reciprocal altruism, not providing for the neediest, and, when an individual did not reciprocate, this produced anger.[22]   This should not be surprising because natural selection did not favor indiscriminate sharing.[23]

Hitler believed in an extreme form of Social Darwinism in which groups were the unit of selection and races were distinct.[24]   Based on this wrong model of human nature, he thought that "the extinction of inferior races was part of the wisdom of nature."[25]   Of course, this view resulted in the extermination of countless Jews and others.

Professors Cosmides and Tooby give three examples of how collectives have failed.[26]   First, the Shuar of the Ecuadorian Amazon created a collective for the cultivation of sugar cane. They would share profits equally, and they levied fines for not working, which were to be subtracted from profits. The fines had no effect. Eventually participation decreased and the venture failed.

On a larger scale, the Soviet Union nationalized farmland, but it allowed 3% of farms to be held privately. This 3% produced 45 to 75% of the vegetables, meat, milk, eggs, and potatoes consumed in the Soviet Union.   Similarly, collectivization in Communist China resulted in the largest famine in history.

In sum, "[s]ufficiently large collective actions decouple reward from effort, initiating a process of declining effort by some, which stimulates matching withdrawals by others."[27]   In other words, "societies dominated by central economic planning (rationally designed to produce increases in general welfare) end up producing far lower levels of welfare than societies in which the private exchanges (not aimed at producing welfare) substantially replace government decision making."[28]   As this book has shown, this is because individuals cooperate to further their selfish interests.

Utopian experiments have failed because they went against human behavior. As Professor Ridley has remarked, "the only lesson to be drawn from utopia dreaming is that all utopias are hell."[29]   Ridley believes that the major cause of the breakdown of utopias is individualism, especially social jealousy.[30]

Most notable of these failures is the classic kibbutzim.[31]   The classic kibbutzim were collectivist, agriculture communities in Israel, where property was held in common and egalitarianism reigned. Children were raised in common, and everyone shared in chores like cooking and cleaning. Today, the classic kibbutzim are disappearing.[32] Members have individuals businesses operating on capitalist principles, families do their own cleaning and cooking, and children are raised by their families.

The classic kibbutzim failed because it went against human behavior.[33] They initially worked because individuals voluntarily decided that the kibbutzim was the best social organization for them, especially considering the great discrimination the Jews suffered in the early- and mid-twentieth century. In other words, they decided that their selfish interests would be best served by the kibbutzim. However, over time, cheating weakened the kibbutzim, and members left because they were dissatisfied with communal life.[34] As mentioned in Chapter Five, mothers decided that they wanted to raise their own children; traditional families won out against communal ones.[35] Moreover, kibbutzim children, who had not agreed to the original social contract, grew into adulthood and doubted the organization and the rules of the kibbutzim because it went against their natural instincts discussed throughout this book. Most importantly, private property was needed as an incentive for work; reciprocal altruism holds together the social structure and overcomes the selfish gene.

Details of how society is regulated should also consider human behavior. As Professor Pinker has declared: "Many atrocities of the twentieth century were committed in the name of egalitarianism, targeting people whose success was taken as evidence of their criminality."[36] Such attitudes (or justifications) were partially responsible for mass exterminations in Nazi Germany, Soviet Russia, Communist China, etc.

Professor De Waal is especially critical of behavioralist experiments, declaring that behaviorism has worked more havoc than any other school of psychology.[37] He discusses experiments in Communist Romania, where thousands of children were raised in institutions in isolation from others. He states, "[t]he orphans were incapable of laughing or crying, spent the day rocking and clutching themselves in a fetal position . . ., and didn't even know how to play."[38]

While concentrating on the innate aspects of human behavior, this study has also shown that there is an instrumental aspect to law. However, as Brian Tamahana has shown,[39] overemphasis on the instrumental aspects of law, which has been advocated both by conservative economists and liberals, can have a destructive effect, especially when it goes against positive aspects of human nature.[40] Forcing an individual to conform to behavior that is foreign to his nature is like forcing a person to speak a language he neither knows nor can understand. Behavioral biology can help with making choices for instrumental rules by illustrating how human behavior actually works, showing how an instrumental rule can be effective at the least cost.

Finally, we should stop blaming the wrong causes for problems. Much guilt has been spread based on faulty models of human behavior. For example, autism is 90% inheritable; it is not caused by "cold" mothers.[41]

This book has attempted to demonstrate how human behavior affects law and law affects human behavior through the prisms of behavioral biology, neuroscience, and related fields. This author does not claim that everything in this book is correct; scientific details change all the time. However, I hope it has shown that legal scholars must reject unprincipled postmodern approaches to law and instead use scientifically-supported models of human behavior.

Notes

1. CHARLES DARWIN, ON THE ORIGIN OF SPECIES BY MEANS OF NATURAL SELECTION 488 (1859).

2. http://www.merriam-webster.com/dictionary/totalitarian (Checked September 1, 2010).

3. STEVEN PINKER, THE BLANK SLATE: THE MODERN DENIAL OF HUMAN NATURE 157 (2002).

4. 7 FREDERICK COPLESTON, MODERN PHILOSOPHY: SCHOPENHAUER TO NIETZSCHE 83 (1963).

5. *Id.* at 80.

6. *Quoted in id.* at 83.

7. Id.

8. *Id.* at 77.

9. KARL MARX, The Criticism of the Gotha Program (1875).

10. COPLESTON, *supra*, at 95.

11. *Id.* at 85.

12. *Id.* at 95.

13. *Id.*

14. *Id.*

15. Leda Cosmides & John Tooby, *Evolutionary Psychology, Moral Heuristics, and the Law, in* HEURISTICS AND THE LAW 188 (Gerd Gigerenzer & Christoph Enge eds., 2006).

16. COPLESTON, *supra*, at 95.

17. *Id.*

18. FRANS DE WAAL, THE AGE OF EMPATHY: NATURE'S LESSONS FOR A KINDER SOCIETY 202 (2009).

19. Professor Ridley has similarly declared, "the focus of economic and social theory is, and must be, the individual. . . . Individuals, not societies, are the vehicles for genes." MATT RIDLEY, THE RED QUEEN: SEX AND THE EVOLUTION OF HUMAN NATURE 11 (1993).

20. Cosmides & Tooby, *supra*, at 196-97.

21. *Id.* at 189.

22. *Id.*

23. *Id.*

24. PINKER, *supra*, at 153-54.

25. *Id.* at 154.

26. Cosmides & Tooby, *supra*, at 201-02.

27. *Id.* at 202.

28. *Id.* at 203. They add: "By prohibiting a given category of interactions, the law throws away local or rapidly changing information about variation in values in a way voluntary consent expressing itself in changing prices does not." *Id.* at 205.

29. MATT RIDLEY, AGILE GENE: HOW NATURE TURNS ON NURTURE 67 (2003) [hereinafter RIDLEY, THE AGILE GENE].

30. *Id.* at 230.

31. The *Kibbutz* in Jewish Virtual Library,
http://www.jewishvirtuallibrary.org/jsource/Society_&_Culture/kibbutz.html (checked September 15, 2010).

32. Ilya Somin, *Formerly Socialist Israeli Kibbutzim Discover the Virtues of Private Property*, on The Volokh Conspiracy,
http://volokh.com/2010/01/26/formerly-socialist-israeli-kibbutzim-discover-the-virtues-of-private-property/ (checked September 15, 2010).

33. *Id.*; PINKER, *supra*, at 257.

34. One kibbutznik has called the kibbutz, "a paradise for parasites." PINKER, *supra*, at 257.

35. Obviously, motherhood and family are not just social constructs. Professor Harris has pointed out that studies have shown that children raised in an orphanage do not receive normal levels of nurturing, and they tend to have social and emotional difficulties later in life. SAM HARRIS, THE MORAL LANDSCAPE: HOW SCIENCE CAN DETERMINE HUMAN VALUES 9 (2010). This may be caused by low levels of oxytocin and vasopressin in the brain's reward system. *Id.*

36. PINKER, *supra*, at 152.

37. DE WAAL, *supra*, at 12-13 (2009).

38. *Id.* at 13.

39. BRIAN Z. TAMANAHA, LAW AS A MEANS TO AN END: THREAT TO THE RULE OF LAW (2006).

40. An example of this is rent control laws, which are intended to help the poor obtain affordable housing. Cosmides & Tooby, *supra*, at 194-95. However rent control causes some owners to not place housing on the rental market or to not build new apartment buildings, which limits the availability of housing for the poor. Owners will generally put their property to the use that gives them a greater return–that improves their survival chances. Cosmides and Tooby suggest that giving housing vouchers to the poor might avoid these

negative effects. *Id.*

41. RIDLEY, THE AGILE GENE, *supra*, at 105.

Index